Eduardo Pavez Goye

Schizoanalysis and Ecosophy

Also available from Bloomsbury

Schizoanalytic Cartographies, Félix Guattari
Deleuze and the Schizoanalysis of Literature, Ian Buchanan, Tim Matts and Aidan Tynan
Deleuze and the Schizoanalysis of Religion, Lindsay Powell-Jones and F. LeRon Shults
Bare Architecture, Chris L. Smith
Deleuze and Futurism, Helen Palmer
Deleuze and Cinema, Felicity Colman
Deleuze and Art, Anne Sauvagnargues
Space After Deleuze, Arun Saldanha

Schizoanalysis and Ecosophy:

Reading Deleuze and Guattari

Edited by Constantin V. Boundas

Bloomsbury Academic
An imprint of Bloomsbury Publishing Plc

BLOOMSBURY
LONDON • OXFORD • NEW YORK • NEW DELHI • SYDNEY

Bloomsbury Academic
An imprint of Bloomsbury Publishing Plc

50 Bedford Square
London
WC1B 3DP
UK

1385 Broadway
New York
NY 10018
USA

www.bloomsbury.com

BLOOMSBURY and the Diana logo are trademarks of Bloomsbury Publishing Plc

First published 2018

British Library Cataloguing-in-Publication Data
A catalogue record for this book is available from the British Library.

ISBN: HB: 978-1-3500-5218-5
ePDF: 978-1-3500-5219-2
ePub: 978-1-3500-5220-8

Library of Congress Cataloging-in-Publication Data
A catalog record for this book is available from the Library of Congress.

Series: Bloomsbury Studies in Continental Philosophy

Typeset by Deanta Global Publishing Services, Chennai, India
Printed and bound in Great Britain

To
Choi Ke Ryang
who deserved much more

Contents

List of Contributors

Manola Antonioli studied literature in the University of Urbino and earned her PhD in philosophy and social sciences from the École des hautes études en sciences sociales. Her research focuses on the intersections between aesthetics, architecture, urbanism, political ecology and contemporary philosophy in the context of the new technologies of information and communication. Her publications include Écriture de Maurice Blanchot. Fiction et Théorie, Deleuze et histoire de la philosophie, Géophilosophie de Deleuze et Guattari, Gilles Deleuze, Félix Guattari et le politique, and with Frederic Astier et Olivier Fressard, Gilles Deleuze et Félix Guattari: une rencontre dans l' après mai 1968.

Hanjo Berressem is professor of American Studies at the University of Cologne. He has authored and edited several books among which are *Pynchon's Poetics: Interfacing Theory and Text*, *Lines of Desire: Reading Gombrowicz's Fiction with Lacan* and, with Leyla Haferkamp, *Deleuzian Events*.

Constantin V. Boundas (Trent University, Ontario) holds M.A. Ph.D. from Purdue, and he is Professor Emeritus of Philosophy and a member of the Centre for the Study of Theory, History and Culture at Trent University. He is the editor of *The Deleuze Reader* (New York: Columbia University Press, 1993); with Dorothea Olkowski, of *The Theater of Philosophy: Critical Essays on Gilles Deleuze* (New York: Routledge, 1994); and of *Deleuze and Philosophy* (Edinburgh: Edinburgh University Press, 2006); the General Editor of *The Companion to the Twentieth Century Philosophies*, jointly published by Edinburgh and Columbia University Presses in 2007; and of *Deleuze: The Intensive Reduction* (London and New York: Continuum, 2009). He organized four now international conferences on Deleuze and Guattari in Canada and Greece. His translations include Gilles Deleuze's *The Logic of Sense* (New York: Columbia University Press, 1990), Gilles Deleuze's *Empiricism and Subjectivity: An Essay in Human Nature* (New York: Columbia University Press, 1991), and, with Susan Dyrkton, Jean-Clet Martin's *The Philosophy of Deleuze: Variations* (Edinburgh: Edinburgh University Press, 2014). Professor Boundas has published essays on Nietzsche,

Gadamer, Ricoeur, Yannaras, Deleuze and Guattari and he is on the editorial board of *Symposium: Canadian Journal of Continental Philosophy*, of *Angelaki: A Journal of Theoretical Humanities*, and of *The Deleuze Studies*. Rowman and Littlefield Press is in the process of publishing his (and Vana Tentokali's) *Architectural and Urbanist Reflections after Gilles Deleuze and Félix Guattari.*

Flore Garcin-Marrou holds a PhD in French Literature from the Sorbonne, with degrees in Philosophy of Religion (Paris Sorbonne) and Theater Studies (Paris Sorbonne nouvelle). Her PhD dissertation, entitled 'Gilles Deleuze, Félix Guattari, between theater and philosophy', supervised by Prof. Denis Guénoun, attempts to restore to theater its place among the other arts and to study unpublished plays that Guattari himself wrote between 1980 and 1990. Many Deleuzian studies are formulated around the idea of the intersection between Deleuze's work and particular disciplines such as music, literature and cinema, but from which theatre is often absent. Her current research focuses on the relation between contemporary philosophy and contemporary theater, as well as on questions regarding theater history. Director of the acting company *La Spirale ascensionnelle*, she has vocally staged *Ritournelles* by Félix Guattari with the voice of poet Damien Schultz (2011 Mains d' oeuvre, Saint-Ouen). She is now Lecturer in Theater and Visual Studies in the University of Toulouse Jean Jaurès. Her last publication, *Les Scènes philosophiques de la marionette* is about Philosophy and Puppets (L' Entretemps edition, 2016).

Gary Genosko is professor of Communication and Digital Media Studies at University of Ontario Institute of Technology. He has published extensively on Félix Guattari, including co-editing *Machinic Eros: Guattari and Japan* (2015), editing *The Guattari Reader* (1996) and *Deleuze and Guattari: Critical Assessments* (2001). He is the author of *Félix Guattari: A Critical Introduction* (2009), *Félix Guattari: An Aberrant Introduction* (2002) and *The Party without Bosses: Lessons on Anti-Capitalism from Félix Guattari and Luís Inácio 'Lula' da Silva* (2003). In 2012 he edited a special issue of Deleuze Studies on 'Félix Guattari in the Age of Semiocapitalism'. He is co-contributor of the Guattari entries in *The Deleuze and Guattari Dictionary* (2013). His recent articles include studies of post-media theory, post-autonomia politics focused on Bifo Berardi and Anontio Negri; his current project is *Critical Semiotic Theory from Information to A-Signification.*

Andrew Goffey is teaching in the Department of Culture, Film and Media in the University of Nottingham. His research is interdisciplinary, in the grey areas between media, philosophy, science, technology studies and politics. His interests include the role of digital technologies, and more specifically, software in shaping contemporary culture. He has broad expertise in contemporary French philosophy, specifically in the work of Gilles Deleuze, Félix Guattari and Isabelle Stengers. He has written many essays on Guattari, governmentality and health care.

Eric Harper is a psychotherapist, social worker and human rights activist currently working in London with homeless persons presenting with both mental health and addiction concerns. Prior to coming back to London he assisted with the founding of the African Sex Worker Health and Human Rights Alliance. His published work includes articles on therapy and human rights, for example, The Therapist's Relationship to the Unknown. Harper, E. Mantis Publications. *Jungian Journal.* 2013 Torture a presence without Absence. Harper, E. The Symptom Online Journal for Lacan.com. Issue 4, 2003. Horror Unmasked: Truth or Fiction. Buur, L and Harper, E. Published by Human Rights and Human Welfare. Vol. 2, No. 1 2002.

Elizabeth Kouki studied psychology in Paris where she lived and worked as a psychoanalyst. From 1976 to 1982, she worked in the La Borde clinic which was then directed by Jean Oury and Félix Guattari. She was a member of the group of psychoanalysts who supervised the publication of the works of Francoise Dolto and has translated into Greek a number of Dolto's writings. Recently, she translated Guattari's book *From Leros to La Borde* for the Koukida editions.

Jean-Sebastien Laberge is a PhD student in the Ecole d'études politiques of the University of Ottawa. With an initial focus, inside the EuroPhilosophie programme, on the Deleuzian appropriation of Spinoza's metaphysics and interpretation of God's genesis in the first propositions of his Ethics, Laberge's current research bears on the relationship between Spinoza's practical philosophy and the work of Deleuze and Guattari. More specifically, he is interested in the connections that may be established between a Spinozist political ecology and the Guattarian ecosophy, and in the significance these connections may carry for biodiversity and cultural diversity.

Oleg Lebedev is a teaching assistant in philosophy at the Université Catholique de Louvain (Belgium). His research interests have focused so far on cinematic realism (especially among French theoreticians and film critics influenced by

Bazin, such as Daney or Comolli), and on the conceptualization of the link of politics and aesthetics proposed by Jacques Rancière. His current research pertains to the theory of subjectivity and individuation in the philosophy of Deleuze.

Katerina Matsa is a psychiatrist PhD, born in 1947, in Greece. She is the former Director and Scientific Responsible of the Drug and Alcohol Clinic (named 18 Ano) of the State Mental Hospital of Attica (Dafni) (the clinic that F. Guattari visited in 1989, coming back from Leros qualifying it as a 'model clinic'). She participated since 1980 in the Movement for the Deinstitutionalization of Psychiatry, against the barbarism of the psychiatric asylum. She is member of the Committee of Action of the 'Union of Hospital Doctors of Athens and Pireus' (EINAP) and honorary Chair of the 'Federation of Unions of Hospital Doctors of Greece' (OENGE). She works now as psychiatrist in two social centres of the Health Network for Social Solidarity in Greece, in this period of humanitarian crisis. She is an active member of the Polymorphous Movement for Mental Health, fighting for the emancipation of mental patients, in defence of their social rights, and a member of a collectivity of action for social solidarity. Activist in scientific, social, trade union and political fields of action, as a Trotskyist. Since 1984, editor of 'Psychiatric Notebooks', which has played an important role in the construction and development of the Movement for the Deinstitutionalization of Psychiatry in Greece. She has published five books and she has participated in many collective works on mental health and addiction.

Charity N. Mwaniki is an architecture graduate and currently a resident artist at Numbi arts. She has exhibited works at Oxford House in London as part of the Somali Week Festival and at the Art Market in Budapest as part of La Grande Migration. Together with Eric Harper, she published *Multiple Dreams. From Hillman to Deleuze.*

Jean-Claude Polack is a psychiatrist and psychoanalyst. He worked in the La Borde clinic between 1964 and 1976. Together with François Paine and Danielle Sivadon he has produced 'François Tosquelles, une politique de la folie', a film-testimony to the work of the famous Catalan psychiatrist who inspired the creation of institutional psychotherapy. He directed the journal *Chimères*, which was founded in 1987 by Gilles Deleuze and Félix Guattari. His publications include La Mèdecine du Capital, La Borde ou le Droit de la Folie (with Danielle Sivadon-Sabourin, Épreuves de la folie: travail psychanalytic et processus psychotiques, and L' obscur objet du cinéma: réflexion d' un pschanalyste cinéphile).

Anne Querrien is a sociologist and political scientist by education, an activist by practice. She participated with Félix Guattari in the foundation of CERFI (centre d'études, de recherches et de formation institutioonnelles), and in the creation of the journal *Recherches* in 1965. She was co-editor of research and practice journals *Education Permanente* and *Vivre en France*, from 1968 until 1972. Full time in CERFI from 1972 until 1979, she participated in research on collective services, especially school and training activities, and participative urbanism. From 1985 until 2010 she was the editor of the journal *Les Annales de la Recherche urbaine*. Since 2000 she is member of the editorial board of the journal *Multitudes*, of which she is co-editor since 2008. Since 2010 she is also member of the editorial board of the journal *Chimères*, founded by Gilles Deleuze and Félix Guattari in 1986. She has published a lot of papers in all the journals mentioned here, but also in others, related to education, training, urbanism and feminism. She is the author of *L'école mutuelle, une pédagogie trop efficace?, Les empêcheurs de penser en ronde/Editions du Seuil*, Paris, 2004.

Andrej Radman has been teaching design and theory courses at TU Delft Faculty of Architecture since 2004. A graduate of the Zagreb School of Architecture in Croatia, he is a licensed architect and recipient of the Croatian Architects Association Annual Award for Housing Architecture in 2002. Radman received his Master's and Doctoral Degrees from TU Delft and joined Architecture Theory Section as assistant professor in 2008. He is an editor of the peer-reviewed journal for architecture theory *Footprint*.

Charis Raptis has been awarded a PhD in Media Philosophy and Aesthetics by the Panteion University of Athens. He has taught cultural and communication theories in the MA Program in Cultural Management at Panteion University and theory and image in the MA Program in Digital Arts at the Athens School of Fine Arts. He is the author of *Poe, Lacan, Derrida: Connections* (Athens: Smili, 2013 – in Greek). He is a member of the editorial board of the Greek journal for psychoanalysis, philosophy and the arts, αληthεια. His research interests and publications centre on Lacanian psychoanalysis, continental philosophy, media theory and their intersection. He works at the Centre of Psychoanalytic Studies of Athens.

Introduction

Constantin V. Boundas

Ce n'est pas l'inconscient que fait pression sur la conscience, c'est la conscience qui fait pression et garrot, pour l' empêcher de fuir.

Anti-Oedipe

The chapters of this book are intended as an introduction to schizoanalysis and ecosophy, accessible to those who know little about these two registers of theory and practice, but also challenging and informative to those better acquainted with them. Fourteen in number, they are organized in two parts: Part 1 (Querrien, Kouki, Polack, Antonioli, Querrien/Goffey, Laberge, Berressem, Lebedev and Raptis) consists of the testimonies of those who witnessed François Tosquelles, Jean Oury and Félix Guattari in the La Borde clinic and saw their efforts to establish 'institutional psychoanalysis'; it includes answers to the questions 'What is schizoanalysis?' and 'What is ecosophy?'; and, finally, it offers a few engagements with subjects central to schizoanalysis and ecosophy (freedom, the eternity of desiring-machines and the place of Lacan in the discussions on schizoanalysis). Part 2 shows schizoanalysis and ecosophy at work (through Garcin-Marrou's chapter on the ecosophical theatre, Harper/Mwaniki's chapter on the production of an anxiety dream space machine, Genosko's description of the skateboard factory of an alternative school, Matsa's chapter on the experiment of institution 18Up, and Radman's meditations on ecosophical ethics).

This Introduction, in keeping with the book's introductory design, is a quick scanning of the texts of Gilles Deleuze and Félix Guattari, the two main characters of schizoanalysis and ecosophy, and a display, in summary form, of the theoretical claims central to those two. It allows the texts of Deleuze and Guattari to speak for themselves and prevents as much as possible interpretations, that is, the show of mastery from telling the reader what to think and, in the case of an edited collection like this one, from instructing the contributors about what they should have written. Most of the chapters forming this book, in their earliest incarnation, were presented in Athens, at the international conference on '*Gilles Deleuze and Félix Guattari: Refrains of Freedom*', held at the Panteion University from 24 to 26 April 2015. During the selection of the chapters, I allowed two claims, made by two of the contributors, Jean-Claude Polack and Jean Sebastien Laberge, to guide my decisions. I thank them both and I quote them here: 'The ambition of [schizoanalysis and ecosophy] is not to combat or invalidate psychoanalysis', wrote Polack, 'but, on the contrary, to extend its range to the critical understanding of our world ... It is thus both an extension and a process ... a metapsychoanalysis'; and according to Laberge, 'if the question is to understand what Deleuze politics entails ... the answer is to be found in the work of Guattari'.

***

Deleuze and Guattari's *Anti-Oedipe*, the first volume of *Capitalisme et Schizophrénie* (Capitalism and Schizophrenia), was published in 1972; the second volume was issued in 1980, with the subtitle *Mille Plateaux* (A Thousand Plateaus). In these two volumes, the critique of psychoanalysis is no longer revisionist only, as it was still with Marcuse, Ricoeur and Habermas. It is broader and sharper, without being dismissive. Guattari's *Les trois écologies* and *Cartographies schizoanalytiques* were both published in 1989, and, unlike works by Arne Naess and the Deep Ecologists, they were not satisfied with the grounding of ecosophy in the deconstruction of man's alleged supremacy over Nature. As Querrien and Goffey put it, 'Schizoanalysis operates across and challenges the segmentarity of life into the registers of the individual and the collective, the therapeutic and the political, the mental, social and the natural', in a way that psychoanalysis had not dared to do; and ecosophy attempts 'to construct ecological problems as directly philosophical and political issues, as problems that were immediately ethical in nature because lacking any technical or technocratic solution' (infra, 88).

By the time Deleuze and Guattari joined efforts to write *Capitalism and Schizophrenia*, the Freudian dissidence in France was already strong. By the time Guattari came to articulate his ecosophy, ecologies of different stripes were stressing the need for the 'sustainable development' of humans inside a Nature understood as a mere container. Sherry Turkle in her *Psychoanalytic Politics: Freud's French Revolution* (Cambridge, MA: MIT, 1981) gives a detailed reading of the nexus of forces behind the anti-psychiatric and anti-psychoanalytic manifestos of those days. For the French dissidents of that time, she claims, the view of the classical psychiatric theory of madness as a lack of rationality and a decrease of one's power to act and to go as far as she or he could go was the result of the conflation of an idealist theory and a 'voluntarist' therapeutic practice that had to be deconstructed. Throughout his archaeological investigations, Michel Foucault had already argued that Freud demonstrated that the transition from the monarchic and juridical notion of power to the 'liberal' one had already occurred and that our having learnt to police ourselves was the result. And Derrida had already expressed his conviction that the cogito, the kernel of rationality, was a moment of total madness. Robert Castel had undertaken to sketch out the evolution of the institutional psychoanalytic structure from a 'corporative craftsmen's organization to a semi-industrial organization' (Castel 1973: 107). In *Le Psychanalysme* (Paris: F. Maspero 1973: 72), he wrote that all analytic relations carry specific social effects that can never be totally neutral and that the new balance of power relations rests on new instances of control and normalization more supple and effective than those of totalitarian institutions.

In the midst of all this, Lacan's return to Freud, despite, or perhaps because of, its profound ambiguity, made him a central player in the French Freudian dissidence. In his return to Freud and the displacement of the subject, the dissidents found the weapons necessary to avert the domestication of psychoanalysis *à l americain* and the sacrifice of its social content for the sake of psychic healing. Moreover, the good and common sense that has been held for the norm in the language of communication found in Lacan's re-description of the unconscious as language was a powerful contester (Turkle 1981, chap. 8).

It was at that very moment that Deleuze and Guattari's writings began to generate an uproar. Their reassessment of desire praised psychoanalysis for its discovery of the desiring production. But then, rather than being a source of phantasms, as psychoanalysis had it, desire, in Deleuze and Guattari's work, was productive of relations and connections, real in its exploits and revolutionary in its rhizomatic multiplicity. Desire was no longer defined by the intentionality of 'wanting to be or to have'; lacking nothing, desire was now defined by its capacity to work out articulations. It was not measured by the extrinsic *telos* of pleasure, precisely because it is desire itself that distributes the intensities of pleasure and strives to stave off the dissipation of those intensities in extension. Desire atrophies, according to our authors, inside the dialectic of subject and object because, given this dialectic, either a fully constituted subject confronts a fully constituted object, in which case desire can only be a relation external to both, or, if desire were to be thought of as a relation internal to both subject and object, subject and object alike, in their effort to establish reciprocal relationships, will have to suffer from a Sartrean haemorrhage of being. It is not strange, therefore, that, under these circumstances, desire is always downgraded to the need of the 'have nots'. The way to prevent this, Deleuze and Guattari suggested, is to think of desire the way Aristotle thought of *energeia* – and not as *kinesis.* A process without *telos*, intensity without intention, desire (like Aristotle's pleasure) has its 'specific perfection' in itself, at each moment of its duration.

Conscious of his proximity to Spinoza, Deleuze submits that desire is not a passive state of being but rather an act, enhanced by joy, facilitating the formation of adequate ideas and striving towards more and 'better encounters' – in other words, desire is the power to annex Being. The necessary distinction between good and bad annexations – good and bad encounters – has of course to be made, but not according to the measuring rod of transcendent norms. It will be made on the basis of the ability of the fabricated encounters and relationships to increase the power to be of their *relata.* Experimentation, rather than expertise, is required, given that 'there are never any criteria other than the tenor of existence, that is, the intensification of life' (Deleuze and Guattari 1977b).

Now, as far as Deleuze is concerned, *Anti-Oedipus* was not his first encounter with psychoanalysis. The *Logic of Sense,* published in 1968, was. This book displays the traces of Lacan's seminar and, despite signs of anticipation, the anti-Oedipus stage has to wait for the years of Deleuze's collaboration with Guattari. The *Logic of Sense* explores the very archaic and deep-seated psychic infrastructure, populated by all sorts of frightening phantasms, the 'theatre of terror' that Melanie Klein discovered and assigned to the pre-Oedipal stage of children's development.[1] The stage is occupied by part-objects – the breast, the finger, the penis, urine and excrement, whose unpredictable behaviour, precarious availability and perennial oscillation between being good and being bad, lack of identity and sameness, are there for all to see. It is evident that already in the *Logic of Sense* the part-object occupies with respect to the integrated whole the place that, later on, the molecular line of escape will claim as its own, relative to the molar; and that Deleuze's disagreement with Klein, despite his welcoming of the part-object, will rest on Klein's decision to qualify the part-object as 'bad', in view of the good, integrated and self-identical whole. Deleuze will concede that the suffering, pain and anxiety that part-objects cause can be very real, without the presence of the self-accusatory delirium of the adult paranoid. Later on, the *Anti-Oedipus* will deplore that the molecule had to be subsumed under the law of the biggest molar formation of all, that is, the master-signifier. Once this step is taken, the deterritorialized and reterritorialized molecular cathexes will be read as perversions, and desire, far from being joy and affirmation, will come to be interpreted as a fetish.

It is the sidelining of the part-objects for the sake of Oedipus and his magic, integrative powers that seals the centrality of the Oedipus complex. Only in relation to molar formations will the part-objects of the molecular order give the impression that they lack in integrity. Only then desire and lack will be associated, and desire, whether individual or collective, will be endowed with goals and intentions, which were not evident at the molecular level. This insertion of negativity and lack are shadows cast upon individuals as well as upon cultures, social and political organizations, law and religion, morality and its sublimations. Freud's ontogenetic and phylogenetic hypotheses were still centred upon the 'real father'; but with Lacan's parental *imago,* with its super-father content, the complex has been intensified and turned into a real transcendental foundation that must now be deconstructed. Whether as the real father or as the father's *imago*, Oedipus is an enormous machine, a reactionary investment, destined to oppress all desiring machines. What the son has to repress is the unconscious of his mother and father and it is the failure of this repression that accounts for the neurotic. That which psychoanalysis takes to be the resolution of Oedipus is the internalization and the acceptance of the complex, and this is what explains its ubiquity in social fields and its transmission from one generation to the other.

It is not therefore hard to understand why the first target of schizoanalysis is the unconscious, the logic of which has been totally misunderstood by psychoanalysts. According to the latter, the nameless principle – the Id – must acknowledge the name of the Subject – the Ego – in order to find its rightful place inside the symbolic order of the Superego. But, schizoanalysis contends, this requirement misconstructs the interplay of the named and the nameless. It blocks systematically every line of escape, sidesteps the part-objects for the sake of integration, and substitutes, with the help of a gigantic hermeneutic machine, for 'the rhizomatic layout of desire the arborescent growth of subjectivity'. Whether this machine operates metaphorically or whether it operates metonymically, desire is always of the Father whose tolerance for part-objects is notoriously low. As a result, psychoanalysis, as it opts for the substantive, shows its contempt for the world-creating abilities of the subjectless and timeless verbal infinitive.

It is in terms of packs, not of masses, that schizoanalysis attempts to understand the Unconscious (Deleuze and Guattari 1987: 26–38). The pack, unlike the mass, is characterized by the smallness of its size and the restriction of its members, its dispersion, variable but non-decomposable distances, qualitative metamorphoses, inequalities, the impossibility of fixed totalizations and hierarchies and the lines of escape of its particles. It has its own hierarchy, but, with it, the leader risks all the time his leadership, instead of capitalizing on it. Even inside its own territory, the pack arranges itself along lines of escape that are intrinsic to it, unlike the mass that appropriates them in order to segment and block them. The pack is molecular, the mass, molar. But, with Oedipus, this reading of the unconscious is lost (Deleuze and Guattari 1987: 26–38). Instead of the unconscious as factory, psychoanalysis loves the ancient theatre. The productive unconscious is being replaced by an unconscious that can express itself only in myths, tragedies and dreams. However, when conceived like a factory, as a social and political space that must be conquered, the schizoanalytic unconscious turns into a substance that must endlessly be manufactured and made to flow.

It will be a mistake to think that it is the reality of Oedipus that Deleuze and Guattari question. What they refuse to accept is that Oedipus is the product of the unconscious itself, especially when the Oedipal unconscious is thought to operate on exclusive disjunctions: one is either a father or a mother, or a child. For them, Oedipus is not the phantasm that haunts the child; it is the (very real) paranoid obsession that torments the adult. The child does not have to become an adult through the forced recognition of the Father's order. The adult has to become a child, with childhood's blocks, or, in their words, 'with the piece of placenta s/he stole, which is always contemporary with them, a veritable material for experimentation'.

In blocking the lines of flight of desire, psychoanalysis disrupts the arrangement of utterances as well. It traps every single statement in advance. The claim is being made that Lacan changed all that. 'Significance has replaced interpretation, the signifier has replaced the signified....structural functions have replaced parental images, the name of the Father has replaced my daddy' (Deleuze and Parnet 1977: 81). Yet, as long as desire is placed between the 'lack of Being that is life' and the satiation of pleasure, psychoanalysts will always be priests and storytellers of an infinite resignation. Deleuze and Guattari concede that this was not Lacan's original intention; it was he, after all, who discovered, below the structure of the unconscious, the 'a' of the machine and the 'A' of the non-human sex. However, those who followed his steps brought Oedipus back again into Lacan's theory by exploring his own ambivalences: it was, after all, Lacan himself who stretched the signifying chains until they met the despotic Signifier, marked by lack and threatening with castration.

Undoubtedly, there has been a change. After the challenges of the 1960s, psychoanalysis abandoned the discredited family model: Oedipus migrated from the familial triangle to the four corners of society, becoming a universal symbol. And again something changed in the theory itself, the moment that the signifier replaced the signified. Psychoanalysis became *index sui.*

It ceased to be an experimental science in order to establish itself as an axiomatic system. This shift, as Foucault has shown, allowed psychoanalysis, through the discovery of the symbolic order, to institute an abstract machine and to articulate an official language (Deleuze and Parnet 1977: 82–3).

From the point of view of schizoanalysis, psychoanalysis is guilty of three paralogisms. First, it makes something forbidden the object of a previous desire, forgetting thereby that there is desire in the prohibition and the oppression. Second, in moving from part-objects to the complete object – the Phallus – it goes on to constitute the total person, after having assigned lack to it. Third, it pretends that it possesses the means to move directly from repression to the nature of that which is repressed, overlooking the fact that the Law issues prohibitions, in order to persuade its subjects that the nature of their intentions has been culpable all along. This is the most secure way to affect the subject with guilt. Once this is accomplished, it is not the desire of sleeping with the mother that is repressed; it is desire itself. Desire threatens society, not because it is asocial, but rather because it is revolutionary (Deleuze and Guattari 1977, chapt. 2, sections 3, 4 and 5, 80–123).

Desire is not repressed by politics so much as it is coded. It produces the very terms that also enslave it. Interests are themselves stratifications of desire. Rather than having to answer the question, 'how does ideology blind people to their real interests?', Deleuze and Guattari give themselves a different task: The questions, how is it possible for affirmative desire to be so often discussed in forms of negation and lack? How is it possible for the desiring machines to want their own abolition? – these questions are now rewritten: How do interests (the products of desire) move against desiring production? It is by borrowing a page from Kant's *Critique of Pure Reason* that Deleuze and Guattari answer this question: They introduce three syntheses, that is, three social and individual processes by means of which desire succeeds in connecting experiences and social formations together. They call them, connective synthesis of production, disjunctive synthesis of recording and conjunctive synthesis of consumption (Deleuze and Guattari 1977, chap. 1, sections 1–3; chap. 2, sections 3–5; and section 6).

In the context of a social ontology that is grounded solidly on relations, the connective synthesis makes multiple, heterogeneous and continual connections of part-objects, not of whole persons or organs. The conjunctions, and … and … and, characterize this style of connectivity and the risk that this process runs is clinical delirium and schizophrenia. The disjunctive synthesis of recording hinges on Deleuze's metaphysics of difference – Being is Difference (differentiation of the virtual and differenciation for the actualization of the virtual). This synthesis is the answer to the (transcendental) question – how is it possible to interrupt the connections (associations) that have been made that could threaten us with a habitual and mechanical repetition, in order for new connections to arise? The answer lies with the disjunctive synthesis upon the recording surface of the 'body without organs', it being understood that this body does not pre-exist the connections and the networks of relations that constitute it.[2] An anti-productive force of repulsion of part-objects/organs freezes (puts out of play) the connections already made for different connections to become possible. What registers on the body without organs are signs of connections that enable us to repeat previous modes of desiring satisfaction, albeit with greater or lesser degrees of variation in repetition. This is how Holland explains it:

> The interplay of desiring production and anti-production generates alternating rhythms of attraction and repulsion between the organs and the body without organs. What is essential is that even while anti-production interrupts productive connections, it at the same time registers their diverse possibilities and ends up multiplying their relations in an open-ended series: either … or … or. (as in inclusive disjunctions)

The organization of social production depends on anti-production. It is in Bataille's notion of expenditure that 'anti-production' finds its origins, that is, in the claim that social organization is always based on the expenditure of excess. Deleuze and Guattari, as a result, will lean on this characterization to repeat that desire has no need of lack as its presupposition. It is anti-production that precludes the appropriation of the fruits of production and opts for deferral. Assigning such a central role to anti-production does not imply the devaluation of the forces of production; it implies that they are given their purpose by the forces of anti-production. Instead of basing their economic theory on exchange, Deleuze and Guattari will choose debt and gift (the Nietzschean influence is evident in this). Debt is owed to a creditor who is in control of the processes of anti-productive distribution and consumption of the excess. We deal with a gift when something in it (or of it) cannot be 'paid back' by means of reciprocation.

'Debt is the name under which relations of social obligation are enforced by anti-production' (Holland). The external limit and the danger of the anti-productive processes is catatonia – the elimination of all connections.

In my discussion of the three syntheses, the schizoanalytic message that all three are present in the psychophysical life of the individual as well as in the life and work of social formations was implicit. It is time to make it explicit. Schizoanalysis does not recognize desiring machines outside the social machines nor does it recognize social machines without the desiring machines that inhabit them. The first thesis of schizoanalysis is therefore this: all desiring investments are social and necessarily related to a historical field. Now, the claim that the individual and the social productions of desire, along with their pathogenies, run parallel to each other is embedded in a longer narrative that gives the schizoanalytic claim its credibility. The narrative makes clear that the captivity of desire called 'Oedipus' has a long genealogy – the genealogy of a contingent, singular and critical universal history: contingent, because its course is the result of totally accidental encounters; singular, because the universality of the West's line of development is singularly different from other lines of development; and critical, because it is written, not from the point of view of the smooth functioning of capitalism, but rather from the perspective of the conditions of its transcendence.

Every social formation has a premonition of the absolute limit that can dissolve it and makes every effort possible to keep it away. The absolute limit that haunts every social formation is the decoded flow of desire that no code can contain and control. Every social formation lives the spectre of the absolute limit both as something that may happen to it and as something that has happened *in illo tempore*. Their endless struggle to distance themselves from this limit has the paradoxical result of planting the limit in their middle. Oedipus is the name of the displaced limit, and in this sense Oedipus is universal (Deleuze and Guattari 1977: 266f). The explanation and defence of bringing to the centre the very thing that one tries to escape is offered by Deleuze and Guattari in their discussion of three basic social configurations: The primitive territorial machine, which inscribes literally codes on the body of the individuals that make it up; the Despotic State, which overcodes what the territorial machine has already coded, referring everything to the immobile motor of the despot; and the Capitalist axiomatic, which is the product of a generalized decoding of all fluxes and of the process of their artificial reterritorialization, underwritten by an abstract axiomatic machine. Here, political economy and the production of the commodity turn into libidinal economy and the production of desire.

In the case of the primitive territorial machine, everything must circulate. Desire should not be allowed to have immediate access to its object. Whatever one produces belongs to the system of anti-production. The incest taboo is governed and explained by the imperative to circulate. In the Despotic State, everything is owned by the despot who imposes an infinite and unpayable debt upon his subjects. He is the castrating Oedipus, but this Oedipus has not yet been internalized by everybody and turned into a 'complex'. Finally, capitalism emerges with two defining characteristics: Constant coding, decoding and recoding aided by a set of axioms that quantify over entities that are qualitatively different and a system of anti-production operating through the market. The constant coding, decoding, recoding of this system is responsible for the double bind and the schizophrenia endemic in it. Family falls prey to the decoding of capitalism since Capital does not tolerate any competitors and becomes privatized. But this privatization is precisely what gives family the social centrality which it has in the capitalist machine. The boss, the manager, the worker, the banker are social persons; but the privatized individuals of the capitalist family are only 'daddy', 'mommy' and I. The social centrality of this impotent family is to reproduce the relations which are reflected in it.

In order to avoid the reading of these formations according to an evolutionist schema, incapable of accounting for the transitions from one formation to the other, Deleuze and Guattari introduce the *Urstaat* hypothesis (Deleuze and Guattari 1977: 217–22). The State exists always already in relation to an Outside and cannot be conceived apart from this relationship. The Outside can be either world machines colonizing the entire space and relatively independent from the State or bands, packs, nomads and minorities that defend their rights to stay segmentarized against the wishes and the pressures of the State apparatus.

Desire's social investments occur in a continuum whose poles are paranoia and schizophrenia. Paranoia is the investment of desire, the molar structures of which dominate and fuse together molecular multiplicities. In schizophrenia, on the other hand, the molecular flows make the molar formations run away, as they themselves run away. Paranoia is the investment of a subjected group; schizophrenia is the investment of a group that is itself the subject. It is upon the surface of the body without organs that the investments of paranoia and schizophrenia take place, but we should not take the body without organs as the substrate of society[3]. Rather, the body without organs is constituted and transformed together with the contingent investments of desire. It is best to think of it as the limit of society, that is, as the limit that haunts all social formations.

Given the nature of the desiring machines and the interaction of the molar and molecular instances, the lines of escape that define every individual and every group can either escape schizophrenically and generate a revolutionary investment of desire or flee the way the paranoiac does and activate all kinds of conformist and fascist investments. The difference between the schizophrenic as a clinical entity and the schizophrenic as a revolutionary subject is that the former runs away, whereas the latter knows how to make that which runs away run away. The difference is between schizophrenia as an entity and schizophrenia as a process.

Schizophrenia – the total decoding of flows – proceeds on the basis of inclusive disjunctions: either, or and both at once. It seems to be the state of desiring machines characterized by the paradoxical simultaneity of fission and fusion. The territorial machine wards off both fission and fusion by playing the one against the other. It recognizes in fission its greatest enemy because it understands dispersion and difference to be the total abolition of the power of its codes. On the other hand it also strives to prevent the fusion and the indifference of inclusive disjunctions, knowing that they would also make inevitable the decoding of the flows of desire. This is why the primitive formations prevent the consolidation of power in the hands of the chiefs, maintaining the latter in a relation of powerlessness over the people. They are not societies without the State, in the sense that they have not yet reached a certain stage in their development. They are societies against the State, in the sense that they try to prevent the kind of fusion that makes the State inevitable. In their case, Oedipus is not running the territorial machine. The conditions for the familial complex called 'Oedipus' are not yet ripe. If, as the Jungians will claim, the incest with the mother that Oedipus tries hard to avert and yet anticipates is the incest with the mother earth and the desire for being reborn from the depths of the earth; the primitive societies repress this desire because they sense that the depths of the earth, not being an extensive and differentiated system, cannot be coded. The absence of the repression of this desire would stand for the generalized decoding of all flows and an absolute deterritorialization.

In the territorial and despotic machines, social economic reproduction is closely related to human reproduction. But the capitalist formation does not revolve around the desiring of a distinct object (earth or despot). It rather aims at the productive process itself. The result is the privatization of families which become unable to give their own form to economic reproduction. But this privatization of the family is precisely what gives family the social centrality that it has in the capitalist machine. Private persons are mere simulacra and only as such acquire the ability to represent the macrocosm of social persons. The boss, the manager and the worker are social persons, but the privatized individuals are only 'daddy', 'mommy' and I. The father represents the despotic sign, the mother assumes a residual territoriality, and the child expresses the sign of impotence and castration. The family closes upon itself, representing and expressing a process over which it is powerless. Its function is to reproduce the relations of production that are reflected in it. The full-fledged Oedipus is here, albeit as the result of prior social investments and not as the cause of anything. The child suffering from Oedipus suffers actually from a social disease. Desire, being expansive and revolutionary, is artificially reterritorialized on the displaced limit and is blocked there.

To sum up: To attract and to avert-part objects allowing them to function is the *raison d' être* of the social machines, with their transformations being the outcome of the radical contingency of encounters and supervening conditions. This is why Oedipus, despite his universality, is not astride on every social formation. In order for his empty space to be filled, a number of conditions must first be realized. And only in the capitalist social formation are all requirements fulfilled and, only in it does Oedipus colonize the space that the other formations were only anticipating and averting.

What is then to be done? Is there, inside social formations, a desire that can ward off the power of codes, overcodes and axiomatic systems? Deleuze and Guattari believe that there is one, and they choose to call it 'nomadic' (Deleuze and Guattari 1987: 351–423). Do we have here the remnants of the Marxist reading of the State in the hands of the ruling class for the sake of its own interests? Are the sedentaries (*alias* the majority or the majoritarians) the State or the State apparatus or the State form? Are the nomads the multitudes or the packs or the minorities whose desires do not coincide with the interests of the State? Should we be able to discern in this narrative the reading of the State and the State apparatus according to Althusser and his 'Ideology and Ideological State-Apparatuses' (*Lenin and Philosophy and Other Essays*)? Would the ruling ideology harmonize the State Repressive Apparatus and the Ideological State Apparatus by interpellating individuals and turning them into subjects? The thing though is that the Deleuzoguattarian nomads do not wish to become the State or to take over the State apparatus, but rather to destroy it or to escape it. To be sure, Deleuze and Guattari agree that the State is an apparatus of 'capture'. Nevertheless, they reject all appeals to ideology because ideology has to assume that there are real interests that are concealed of the individual who awaits liberation from the imposed illusions of culture. And the alleged antagonism of classes does not hold the key to universal history. Which does not mean that schizoanalysis denies the existence of dominant classes. But to read universal history from the perspective of the class struggle is to read it from the point of view of the bourgeoisie which thinks of itself as the one universal decoding and decoded class. For Deleuze and Guattari, the real opposition is between one class and those who are outside class, that is, between capitalists and schizophrenics.

As I said already, rather than appealing to an ideological blindness responsible for people's love of their chains, schizoanalysis maintains that, inside the social investments, the unconscious libidinal investment, whether of an individual or of a group, may be different from the preconscious investments of class and interest. Naturally, our interests predispose us to invest libidinally in certain part-objects; and our libidinal or molecular investments direct our goals and interests, our molar preferences. It is nevertheless the lack of coincidence between the two investments that accounts for the case of oppressed individuals or groups loving their chains. The concept of ideology explains nothing. It is rather a question of a non-revolutionary molecular investment (Deleuze and Guattari 1977: 104–5).

We can, at this point, return to the question we raised above: What is to be done? We ask, how can we escape the capturing tendencies of the State that fence us in and suffocate us? And schizoanalysis replies: By taking the line of escape of the nomad and the masochist. The course and the direction of this line is best understood, as François Zourabichvili argued, by taking into account the simultaneous presence in the work of Deleuze and Guattari of two attitudes – subversion and perversion.[4] Their subversive tendencies tend to cluster around the concepts minority/majority and nomad/sedentary, developed in *A Thousand Plateaus* in an attempt to rally together those in a position to stand against the State's capturing forces. Although the tactical significance of nomadism brings to mind guerrilla warfare, their quest for nomadic tendencies is broader than it initially appears. It involves minor, transformative forces (of life, politics, thought, artistic creation) capable of escaping the sedentarity and stratification so dear to majorities. 'Sedentaries' are the State or the State apparatus or, rather, the State form. 'Nomads' are those whose investments of desire do not coincide with the interests of the State. The nomads do not want to become the State or to take over the State apparatus – not even temporarily. Rather, they strive to dismantle it or to escape it. 'Nomadic' are called the minority forces – better still, the minor tendencies – that are also designated as the 'noumena of history', because they belong to the events of virtual becoming, rather than to the states of affairs of actual history. Nomadic sciences deal with material and forces, rather than the matter and form of the hierarchical and hylomorphic sedentary sciences. The singular, not the universal or the essence, is their objective. Deleuze and Guattari hypothesize that nomads (or nomadic tendencies) have the ability to ward off the encroaching forces of the sedentaries. In fact, they recognize them as the inventors of the *war machine* that is required to 'make the steppe grow' and to trace the lines of escape of their nomadic trajectory. The State, they say, wages war in order to conserve its integrative power; the Nomad wages war because her lines of escape are blocked and her deterritorialization, prevented. When all is said and done, the nomad is the one who tries to prevent the social sedimentation of desire from blocking the connective process of the production of desire. Nomadic lines of escape are lines of subversion and transformation of the well-organized and smoothly functioning institutions of the sedentaries.

But there is another side to Deleuze and Guattari's take on the political – a take that Zourabichvili qualified as 'perverse' (Alliez 1998: 357). With respect to Deleuze and Guattari's subversive tendencies, the emancipatory interest manifests itself in the question 'how best to escape', without being deprived of weapons or of the artifices needed on the line of deterritorialization. The question of the best means available for escaping, in turn, leads to Deleuze's 'perversion'. Perversion finds its theoretical support in Deleuze's discussion of sadism and masochism and his repudiation of the conventional wisdom that sees in masochism the mere inversion of sadism. The sadist, argues Deleuze, is still steeped in the language of the law; his feat is that, in opposing the deduction of the law from an alleged principle of the good, he chooses to subvert the old law ironically by maintaining its form, while, at the same time, replacing its content with precepts deduced from a principle of evil. *A contrario*, for Deleuze, the true bearer of the emancipatory interest is the masochist, for she or he chooses to pervert the law by submitting to it humorously in order to savour the pleasures that the law prohibits and punishes.[5]

Despite all the reservations that schizoanalysts harbour towards actual democracies, their option for the becoming-democratic, inscribed in the politics of a universal brotherhood *à venir*, is unmistakable. In Deleuze's story, the people (to whom the schizoanalyst appeals) are missing; a 'new people and a new earth *à venir*' gives Deleuze and Guattari's political posture 'a purposefulness without purpose' – provided, that is, that the clarion call for a new people and a new earth is not heard as a teleological anticipation with messianic aspirations.

Schizoanalysis did not designate or name the people to come or the new earth. It does say, though, that the new 'race' exists only as an oppressed race. It will always be inferior and minoritarian, never to be defined by its purity, but rather by the impurity conferred upon it by a system of domination.

In my view, the ecosophical agenda of Guattari finds its best fit here because as Laberge claims in his chapter of this book, the nomadism of schizoanalysis finds in the theoretical and tactical programme of ecosophy its concretization and its completion. With Guattari's ecosophy the issue is no longer how to manage better than before our old needs but, rather, the search for new ways of living, new modes of subjectivity and new geopolitical relations. Ecosophy is more than a concern for the environment, it is an ontological and epistemological system characterized by feedback loops and non-linear causality. For the articulation of this ecosophy, Guattari will appeal to a politico-aesthetic paradigm where 'aesthetic' will come to designate the artful exploration of new possibilities, and the continuous reinvention of our lives in the spirit of resistance, which, for him, is the defining characteristic of the art. This politico-aesthetic paradigm will scrutinize traditional notions of selfhood, the proliferation of global capitalism, and the expansion of digital media and will stimulate the articulation of an ontology in line with ecological concerns.

However, the experimentation for the sake of new modes of living requires the knowledge of who one is, of the existential territory he or she occupies and the availability of machines for the desired transformation. Every project requires the invention of a specific apparatus, suitable to the collective assemblage that will put it to work. Guattari's cartographies of desire or what Hanjo Berressem in this book calls 'Guattari's fourfold' is the ecosophical response to this requirement. This is what Querrien and Goffey, in their chapter, have to say about this response:

> [Guattari's] ambition was to give everyone the means to orient themselves in the trajectories of their lives, to enable others to get a vision of this to facilitate a collective apprenticeship to the transformation of existing social coordinates. Guattari … felt the need for a method of visualisation, one that would allow for grasping of the history of the world in all its dimensions (infra).

To the extent that, as Gary Genosko, writes 'subjectivity is a group phenomenon' and the subject is the residue of the social machinery in which he or she participates, everyone needs to know *the flows* that individuate him or her, and the *existential territory to which they* belong. But in order to be able to modify it, the learning of *political theories, ideologies, practices and disciplinary references,* along with the invention of *new machines,* is required. Without the coordination of 'Guattari's fourfold', the extension of the potentialities made available will not be possible.[6]

It follows that when we refer to Guattari's ecosophic proposal, it is a mistake to think of ecology in the singular. Ecosophy requires the cross-fertilization and the criss-crossing of many ecologies. 'Transversality', says it best; mental ecology **and** the ecology of the media **and** the ecology of urban practices **and** the ecology of nature for the sake of the discovery of existential territories and common spaces. The desideratum of this transversality, its political implications, according to Laberge (see below), of the Deleuzian heterogenesis, is a dissensual democracy, a crowned anarchy – 'a Federalism understood as the politics of multiplicities'. It is not a consensual democracy that this Federalism envisages; it is dissensual because dissensus is essentially 'a call for the revival of individual competence as a social force – an unpredictable and untamed criss-crossing of dissident subjectivities, with no leader directing their activity' (Laberge). Pluralism and multiculturalism are often grounded in the tolerance for the other's point of view, but dissensual democracy is grounded in the conviction that the other's point of view enriches my own.

Notes

1 Melanie Klein, *La Psychanalyse des enfants* (Paris: Presses Universitaires de France, 1932). See Gilles Deleuze, *The Logic of Sense* (New York: Columbia University Press, 1990), 187–9.

2 Eugene Holland, *Deleuze and Guattari's Anti-Oedipus, Introduction to Schizoanalysis* (New York: Routledge, 1999).

3 See Gilles Deleuze, *Masochism: an Interpretation of Coldness and Cruelty* (New York: G. Braziller, 1971).

4 Francois Zourabishvili, 'Deleuze et le possible (de l' involontarisme en politique)', in *Gilles Deleuze, Une Vie politique*, ed. Eric Alliez (Le Plessis-Robinson: Les Empecheurs de Penser en Rond, 1998), 335–57.

5 See Note iii and note iv.

6 (See John Tinnell, 'FCJ-121 Transversalising the Ecological Turn: Four Components of Félix Guattari's Ecosophical Perspective' http??eighteenfibreculturejournal.org/2011/10/09/fcj-121- transversalis (accessed 4 June 2017).

References

Eric Alliez (1998), *Gilles Deleuze, Une Vie Philosophique*. Le Plessis-Robinson: Less Empecheurs de Penser en Ronde.

Gilles Deleuze (1971), *Masochism: an Interpretation of Coldness and Cruelty* (New York: G. Braziller).

Gilles Deleuze (1990), *The Logic of Sense*. Translated by Mark Lester and Charles Stivale. Ed, Constantin V. Boundas New York: Columbia University Press.

Gilles Deleuze, and Félix Guattari (1977), *Anti-Oedipus: Capitalism and Schizophrenia*. New York: The Viking Press.

Gilles Deleuze, and Félix Guattari (1987), *A Thousand Plateaus. Capitalism and Schizophrenia*. Minneapolis: Minnesota University Press.

Gilles Deleuze and Claire Parnet (1987), *Dialogues*. Translated by Hugh Tomlinson and Barbara Habberjam (New York: Columbia University Press).

Guattari, Félix (2000), *The Three Ecologies*. Translated by Ian Pindar and Paul Sutton. London: The Athlone Press.

Guattari, Félix (2013), *Schizoanalytic Cartographies*. Translated by Andrew Goffey. London: Bloomsbury.

Eugene, W. Holland (1999), *Deleuze and Guattari's Anti-Oedipus: Introduction to Schizoanalysis Anti-Oedipus*. New York: Routledge.

Melanie Klein (1932), *La Psychanalyse des enfants*. Paris: Presses Universitaires de France.

Part One

1

An Interview with Constantin V. Boundas*

Anne Querrien

CVB: Anne Querrien, you have been witness to the early days of schizoanalysis, to the role that Félix Guattari played in the La Borde clinic, you have been a participant in the new enlightenment of the 1960s and a champion of the need for a new schooling and a new revolutionary pedagogy. Could you talk a little about yourself, the lines of escape that brought you to your dissident form of Marxism, to the institutional researches, to Guattari and to the revolutionary pedagogical movement?

AQ: I met Félix Guattari in 1965. He was leading a group of dissident activists of the communist party called *La Voie Communiste*. The group came together during the war of Algeria in order to offer support to the Algerian revolutionaries and to go beyond the refusal to participate in the war (desertion, insubordination), which was then the standard position of the militants of the Left. The Algerian War was over in 1962, and the new powers in Algeria had no need for the advice of the French militants of the extreme Left. The struggle within the group of *La Voie Communiste* was very violent between those who thought the revolution in France an impossibility and those who, like Félix Guattari, thought it possible, but on condition that it be built upon new and different foundations. Being much younger than the militants of *La Voie Communiste* (fifteen years younger than Félix Guattari, and three years younger than the youngest members of it), I had followed from some distance the struggle against the war of Algeria, but my desire to revolutionize the social relationships was grounded in my participation in the student syndicalism, where the cleavage present in *La Voie Communiste* was equally visible. For many, the role of the communist militants was to control the bureaucracy of the syndicate and eventually to draw personal advantages for the sake of their social mobility. I was of the opinion that the union, in organizing the student body, should aim at opening the university to all, to give up its meritocracy and to participate in the transformation of society. I was one of the few women to be accepted into the ranks of the Parisian and national leadership of the syndicate. I was a student in the Institute of Political Studies, the attendants of which were, generally speaking, moderate, but I shared the more leftist ideas of the students of the other schools. I was coming from a family of high public servants and I had the means to study and also to be involved in the work of the union. Very soon I was promoted to president of the Parisian section of the National Care Organisation of French Students (MNEF), and later on, vice-president of the national office, with responsibilities over mental health and family planning. At the same time with my bureaucratic ascension, I began to attend the meetings of Félix group, the members of which were student-comrades of the Communist Union of Political Sciences, the Economic Sciences and the Faculty of Law. The problems of the mental health of students were considered to be both collective and individual and the UNEF (National Union of French Students) activists agreed to deal with them within the framework of institutional psychotherapy. On the other hand, only the group surrounding Félix was ready to extend over as many social fields as possible the professional and political presence initiated in the La Borde clinic and the psychiatric hospital of Saint Alban. The claim that it is the institution that must be cured first and not the deviant behaviours was inadmissible to militants who were anxious to distinguish themselves from the insane and the bad apples. To endlessly undertake the transformation of institutions in order to render them functioning and welcoming to everybody was considered to be an error in judgement in all places of meritocracy, including those on the Left.

My sliding from my family's left-wing Christianity to Félix's *La Voie Communiste* took place slowly. In the last class of my lycée, shocked by the death of eight communist militants, killed by the police during a demonstration for peace in Algeria, I joined the anti-fascist committee of my school. Afterwards, during the first year of my undergraduate studies, I decided to participate in the discussions of the circle of the union of communist students. But syndicalism was rather what attracted me, ever since I had been told that my grandfather had granted customs officers and eventually civil servants the right to form syndicates, having suggested that his colleagues work to rule, and as a result bringing about a considerable bottleneck effect on the nation's borders. Members of my family were friends of the Dominicans who supported theologically the worker-priests. My father often quoted Marx and Lenin, even Stalin, in a rather humorous way. When I was fourteen, I began to borrow these authors from his library and became acquainted with them on my own. Reading the *Communist Manifesto*, I chose to study sociology, with the plan to adapt Marx to our times – a plan which was given the blessings of my parents' Dominican friends. My Marxism was therefore dissident from the very start and ready to join that of Félix. My parents were following my peregrinations closely. Fifty years have gone by and my father still publicly affirms that his method of thinking is schizoanalytic, meaning a revised Marxism where the opposition of contraries goes on ad infinitum without a third power ever presiding over the conflict. I was then ready by my early training to meet Félix and to participate in his endless struggle against the established order.

I was introduced to him in 1965 as someone capable of composing the text he needed for his break away from *La Voie Communiste*. The activists to whom he was opposed used to think that only the working class, in the original sense of the term, was entitled to be revolutionary and that, given its integration into the society of consumption in France and the other Western societies, the only thing left was to trail behind the big Soviet brother and to obey his orders. Given the brief experience of La Borde and the institutionalist movement of psychiatry, Félix was proposing a very different hypothesis and was trying to organize all those who were visiting La Borde, looking for different perspectives. This is how the break from *La Voie Communiste* took place to give birth to the *Fédération des groupes d'études et de recherches institutionnelles* (Federation of Groups of Studies and Institutional Researches (FGERI)). The simple idea behind this federation was that in every domain where intellectual labour is deployed – and the labour of the manual worker is also intellectual labour – the workers encountered forces that Félix called forces of anti-production, that is, social forces that prevented them from reaching the best possible realization of whatever it was they planned to do. Exploitation showed itself in the practices of throwing obstacles in the way, of putting on the brakes and of repression, even during the course of productive activities, in an attempt by the dominant society to manage everybody's time and to prevent them from enjoying the freedom of enjoying a variety of things. For example, innovative pedagogical ways proved that only half the obligatory hours of schooling were necessary for teaching the things we do and that, paradoxically, 'putting on the brakes' blocked learning. The same situation prevailed in the factory and the office and the neurotic or psychotic collapses testified to the omnipresence of this realm of anti-production. In this way, bringing thematically working groups to bear on other blocked professional practices, we would come to imagine avenues of transformation, we could take care of institutions and, by transversally exposing working groups to the issues of different thematics, we would be further ahead with their elaboration. The journal *Recherches,* issued after the *Cahiers de la FGERI*, published the texts produced by these working groups.

Our space was diverse; it included a dissident workers' group of the communist cell of Hispano-Suiza – a factory that made airplane engines in La Garenne-Colombes. La Garenne-Colombes was the commune where Félix spent his childhood and where he had made solid friendships. There was also a group of school teachers led by Fernand Oury, the older brother of Jean Oury, the founder of La Borde. Fernand Oury was a disciple of the progressive pedagogy of Célestin Freinet, but he disagreed with the ruralism of those who were now applying it, and wanted to create an institutional pedagogy for the suburbs. I was interested in this group, despite the fact that I did not have an adequate professional practice that would allow me to become a member. However, my association with its members prompted me to make the school an object of study and to raise the question of anti-production in schools that use the strong students to persecute the poor ones, instead of mobilizing them to assure that the poor ones learn too. There were also architects among us, whose profession was very much contested in those days. There were film makers, physicians and one group called Grobofega (Groupe of Left-wing women) who supported militant women in their struggle for the rights to contraception and abortion, and monitored the global diversity of practices in this domain. FGERI was a kind of cultural porridge, not explicitly revolutionary, in the sense of a communist, Trostkyite or Maoist organization. It was rather a point of reference that in March '68 welcomed the movement of March the 22nd, and allowed it to start again, past 8 May – the day that the 'serious' organizations wanted to put an end to it.

CVB: For a quick characterization of Guattari's life projects, a reference to Marxism and to 'institutional research' will do for starters. We should perhaps focus on his Marxist choices first. Unlike Deleuze, Guattari had roots in some forms of the Marxist praxis long before the explosion of the 1960s. Would you like to offer us your understanding of these choices as they were made in the context of the struggles of the Left of those days?

AQ: I came to know Félix Guattari in 1965, when he was thirty-five years old, and I have never tried to learn things about his past in any detail. His affiliation with the movement of the youth hostels impressed me because in the 1960s these were still meeting places for the young, allowing us to carry on with our endless discussions in a situation where boys and girls could mingle. The girls, in student unions, were few and easily reduced to silence. I knew that he was associated with the Communist Party early on, despite the fact that his lower middle-class social origins should have kept him away. I knew that he had been shocked by how the Communist Party treated the directors of Tourism and Labor and Labor and Culture with whom he was acquainted.

His Marxist and Trotskyite readings formed his criticisms of the Stalinism, the Communist Party and its inefficient involvement on behalf of the Algerians. His texts for *La Voie Communiste* were published under the pseudonym Claude Arrieux. His precocious love of philosophy was visible in the collection of books that decorated his desk, although, my memory tells me, his pharmaceutical studies were noticed much more than the beginnings of his philosophy *license*. He was a member of the Sorbonne cell of the Communist Party where he became acquainted with his anthropologist friends. His in-depth reading of Sartre seems to precede his reading of Marxist texts; with respect to the latter, he never assumed the posture of submission to the master that characterized the members of the Althusserian school. The texts were no more than background material, quotations were used during presentations as a useful backup, never in the form of commentaries or textual exegesis. Their reading was free. Félix poured over the different Trotskyite currents that weighed on various forms of support brought to the Algerian struggle. He discussed the tactics that must be pursued against the background of the Communist Party's stagnation due to the Stalinist doctrine of the revolution as the affair of one country only and especially against the background of the unforgiving politics of the total exclusion of the non-submissive militants. The readings of Marx, Lenin and Mao were, in this case, the support of local tactical choices: the more one was capable of drawing out of them an incontestably strong argumentation, the more they were considered worthy of approval. Guattari never made himself the flagbearer of any orthodoxy. His own brand of militantism, theoretical and practical, was forged in 1945 and the years after within the movement of youth hostels and under the guidance of his teacher, Fernand Oury.

Fernand Oury was a follower of Freinet's method, a method that helps students acquire knowledge, under the supervision of a teacher. In this movement Félix befriended the brother of Fernand Oury, Jean, who had just begun his studies in medicine and was an anarchist sympathizer. A few years later, Jean became a psychiatrist in the Loir and Cher where he established the La Borde clinic in order to avoid restrictions of the budget and the imagination. Jean did his internship in the Saint Alban hospital in the south of France with a Spaniard anarcho-communist psychiatrist, François Tosquelles. Tosquelles, with the help of patients, physically brought down the walls of the asylum and transformed the psychiatric institution into a place of life, with a self-managed club for the inmates and their associates, who also managed the place with the help of the medical and administrative hierarchy. The institution was turned into a curing place, facilitating the comings and goings of patients from and to the world beyond its walls. The expression 'institutional psychotherapy' will be invented in order to designate this new practice whereupon the institution itself must be cared for in order to be enabled to heal its patients. This psychiatric practice requires a special attention to the way the local community functions and an exposure to events of the world which could be linked with the lives of the patients. In La Borde, Jean Oury undertook the management of the local psychiatric community and entrusted his friend, Félix Guattari, who had by this point joined him, with the care of this connection to the world outside. The link with the outside took on the form of the communist activism of the party and its adjacent organizations, even when these organizations had a different orientation. The connection nevertheless was built in accordance with the general psychoanalytic thought of the day, but mainly in accordance with the seminars of Lacan. It was carried out by means of many special experiments, both in the arts and in the human sciences.

In the midst of a variety of practical and intellectual experiments, Félix Guattari developed a special affinity for the synthesis and the constitution of a collective environment with a limited hierarchy and with loose rules of association – together with Gilles Deleuze, they would refer to it later on as *rhizome*. Guattari, as early as 1965, named it FGERI. He repeated thereby on a grand scale the *Fédération des groupes d'études de lettres* that dominated the Left of the National Union of Students in France. Guattari's journal, which started in 1951, is kept together with his archives in the *Institut pour la mémoire de l' Édition contemporaine* (IMEC) in the Abbey of Ardennes in Normandy. It refers to the militant activities of the Trotskyite revolutionary youth movement, and especially the psychoanalytic and psychiatric readings that his friend Jean Oury had recommended. Félix seemed to have assimilated Marxism earlier, from 1945 to 1950, in other words, when he was between fifteen and twenty years of age, as was typical with all the French revolutionaries at that time. Lenin's writings occupy a privileged place because he had instituted the revolution, discerned the reactionary nature of the State and denounced imperialism against which the young militants were fighting in their effort to support the Vietnamese and the Algerian revolutionaries. Guattari's writings in *La Voie Communiste* do not always quote Marx's texts, the way the Althusserians would do later. Arrieux, alias Félix Guattari, is a merciless record-keeper of the errors made by the French Communist Party and the party of the Soviets.

CVB: In 1960, Jean Oury in bringing together a group of psychiatrists creates the *Groupe de Travail de psychologie et de sociologie institutionnelles* (GTPSI). Félix Guattari joins the group the following year. What was the purpose and the function of that group? How does the qualifier 'institutionnelles' guide the group discussions and work? How does the Sartrean 'we-subject' influence the members of the group to think about a '*groupe-sujet*'? Is the inevitability of Sartre's alternation between we-subject and us-object prevented in favour of the auto-valorization of the subject? Could you discuss at some length Guattari's role in the '*recherches institutionnelles*'?

AQ: In 1960, the ideas that the institutional psychotherapy was defending since 1945 became official ideas for the World Health Organization. The WHO declared that mental health patients should no longer be incarcerated in hospitals or have to remain there until their death because the conjunction of medications and psychoanalysis has made their care possible in a more natural environment – a place to which they should return after short periods of hospitalization following a crisis. This new stance was a formidable opportunity for institutional psychotherapy which until that time was very much in the minority. But it also went against the actions and the traditional beliefs of those convinced of the virtues of the separation of mental health patients from their familial and social context. On the other hand, there was a great risk – and this risk was later on proven to be real – to see the medical and behavioural care win the day for the sake of avoiding hospitalization and achieving the greatest economy possible. Under this mode of caring, the submissiveness of the patient and the following of orders are the only things aimed at so that the patients are not given the possibility to trace their line of desire freely. The few psychiatrists adhering to institutional psychotherapy had to stick together to preserve the theoretical elaboration and the practical reflection that sustained their work. The GTPSI was at the time understood as a discussion group: each one was to bring his or her own thoughts and questions on a topic that had been decided beforehand or had sprung up along the way.

The fundamental rule of the GTPSI was to discuss at length every single problem raised during the practices (*ne pas s'en laisser passer une*). Tosquelles's talk, his accent, his wordplays and his Catalan French, cemented this group, which turned out to be a professional brotherhood of sorts, despite the divergence of points of view, the responsibility for which was created by the difference in the points of origin of its members. The GTPSI met between 1960 and 1966 fourteen times. All sessions were transformed through notes, recordings and transcripts, made by Brivette Buchanan, who worked with Jean Oury in La Borde. The *Editions D'Une* in Paris are now in the process of publishing these meetings and have already released four. In the beginning, Félix Guattari did not participate in the meetings, either because he was prevented by his Parisian militant activities in *La Voie Communiste*, or because he was keeping himself apart from what looked like a club of physician-directors of psychiatric teams. However, according to what passages in the first collection show, the GTPSI members often mobilized linguistic and Marxist references and their thoughts were clearly political. Indeed, GTPSI, with Félix Guattari and Jean Oury together as the driving force, originated a petition against the psychiatric politics of the French government, because the government was aiming at the industrialization of the construction of psychiatric hospitals all over France, the very moment that WHO was arguing that they should close.

Now, and this was true of all groups, the GTPSI did not always work well, the threat of corporatism was ever present. During that time, inside the student circles and the worker syndicates, workgroups were formed and understood as a revolutionary potentiality, under the influence of psycho-sociologists. Sartre himself dedicated important discussions to the free production of subjectivity that would allow groups in fusion to go through the multiple in order to bring about the community. In the 1960s, Sartre was a reference common to all French intellectuals of the Left, even if they had not spent time with his theoretical works at any length. The thought of Félix Guattari on subject-groups and subjected groups is clearly derived from Sartre's writings on the question of how it is possible for a collectivity to escape the practico-inert. Dealing with groups would attract Gilles Deleuze's attention, along with Félix's challenge of his structuralism in *Machine and structure* (initially a note of his reading of Deleuze's writings for the journal of Lacan's school; it ended up as a celibate text because of its rejection by the Lacanian family). At the same time as *Anti-Oedipus*, Guattari's *Psychoanalysis and Transversality* was published, a collection of his writings, intended to promote institutional analysis. It was prefaced by Gilles Deleuze's 'Three

Group-Related Problems', where Deleuze spoke of Félix as the one whose work was dedicated to groups trying to secure for themselves a revolutionary becoming. This thoroughly political text of Gilles Deleuze presents Félix Guattari's political credo.

Is it even possible to overlook the State's role in every dead end that the libido has been led to by being reduced to investing itself in every single, intimate image of the family? How can we believe that the castration complex will be able to find a satisfactory solution for as long as society entrusts it with the unconscious role of social regulation and repression? As Deleuze explains it, Guattari's distinction of the subjected groups from the subject-groups as well as the risk of going from the one to the other sheds light on the objectively counter-revolutionary role that institutions created by the Soviet revolution and by the pro-independence leaders of the third world were asked to play and suggests some of the conditions for the construction of war machines that could successfully work against the State apparatus. The notions that Guattari proposes 'have a precise practical orientation: introducing a militant political functioning to the institution, constituting a kind of "monster" which is neither psychoanalysis, nor hospital practice, even less group dynamics, and which is everywhere applicable, in the hospital, at school, in a militant group – a machine to produce and give voice to desire, and the collective arrangement of enunciation of an institutional analysis' (Deleuze 1974: 201). And Deleuze adds: 'What comes into play here are Guattari's problems concerning the name of cured-curing capable of forming group-subjects, that is to say, capable of making the institution the object of a genuine creation where madness and revolution each reflect, without combining, the face of their difference in the singular positions of a desiring subjectivity' (202).

CVB: Championing the transformation of the traditional school along the lines of revolutionary pedagogy was your own contribution to the domain of institutional researches. You made the school and its history the object of your investigations. What did you find in mutual schools and in the pedagogical innovations of Céléstin Freinet that could serve as an alternative to the traditional schooling?

AQ: In the work that I did for CERFI (the Centre for Institutional Studies, Research and Development), I studied the history of school in order to try to understand the source of that which everybody, especially in France, considers to be a mess: the school that a century ago was able to assure, however limited, a social and intellectual improvement of the entire population is now incapable of giving the same hope to new generations. I searched therefore the archives and the satirical publications of the nineteenth century that had focused on this subject and I happened by a very violent challenge involving people of the church, politicians and businessmen and revolving around a model of school called 'mutual school' that was developed in France in 1816. In the beginning, these schools were created by the government in order to offer schooling to a number of pupils who did not attend the school of the Brothers of the Christian schools. However, very soon the mutual schools, where the more advanced children helped the others to learn, were teaching much more efficiently than the Christian schools of the Brothers; the former pupils of mutual schools were able to argue against the heads of their factories. The 1830 revolution was punctuated by the cry 'stand up with the mutual school, go down with the Ignorant Brothers!'

As soon as Guizot, who was a Protestant, and supported the mutual schools at the beginning, became minister of public education and then prime minister, he never stopped trying to suppress them. The Normative Schools for Teachers (*Écoles normales d' instituteurs*) were created in 1837 by the State in order to train lay instructors in the method of the Brothers of the Christian schools. As for the Brothers themselves, they were exempt from training. The teachers' union recommended the mutual method in its Teachers' Journal, but families with children in mutual schools could be excommunicated. In the fifty years of a bitter fight, the mutual method was almost uprooted, it survived only in Brittany where my two grandfathers were able to take advantage of it. It reappeared in the *Bourses du Travail*, and in the choices of social and syndicalist pedagogical movements.

The African American movement picked up the mutual method with the formula 'Each one teach one!' The mutual method is a group practice, based on the power of the group to act, which Jean Baptiste de la Salle, the founder of the order of the Brothers of the Christian schools, had also noticed. We no longer learn all alone, under a private tutor, as the nobles and the rich of yesteryear used to do. We learn together, as we listen to others, as mutual schools did, by helping others succeed when they could not make it by themselves. The main difference between the two schools is that the traditional school exists in order to rank students according to the difference of their performance, whereas the mutual school exists in order to help everyone learn according to their own rhythm with the help of others. In each subject, the leaders may be different, with respect to their differences in performance, but the goal is that we all succeed. The school that took its name from Freinet, between the two wars, took on some of the ideas of the mutual school. Soon though it fell victim to inquisitions, and to the thirst for knowledge that it was itself instilling in the kids. Having learnt to write texts based on their own experiences and those of others, the students decided to renew their experiences by going out into the streets and conducting research by themselves. As a result, the antique dealers of Saint Paul de Vence, to whom the students went for their investigations, wrote to the minister immediately, complaining that the local teacher was not following regulations. Célestin Freinet himself, who was a militant communist and syndicalist, was excluded from national education. He was obliged to continue his work privately by creating a research and training institute for innovative teachers. After the Second World War, Fernand Oury was motivated by Freinet's technique to teach college students natural sciences according to the mutual method. His student Félix Guattari became totally fascinated and followed him into the youth hostels, the organization of groups and the grand Outside.

Unlike Ivan Illich who proposed a society without schools, in other words, a system of education where apprenticeship goes on in accordance with the privileged relationship between two, as in the old case of the private tutor, the 'freinetists', just like the friends of the mutual school, built on the considerable progress made by the availability of space dedicated to apprenticeship, to the exchange of knowledge, to the emergence of new desires through contact with others, the lived experience of the group and the experience of relating to others. Naturally, this space needs to be regulated, but this can be done without the silence or the control of parents to whom student notebooks are being submitted, as happened with the Brothers of the Christian schools and even with today's French schools. A group of children may be open to learners of different ages, the way that mutual schools were set up in the Napoleonic armies. They can be organized so that under the direction of an instructor they could pursue a collective task, like, for example, the making of a book in Freinet's class or the realization and release of a research project or whatever else one can think of.

All those dedicated to the new pedagogies say that, in three hours a day, pupils could cover everything that the school programme expects, and that the rest of the time, the remaining three hours, could be given to learning about subjects proposed by the members of the group or by different partners. Today's revolution in numbers permits us to see a different way of having schools. It allows the young to work together with people who are older. Some municipalities have themselves made proposals, but these, unfortunately, are limited by the national will to restrict the abilities of the students at the minimum necessary for a passive citizen. Needs are being expressed, even by the business world, needs for different skills, for more autonomy and more initiative, but these are not needs that express a more revolutionary spirit, and this explains the reluctance of authorities to take risks. Many initiatives try to make the school evolve beyond its limits, to introduce concerns, other than the reproduction of inequalities and the separation of classes. They compete for the formation of a new model for an open school, for a new space for the apprenticeship of all, and for a new space for the expression of desires. But they bump up against the European politics of austerity and have to think of ways to circumvent and to subvert the status quo, by means of a different local economy and a different way of enlivening our schools.

CVB: The founding of the FGERI helped to frame the merging of Marxist analysis of production with institutional psychotherapy, and demonstrated the theoretical strength and the empirical application of the notion 'transversality'. It will be useful to try to explain the character of the merger and the diagonal direction of transversality. Perhaps, as you tackle this question, you may want to situate the *Neuf thèses de l' opposition de Gauche* (Nine Theses of the Left Opposition) in the articulation of the merger.

AQ: Learning the elements of Marxism was for the members of the FGERI, and for Guattari himself, part of their first years of militantism inside the union of the communist students. With the exception of a small group of students in the *École Normale Supérieure* around Althusser, reading Marx was not the issue. The Marxist analyses of social classes, which asked for the leading role of the working class and of its party to be recognized, seemed a little hollow when the most interesting Marxist sociologists of the day were alerting us to the rise of a new working class of technicians that had no place inside the Marxist scheme, although it had an ample presence within the Soviet Union. The young doctors, architects, educators and teachers that FGERI brought together were champing at the bit, trying to invent new professional practices to better serve the working class, immigrants and everybody else. Their presence in the FGERI was pragmatic enough. As the image of the GTPSI, they undertook the task of facing critics and the professional practices that were then emerging, to allow them room to wonder, and to create spaces of freedom and discussion outside the established professional norms. Thanks to the diversity of its members, FGERI had indeed assumed a transversal role, in its search for the association of ideas of different domains. The notion of transversality was coined by Félix Guattari within an intra-institutional context, meaning that in an institution sufficiently hierarchical, like a psychiatric clinic, with its horizontal organization and various groups, we must recognize that there can be no change unless within the project of change itself, the individuals are related in a diagonal way, with respect to the verticality and horizontality of the institution. Félix maintained that neither the revolution from below nor the technocratic change imposed from above had a chance to succeed. What is needed is a politics of alliance with projects which involve all the aspects of the institution. Félix's transversality is a very precise politics that FGERI and CERFI-FGERI's area of studies were able, on the invitation of the movement, to carry on for a while after 1968, but without being able to sustain it past 1974. The definition of the institutional analysis given by Gilles Deleuze in his preface to Félix Guattari's book corresponds to the position that CERFI adopted in the various areas of its own intervention. For example, the programming of collective teams and the study of the evolution of cities, the welcoming of children in society, or the professional formation of adults and the institution of schools; placing analytical groups in the centre of interested groups, seeing desire surge as these groups are brought together, and proposing local reforms against misery, depression or the mere lack of initiative. Unlike agencies of management or of psychological training that tackled the same problems, CERFI's proposals were always directed towards the life of the group rather than the strengthening of the ego of the few against the alleged opposition of all. However, with such appeals to real life, the lack of stable teaching positions, the signing of contracts with businesses or training institutions, CERFI paid a big price, earning the enmity of other militant Marxists who were used to working as individuals to earn their salary but who lived their theoretical and political activities in different ways.

At the end of the war in Algeria, in 1962, there existed a student circle that, with respect to the Communist Party, was designated as leftist. It included many different currents, which to various degrees participated in May '68 and before that in the syndicalist struggles of students. The originality of this current whose driving force was Félix Guattari was that it did not owe allegiance to any theory or practice, to orthodox, Trotskyite or Maoist communism, to their stereotypical answers to every question or to their refusal of every possible autonomy to the student and intellectual movements. Guattari's group, a kind of think tank, was bringing together Marxism and Lacanian psychoanalysis, and searching for any odd manifestation of desire. It was open enough but, at the same time, standing apart from other groups, maintaining its own autonomous judgement about the international workers' movement, and especially the Maoist one. The Nine

Theses of the Left Opposition (*Neuf thèses de l'opposition de gauche*) were in my opinion a point of reference inside this rather confused extreme Left. But it was a way to stand up and be numbered when the other members of the old group of *La Voie Communiste* were asking to limit the role of the students to a force supporting the Communist Party, and to stop indulging in revolutionary dreams when everybody else was lowering the flag of the revolution.

CVB: Was the becoming worker, a notion that had captured the imagination and guided the choices of the militants of the 1960s and 1970s, a mere reflection of a fashionable (for that time) Maoist slogan or was it also expressing indigenous needs and emancipatory thrusts of the French Left struggles? How much did the becoming worker condition the implementation of the 'grid' in La Borde? Are there, in your opinion, conceptual and practical links between becoming worker and becoming minor?

AQ: The Maoist militants developed an essentialist concept of the desire to becoming worker which was attractive to the students at the time to the extent that their numbers, although still limited, had begun to surpass the possibility of their participation in shaping the direction of society. We were looking at the Russian students who had turned to the people and whose lot was not exactly enviable, having failed to put their training and education to the service of the revolution. Maoist students 'planted themselves' in factories, taking advantage of the fact that vacancies were much easier to come by then than it is now. They thus became acquainted with the working conditions in all their harshness, with timetables, and the extremely individualizing organization of the workplace, in short, with conditions that were not encouraging transformation in any way. Moreover, as Robert Linhart had made clear in his book *The Assembly Line* (*L' Établi* (Paris: Minuit, 1978)), the student who takes the place of a worker, no matter how harsh the work is, has other intellectual and militant reserves over the worker who knows only his or her job. The experience may be interesting and formative, but it does not allow the formation of a new revolutionary enunciative assemblage. Paradoxically, meetings outside the work space allow this formation more often, and the militant workers are interested in the stories and the theoretical analyses of the militant students. In the last analysis, by doing the work for which one is competent, intellectuals and workers are able to participate in a common productive labour. In this way, the becoming worker, therefore, of the student is not the labour of the manual worker, but rather a labour of assemblages and the linkages of a common becoming, according to the model of the orchid and the wasp that Proust described and Deleuze and Guattari adopted. Such a common becoming is completely different from the becoming cadre for the sake of which university studies are supposed to prepare us, and which was denounced by the sociology students of Nanterre University in 1968. Nevertheless, the lack of transformation of French society after '*Mai 1968 n'a pas eu lieu*' (May '68 didn't happen), as Gilles Deleuze and Félix Guattari have said (Deleuze and Guattari 2006: 233), just might force us to conclude that the student activists of 1968 have indeed become cadres. But a careful study of the becoming of the members of the March 22nd movement, for instance, will show that this is not always the case. The question of relationships preoccupies these old militants much more than their individual promotion.

In the years before 1968, we could already sense the grand transformation of society in the direction of a 'society of control'. The latter allowed greater initiative, but along well-charted roads did propose that everyone become an 'entrepreneur of himself', provided that this entrepreneurship keeps us in the role of a cog in the system of production, be it cultural, educational or social. New generations entered the workplace and the FGERI after 1968. The idea of building collective arrangements of enunciation for professional practices was recuperated mostly by the proliferation of professional formations and by the constant increase of evaluation practices, which brought about the hierarchization of whatever successes there had already been made. As a result of the growing number of wage earners, which now includes cultural professions, becoming worker has lost its fiery, manual and revolutionary horizon, turning towards obedience and negotiations. It lost its artisanal aura that once emphasized its confrontation with matter. Nevertheless, it kept its sense of solidarity which is still expressed, for instance, in the struggle for pension.

La Borde's 'grid' is a good example of the becoming worker, transversal as it is to statutory categories. According to Guattari, the notion was born in a crisis situation where the numbers of qualified nurses were not sufficient for the upcoming weekend. Félix therefore strengthened their numbers by adding housekeepers and student interns, creating thereby a new transversal category: care/leadership/housekeeping. Here, each category had its responsibility but the persons of all categories revolved around a global post – CLH. The CLH teams, each one of which comprised three persons, could have had any initial qualification whatsoever, but they were expected to fulfil all three tasks. There was a bit of grumbling from the nurses but since this arrangement allowed them to have a break on the weekends, they let it go.

The grid associates the various functions – CLH, kitchen, workshop, work group – with the different spaces of the clinic, and therefore with names of persons, asking them for half-a-day service. The office responsible for the grid was told to rotate the groups of persons neither too often nor too infrequently. Recently, I was told that there also existed factories which were managed in the same way. It seems that this kind of rotation and deterritorialization of persons actually works well as it creates a more fluid ambiance and gives fewer reasons for discrimination than fixed communities.

As La Borde's grid shows, this practice of rotation, this becoming worker with all possible qualifications, was occurring in a horizontal way inside the institution. The desire among labourers was connected to acting in conjunction with others – in our case, with the participation of patients, elsewhere of users. The question was not one of preparation for a career, in which case one could display a list of acquired competences in order to be elevated to higher levels of leadership. It was the kind of functioning that presupposes pleasure in functioning inside the desiring machine, inside the group, and not in a narcissistic domination of others. It was felt that collective work, transversal to several categories, was able to offer new insights on the clinic, the hierarchy and the many groups of the clinic. During the 1960s, the word 'worker' was much more appreciated than it is today where the politicians have abandoned any reference to work and picked up the word 'citizen'. Work used to refer to solidarity, and to team competence.

CVB: It would be useful to talk a little about Lacan in La Borde. François Dosse tells us that 'the entire team of La Borde was acquainted with Lacan's couch'. But we would like to know more about the ways in which Lacan's rereading of Freud influenced the theoretical and clinical work of La Borde. Would you say that Guattari's 1969 essay, 'Machine and Structure', constitutes a significant step away from Lacan and an anticipation of a more mature articulation of schizoanalysis?

AQ: As far as I know, Lacan has never been in La Borde, but most of La Borde's staff – and not only the physicians – were in analysis with him because he was one of the rare analysts to think that psychoanalysis was a possibility for psychotics, whereas Freud had thought that it could only benefit neurotics. On the other hand, Lacan seems to have had a vivid interest in the use of psychoanalysis within institutions, inside relatively closed communities where the effects of desire could be moved from someone to someone else and where the analyst would be surrounded by an entire group of people. Lacan was not a closet psychoanalyst. When I came to know it, in 1965, La Borde lived literally to the rhythm of Lacan's seminar, the entire medical team was running to attend it. Lacan's linguistic researches and the works of Saussure and Troubetskoi were shared by the team of the clinic. Félix Guattari, however, had begun to raise questions on the limited character of these linguistic researches and also about the definition of the unconscious in terms of the signifier. The questions, as always, were raised for pragmatic reasons: these things did not work well in therapy and Félix was already in search of something else. He was, of course, keeping Lacan aware of these developments and it was Lacan who told him to read the *Logic of Sense* and *Difference and Repetition*, and to write a review for the journal of the Lacanian school. It was the small managerial group of the review – the daughter of Lacan, her husband and the friend of the husband – who turned down the '*Machine and Structure*', not so much because of its content but rather for the simple fact that their group had not participated in May '68, whereas Guattari had invested all his energy in the March 22nd movement. '*Machine and structure*' moves away from structuralism, and therefore from the linguistic researches that Lacan was pursuing, although it does so in the way that Lacan himself would follow up later on with his '*synthome*'. However, '*Machine and Structure*' moves away especially from a literary style that was precious to some classes at the time. Félix Guattari offered a schizoanalysis for all, whereas Lacan wished to maintain psychoanalysis as a family affair and as the practice of the elite.

CVB: On which war machines and lines of escape could the micropolitics of the 1960s and the 1970s be counting on and construct? Has Guattari been sufficiently attentive to the need to prevent the line of death from turning into a line of abolition and the war machine from being captured by, and kept inside, the precinct of the State?

AQ: The notions of the war machine and lines of escape are directly opposed to the notion of the State Ideological Apparatus that Althusser proposed around the same time in order to designate the political struggle of intellectuals opposed to capitalism and to discuss the niche reserved for them. For Deleuze and Guattari, revolutionary militants are not merely pieces in a boardgame with rules of movement defined by the system, as happens in chess; they are pawns, one equal to the other, in the winning collective arrangement of the game Go. The struggle against the State is one struggle of evasion, of ruses and uprisings, not at all a frontal battle for the conquest of the centre by means of the electoral vote because this centre, the State apparatus itself is, as its name suggests, an apparatus for the retention of the State, and an obstacle to becoming-revolutionary. The war machine is eccentric in relation to the State, and has lost the war from the start, if it believes that it can take over the centre. Its own fight is of a different nature by offering meaning as it influences the forms of life to change, and by building relationships, especially with minorities, which, inside war machines, conquer their equality. This equality is completely reversible when the war machine disappears under the strata of the State apparatus, as, for example, is the case of the Algerian state. In war machines, each one knows what he or she has to do, they do not require directives to realize the collective work. The birth of a war machine presupposes a growing absence of discipline within the State apparatus but also the challenge of the hierarchy. The war machine refuses to recognize the limits that the State apparatus assigns to territories; it is deployed on the borders and even beyond them. It toys with overstepping boundaries, it multiplies problems, it looks for innovations. It has an intrinsic limit, expending mental and physical energy instead of the consumption of resources because it has the ability to function in a state of sobriety.

The institutional psychotherapy that Jean Oury and Francesco Tosquelles practised was such a war machine against State psychiatry – a machine that was meant to ply State psychiatry to the demands of mental health patients for freedom and creativity by means of behaviours that were not explicitly anticipated by Jean Oury's perspective. For example, having been appointed psychiatrist in the clinic of Saumery in the Loir and Cher department, Oury took fifteen patients on foot through the countryside in search of a new care place, one that would be more satisfactory. This is how he came to La Borde and created an encampment for his battle. In accepting Félix Guattari to La Borde, he was able to push back the frontiers of his clinic and to endow it with a system of external, open and cumulative relationships. Likewise, Tosquelles broadened the space of Saint Alban through its politics of training groups, not only those of psychiatric nurses but also of educators, and by organizing a circle of innovative psychiatrists throughout France. The politics of expansion reached its limits when Félix Guattari expressed his wish to include in the circle Alternatives to Psychiatry the British anti-psychiatrists, the practitioners of family therapies and some sociologists who were critical of psychiatry. Jean Oury thought that the successes of institutional psychotherapy should be protected, including the community formed in La Borde. He adopted Lacan's thought against these new barbarians who had the inclination to limit their practices and their discourses to a mere negation of whatever was built in the past. The war machine of institutional psychotherapy was then transformed into a small localized state, the diplomacy of which was not enough to guarantee a defence of psychiatric spaces marked by psychoanalysis. This evolution was perceived as a generational issue – the leaders of institutional psychotherapy had turned old and, in some cases, had been deceased. But it also reflects the transformation of relationships within a movement that no longer attempted to conquer its domain, but was already in retreat.

The revolutionary political groups, which rose up in 1968 but were already swarming in the shadows beforehand, may also be seen as war machines turned against the capitalist State apparatus. We have already seen the limits within which the actions of these groups were kept, thanks to the competition among them, their condemnation by the Communist Party and the actions of the police. They escaped their semi-clandestine state only when their journals began to circulate, and even then the strict control of their writings hardly allowed them to increase the number of new militants. The dispersion of their members was consigning their ideology to their newspapers, their main indication of any mobilization, and this ended up favouring a very coded language. Despite this closed character, their circulation seems to have reached farther then than it does now. Despite their aggressive vocabulary, they looked like small states inside the State, like closed communities in retreat.

My impression is that the main war machine at that time was the growing rhizome of scientific research, the development of science and the formation of the open. We were faced with a real aspiration towards new institutions, an aspiration that will increase exponentially with the May '68 movement, and a little after that it will be captured by the government. The political movements of the Left had not given a concrete form to these aspirations. Women would become more visible in the May '68 movement, without any significant impact though on its directions, with the exception of the March 22nd movement which was the most informal of all. The movement for the liberation of women would reappear in 1970, but the character of the war machine against the State was taken up only in the well-defined cases of the freedom of abortion and the reimbursement for expenses related to contraception. The movement stressed the need to raise individual and collective consciousness, helped women to free themselves from submission and encouraged the public presence of female artists and writers to testify to the equality of men and women. Recently, a group called *La Barbe* haunted the management of big businesses in order to point out their misogyny. Unfortunately, their discourse that stigmatized the fact that only a small number of women have succeeded in this world of power turned out to be annoyingly repetitive and the group disappeared from the public arena. With respect to homosexuals some publications showcased the existence of groups that could be compared to war machines but the affirmation that all humans are perverse, each in his or her own manner, in *Recherches* and by the *Homosexual Front for Revolutionary Action* in 1973, was censured. To this day, the movement has not created new forms of life that could also be shared with those outside. Different viral forms, AIDS first, and the sort of conformity that the demands for same-sex marriage imposed broke up the movement and restructured it as a defensive watchtower.

We can see that the forces of uprising and the models of reference come from the outside, from Vietnamese, Algerian, Cuban, Chinese, Latin American or African American initiatives. The energy drawn from the outside has been converted to a force of resistance against the boredom and death that ooze from the post-colonial State apparatus. They are not followed by an increase of successful researches for new forms of life and expression. The State apparatus forced them to enter a new order of commerce and advertising, thus marginalizing desire more effectively than ever before. It is this transformation that the open letter of Guy Hocquenghem '*A ceux qui sont passés du col mao au Rotary*' (for those who moved from a Mao shirt collar to Rotary)has denounced.

Towards the end of the 1970s, managers of publishing houses incited the mediatic appearance of the 'new philosophers' with the explicit intention of ridding the public space of Foucault, Deleuze and Guattari. The death drive no longer comes from the outside, like the movement of life had come before it, but from strata, central to the establishment; it forms the black hole of the literary success stories that becomes the main incentive for many candidates to think. There is nothing that one can do against such a strange attractor, except to find the tangent of an escape route.

All the work that Deleuze and Guattari did together states clearly that, when it comes to becoming, there is no guarantee, that it is necessary to always remain alert in order to trace our line of life with the help of whatever happens. Deleuze and Guattari were divided, like Romain Roland that Gramsci quoted, between the optimism of the will and the pessimism of the understanding. They used to remark with irony that in terms of stupidity and darkness the real often surpasses fiction and that as a result we should always expect the worst. Guattari sometimes liked to linger on in front of the explosive vision of Antonioni's *Zabriskie Point*, whereas Deleuze counselled prudence in order to stave off the psychotic crisis. The abolition reigns beyond what we are capable of seeing, so that we would like to go there and see for ourselves. For Guattari it is outside and for Deleuze, underneath. For Guattari, we have just to let ourselves be dazzled and then hopefully recover from it. In Deleuze's case, we must dig for it. This appeal of negativity, when nourished by the refusal to work, can be seen as a surrender to the death drive. But without ignoring it, Deleuze and Guattari's work is an attempt to get rid of it and to go on resisting and creating over and over again.

Be that as it may, there is still one point to discuss. What is '*une ligne de fuite*'? Is it a line of abolition, 'of escape' or is it rather a line of escape from danger, like the path that an animal will take in order to leave alive the scene where it was not able to realize its project? I wish that we wouldn't translate '*ligne de fuite*' as 'line of flight', which evokes the image of a take-off for the great blue yonder, and that we translate it into English as 'line of escape', to let it designate the becoming animal, and the finer possible and meticulous explorations of the plane of immanence, the continuous exploration of the imperceptible. In this way, an entire pragmatism of open escape would be able to find the matter, the space and the time to develop. The philosophy of Deleuze has given us the ability to feel the force of the infinitely small, the imperceptible and the different. This is what Félix Guattari was translating in his own language as 'molecular revolution' – the title he gave to the book that collects his militant articles.

At the molar level, power relationships will always favour power and its capacity to harm, whatever this power might be. The State can always call for more police and even more army forces, as we see these days in France. But change always occurs at the molecular level, as the invisible creation of new connections between sexes, between forms of life and modes of communication. History does not have to be seen from the point of view of power; it is being made by the movement of life and by intersecting lines of escape, which pre-exist and have to be endlessly actualized.

References

*First published in Deleuze Studies 10: 1 (2016): 395–416.

Deleuze Gilles (2006), 'May'68 didn't happen,' in David Lapoujade (ed.), *Two Regimes of Madness. Texts and Interviews 1973-1993*. Translated by Ames Hodges and Mike Taormina. New York: Semiotext(e).

Deleuze Gilles (2004), 'Three Group-Related Problems', in David Lapoujade (ed.), *Desert Islands and Other Texts 1953-1974*. Translated by Michael Taormina. London: Semiotext(e).

2

A Personal Testimony

Elisabeth Kouki

During the Second World War, the Saint Alban psychiatric hospital (in central France) was revolutionized, thanks to the presence of the Catalan refugee François Tosquelles, the 'red psychiatrist', who had arrived there fleeing the Franco regime in Spain. The surrounding walls of Saint Alban were broken down, the doors opened, the bars of the windows removed. All patients and the nursing staff (basically made of nuns, but also two peasants and a few members of the Resistance) were clearly integrated into the everyday life. They played an active role in the Resistance by providing shelter to Jews and partisans (a lot of intellectuals and artists among them), and by operating an underground press. They were linked with the mainly farming local society in the same struggle for physical survival. During wartime, with the exception of those at Saint Alban, some 40,000 mental patients died all over France.

This context had a considerable impact on both the hospital organization and the therapeutic process, promoting, inter alia, a collective autonomy of the patients, through outdoor activities, the creation of a club, their own gazette and so on. One could find there something like a *programmed coincidence*[1] – a propitious sociohistorical conjuncture for the development of collectivities, the invention of mechanisms and the creation of micro-institutions inside the institution. In other words, as Guattari put it, one could find there *a new attitude; a new militant approach to mental illness was born.*[2]

Jean Oury had spent two years (between 1947 and 1949) in Saint Alban as an intern in psychiatry, being trained by François Tosquelles. Later, he continued his Saint Alban experience of institutional psychotherapy[3] by acquiring the Château of La Borde, near Blois, and founding his own private clinic. La Borde opened in April 1953. In 1955, Oury asked his long-time friend and Trotskyite comrade, Félix Guattari,[4] to join him and to coordinate the clinic's internal management and its external relations. The two then agreed to share the field of responsibilities: the medical ones were under Oury, the institutional under Félix.[5]

Félix was an inveterate activist throughout his life, fond of the nomadic way of thinking, defending all kinds of minorities, close to a variety of subversive political action. Repeating practices established in Saint Alban, La Borde was offering refuge to Algerians fighting against the French Occupation of their country. Later on, before and after the May 1968 events, hoards of highly politicized Frenchmen as well as people from other countries invaded the clinic, anxious to learn from this particular institutional adventure. It was, after all, the same logic behind the need for the healing and the therapy of the institution treating the mentally ill – Tosquelles used to talk about the need to treat the institution's pathogeny – that applied also to political organizations. The latter have their own pathogenies and illnesses as well – a high incidence of dogmatism, for example, and the reproduction within their own precincts of the social alienation that they are trying to eradicate. Oury was often upset at these agitators – the waves of 'barbarians' –[6] who invaded the clinic, but Félix stayed in La Borde until his 1992 death and, as a result, one way or another, the institutional psychotherapy (Oury) or the institutional analysis (Guattari) went on.

Félix talks about all these years in his somehow autobiographical text, which also gave the title of the book *De Léros à La Borde*.[7] He discusses how, in La Borde, he came to grips with psychosis and the impact that institutional work could have upon it; how it is shaped by the actual work and organization inside the institution; how the clinical and the political approach to it are inextricably linked together. Oury, for his part, argued in a similar way: unlike other branches of medicine, psychiatry deals with the entire existence of whomsoever it treats, it is a veritable anthropology and belongs to the field of philosophy and metaphysical thought.

The experiment[8] of La Borde – with its graceful and tough moments, its dead ends and the search for mechanisms and lines of escape able to prevent those dead ends – represents a vivid example of thinking together for the sake of effective action and for the elaboration and application of some of Guattari's concepts and ideas. I am thinking as an example of the distinction between 'subject' and 'subjectivity'. Félix had been analysed by Lacan and he was himself an analyst, but he was also an innovative and critical thinker of the psychoanalytic theory. In response to the Freudian unconscious, he proposed the machinic unconscious, which opens up widely the psychoanalytic domain to the winds of the historical, the social and the political and puts the production of 'subjectivity' on the right foundations. By 'subjectivity', Guattari refers to the way someone assumes and makes her own and lives any process that takes place in a large or restrained social context. Everyone has the choice to accept and follow, without any resistance, the main tenets of the subjectivity proposed to him, or, alternatively, to adopt some of its components in order to come up with a singularity, uniqueness and creativity of their own. I am also thinking of the distinction Guattari makes between 'subject groups' and 'subjugated groups'. The 'subjugated groups' structure is vertical and pyramidal; centralization characterizes their members' relationships. On the contrary, 'subject groups' are characterized by transversality. They themselves give meaning and limits to their members' existence.

I am also thinking of the concept of transversality that was forged in the early 1960s and further elaborated on later. The basic task of La Borde, according to Félix, was to cultivate and instil the sense of individual and collective responsibility as the only alternative to the bureaucratic routine and passivity generated by the traditional hierarchical systems. It was therefore necessary to move gradually towards the deconstruction of the old doctor–patient relationship, and also of the relationship between medical staff and service personnel. The work of the service personnel had to be integrated in the medical work, and, reciprocally, the medical staff had to be drafted for tasks such as cleaning, cooking, dishwashing and maintenance.

Oury seems to be following a similar pathway when he advises everyone to distinguish, on a daily basis, status from function and role: 'in a hospital, if someone is known under the status of being a cook, his function will be the cooking. However, his role is always the one the patient gives to him. And sometimes he will be astonished to discover the kind of role he is invested by the patient'.[9] That is why, Oury concludes, the cook should not be confined in his or her job title; contrary to what health services require, she must never close the kitchen's door to the patients.

According to Oury, Félix was highly qualified to assume the lead and the responsibility in the collective adventure that combined political and psychiatric militancy, made all spatial boundaries permeable and encouraged the free involvement of all patients. 'In a few months', Félix wrote, 'I contributed to the creation of a secretariat, to patient–staff parity commissions and sub-commissions, to a coordination office, to several types of activities: local newspaper, drawing, sewing, the chicken coop, horticulture, theater, puppet theater, pottery, etc.'[10] Every kind of workshop, meeting, assembly, every day, in every unexpectable corner of the clinic formed a large constellation of dynamic spaces – all of them emanating from the club. The club was organized like any other association and its mixed composition was reminiscent of the Saint Alban experience. The complexity of the entire setting required that everyone's real presence and vigilance facilitate mobility, and an openness always to heterogeneity, multiplicity and fluidity – all of them being parameters for the creation of an atmosphere, an ambiance, according to Oury's favourite notion regarding the treatment of psychosis.

***

From my diary

The Château of La Borde is situated between Blois and Cour-Cheverny, less than two hours' journey to the south of Paris. That afternoon of September 1976, a car of the clinic was expecting me at the Blois train station. I realized right away that the driver was a patient. As it turns out, the cars connecting La Borde with Blois or Cour-Cheverny are driven exclusively by patients. Patients also hold the posts at the telephone switchboard. It became immediately clear to me that notions like outside/inside did not work there.

In the heart of Sologne, in an open field of the forest, the Château of La Borde and its neglected park do not remind of the famous castles standing along the Loire River.

When we arrived, the driver held my luggage and I followed a 'pilot-fish' who showed me the different places of the domain. 'Pilot-fish' is the name of anyone, who, having lived on the premises for a long time, welcomes and guides the newcomers and monitors potential patients, student trainees, etc in the clinic. My own guide, that day, was also a patient. In the weekly meetings of the commission, the 'pilot-fishes' take their lunch together and talk about their responsibilities and experience. Welcoming the patient is actually the first, and most important, step before her admission to La Borde: it is only afterwards that the patient will give her agreement to stay for treatment.

In front of the Château, like a big square or a market place, there is a large area covered with grass where, during the summer, performances and classical plays are presented, having been prepared in patient and staff workshops during the year. These represent real cultural events for the neighbouring villages.

The Château is surrounded by a forty hectares park, without fence, where, among the trees and bushes, several paths lead to a chapel (which now is the library), a little lake and a wooden house, a daycare for the children of the staff and sometimes of the patients, a chicken coop, the horse stables, the vegetable garden, the telephone switchboard, Oury's house, the beauty salon ('kalothérapie'), the pharmacy, etc.

Patients live in the first floor of the Château and the surrounding outbuildings, in four sectors: the 'Château', the 'Park', the 'Extension' and the 'small woods', with each of these places hosting about thirty persons. Nobody is obliged to stay confined to her room or sector. Quite the contrary, one of La Borde's basic principles is the freedom of movement. Patients can easily change sector whenever they want to; they can walk and go around absolutely everywhere. There is no door locked.

Located in the ground floor of the Château, are the kitchen, the large dining room and, next to it, the Big Salon, the so-called Rue de Rivoli because of its arched windows. Here an open fireplace and a bar that sells soft drinks and cigarettes are also to be found; the bar is run by the patients.

When we had finished visiting these quarters, it was evening. The sound of a bell was announcing the dinner time. I joined a group of people that had staff members and patients alike. The only difference is that some take drugs, others may be not; some have a daily obligation of at least eight hours service, others are encouraged, albeit free, to participate in a workshop (or just to be there), in the meetings, in an administrative task or to assume some other responsibility. Some are remunerated by the clinic;[11] for others, a sum is paid to the clinic by the Social Security and payments or salary for their task are deposited to the treasury of the club.

That first night, one of the monitors offered to be my host. The next morning, I went to the coordination office where they gave me a room in one of the Château donjons. I was integrated into the Park Sector and into 'The Lost' (*les Paumés*), one of the base therapeutic units, usually composed of four or five monitors, one doctor and about ten patients.

Day after day, I memorized the names of the parity commissions, meetings and workshops. Long ago, Marie Depussé remembers,[12] there was a long debate about the name of a new repairing bike commission; they finally decided to call it RAM. They all knew what RAM deals with, but they all ignored or had forgotten what RAM meant. It had perhaps something to do with the verb ram*ener* (to bring for reparation). There was an acronym for all that happened in the clinic: MCB (medical coordination bureau), CAH (care, animation, house-cleaning),

DASC (daily activities sub-commission), WAG (weekly activities grid), MJG (management joint group), BTU (basic therapeutic unity), etc.[13] Was it because it made it easier to remember them? Or, may be, it was because the acronymic naming neutralizes the weight of the full utterance of the words? At any rate, all these commissions and groups were coordinated by the Friday group of groups.

During the six years I stayed there, I was 'gridded' on a weekly basis. The Grid is the most important element of the institutional psychoanalysis, the instrument that Félix put in place to make transversality work. It is a many-line organogram (managed by the WAG commission) that structures time and shows, in a task rotation that includes everybody, the persons responsible for such or such a thing on a given day or in a given week.

And then, time was passing with the same-yet-different rhythm. Sometimes I was in the kitchen, sometimes in the pharmacy, the MCB or the DASC. Tasks were always renegotiated, temporary, alternating, shared and in a flexible diversity.

It was very difficult for me to create my own workshop activity, until the day when, during a group of groups, under pressure from the assembly, I dared say that I would like to practise ceramic sculpture. Immediately, they directed me to whoever could teach me the basics; they gave me a place to work and a budget for my needs. It did not take long for me to start my workshop. But still I was frustrated because, a few months after I had opened up, I was still alone. I decided therefore to be done with it, to close the workshop down and to declare my intention in the next group of groups. They listened to me carefully and then Félix gave me an argument that persuaded me to go on. He asked me whether I conceived the workshop for myself or for the patients. I answered that it was both for me and for them. 'Not at all', he said, 'it is only for you, you told us that it was your old wish to be initiated in ceramic sculpture. You stay there and practise for yourself'. So I did, and then, as if by magic, a few days later, a patient came to work with me and after him, another, and then others...

Notes

1 The cherished formula of Jean Oury.

2 Guattari (2015: 59).

3 It was Georges Daumézon who invented this name.

4 Félix Guattari had participated in the youth hostelling movement, and been in contact with Fernand Oury; he was fifteen years old when he first met Jean Oury, the brother of Fernand.

5 As we all called him spontaneously.
6 According to his own expression.
7 One can read this text, in a shorter version, under the title *La Borde: a Clinic unlike any other* in Guattari (1995a).
8 I use deliberately the word 'experiment'. In my view, it underscores the improvised, situated and conjectural nature of what takes place in the everyday life of the clinic.
9 Oury is referring to the many kinds of patients' transference to persons, animals, objects, etc. It is a question here of the transference of the details. The *detail* is a favourite notion of Oury.
10 Félix Guattari (2012). And he adds: 'One can count about forty different activities for a population consisting of just a hundred patients and seventy staff members'.
11 The monthly salary, of about today's 250 euros, is the same for all staff (the monitors). For the doctors, it was less than a third or a quarter of what they would normally receive elsewhere.
12 Marie Depussé lives and works as a psychoanalyst at La Borde since 1962. She has written many books on the clinic. She has also written the Introduction of *De Léros à La Borde.*
13 In French: BCM, SAM, SCAJ, GHA, GPG, UTB.

References

Dosse, F. (2007), *Gilles Deleuze Félix Guattari, Biographie Croisée*. Paris: La Découverte.

Dosse, F. (2010), *Gilles Deleuze and Félix Guattari: Intersecting Lives.* Translated by D. Glassman. New York: Columbia University Press.

Guattari, F. (1972), *Psychanalyse et transversalité*. Paris: François Maspero.

Guattari, F. (1977), *La Revolution Moleculaire.* Paris: Recherches.

Guattari, F. (1984), *Molecular Revolution: Psychiatry and Politics*. Translated by R. Sheed. London: Penguin.

Guattari, F. (1992), *Chaosmose*. Paris: Galilée.

Guattari, F. (1995), *Chaosmosis: an ethico-aesthetic paradigm.* Translated by P. Bains and J. Pefanis. Sydney: Power Institute.

Guattari, F. (1995a), *Chaosophy.* Edited by Sylvère Lotringer. London: Semiotext(e).

Guattari, F. (2012), *De Léros à La Borde*. Paris: Lignes.

Guattari, F. (2015), *Psychoanalysis and Transversality.* Translated by Ames Hodges. London: MIT Press.

Γκουατταρί, Φ. (2015), *Από τη Λέρο στη Λα Μπορντ*, μετάφραση Ε. Κούκη. Αθήνα: Κουκκίδα.

Polack, J.-Cl. (2011), 'Analysis, between Psycho and Schizo', in É. Alliez and A. Goffey (eds), *The Guattari Effect*. London: Continuum.

3

What is Schizoanalysis?

Jean-Claude Polack[1]

‘What is?’, in an essay title, arouses legitimate suspicion. This fragment of a question contains a promise of exhaustiveness which, clearly, cannot be fulfilled. Not being a philosopher, I do not feel I am being invited here to make an inventory of, clarify and explain the concepts forged, individually or together, by Gilles Deleuze and Félix Guattari. Some of my friends have begun to do that, combining precision and pedagogy.[2] I must therefore substitute ‘how?’ for ‘what is?’, and speak of a genealogy rather than an essence.

Since its appearance the term schizoanalysis has constantly caused surprise or provoked bizarre definitions: analysis of schizophrenics, analysis by schizophrenics, dissociative or dissociated analysis. Deleuze and Guattari never wanted to explain, even succinctly, the subtitle (*Revue des schizoanalyses*) given to *Chimères* in 1988. This plural noun made its way in a multitude of differentiated fields whose tracery sketches out a theory of Desire in which the clinical experience of psychosis and the revolutionary project are essential markers. These two requirements were at the heart of the work of institutional psychotherapy that I shared with Félix and Jean Oury in the La Borde clinic, in Cour-Cheverny, between 1964 and 1972.[3]

The references of schizoanalysis to the works of Freud and Marx are evident; but the syntheses that emerge from their comparison are not merely philosophical articulations of concepts and definitions. Schizoanalysis aims from the outset to test pragmatically, in diverse, but never watertight domains and disciplines, a theory of the Unconscious deeply rooted in the determinations of the socius and politics. The two terms – Capitalism and Schizophrenia – accompany the titles *Anti-Oedipus* (1972) and *A Thousand Plateaus* (1980).

The Freudian ambition

The programme is reminiscent, paradoxically, of the History of the discovery of the unconscious, the complexity of which Ellenberger (1970) once described in almost a thousand pages. The Canadian psychiatrist, armed with encyclopaedic knowledge, shows how psychoanalysis gradually emancipated itself from the domains of magic, belief, magnetism, hypnotism or forms of psychotherapy that preceded it, creating a new method of treatment and bringing to a close, by going beyond it, Pierre Janet's era of 'dynamic psychiatry'. We can only understand this invention by portraying an epoch, with its geopolitical changes, its armed conflicts, its economic and social life, its philosophical currents, beliefs, hypotheses and scientific advances, as well as its literary and artistic creations, the multiform ensemble of which produces what Freud called *Kultur*, translated today by Civilization. In doing so, we must abandon the hypothesis of a structure and its dialectical evolution in favour of singularities, heterogeneity and multiplicity. The author, without having the explicit intention of doing so, anticipates the effects of a proliferating evolution of psychoanalysis and its process (Ellenberger 1970).

Freud himself, notwithstanding the immensity of his *oeuvre,* recognized the obstacles that he could not overcome. The term *Metapsychology* condensed, in 1924, several articles written in the preceding years, including five essays of a theoretical systematization of the Unconscious and of the neuroses that remained incomplete. A few years later, he had already begun modifying elements of it.

Throughout his life (his correspondence, in particular with Jung, Abraham and Ferenczi attests to this) he never ceased to manifest his project of understanding psychosis and of evaluating History, without, however, treating what he calls 'discontents in civilization' and the enigma of 'dementia precox' as part of the same question. Before his five-day visit to the Burgholzi Hospital in Zurich, Freud insisted, in a letter dated 13 August 1908, that Jung should 'make a few personal concessions' to his theory, and manifested clearly his concerns:

> My selfish purpose, which I frankly confess, is to persuade you to continue and complete my work by applying to psychoses what I have begun with neuroses. With your strong and independent character, with your Germanic blood which enables you to command the sympathies of the public more readily than I, you seem better fitted than anyone else I know to carry out this mission. I'm fond of you but I have learned to subordinate that factor. (McQuire 1994: 81)

We are entitled to suppose that the rupture between Freud and Jung, which was long attributed solely to their different appreciation of the 'sexual factor' in the

Unconscious, unfolded partly against the backcloth of a disavowed ideological disagreement, which this letter, with the phrase 'Germanic blood', touches on prudently.

Freud's socialist engagement was discreet. As a member of the B'nai B'Rith, whose orientation is more masonic and humanitarian, he remained at a distance from Sionism. But 'Thoughts for the Times on War and Death' (1915b), *Group Psychology and the Analysis of the Ego* (1921c), *The Future of an Illusion* (1927c), *Civilization and its Discontents* (1930a) and *'Why war?'* (1933b) are political essays in which, for better or for worse, the effects and ruses of the Unconscious emerge.

The Frankfurt School, founded in 1923 (sixteen years before his death), was long considered as the space and the moment of a philosophical elaboration of Freudian–Marxist inspiration. The history of its successive institutions and of their migrations in times of war, however, temper this appreciation. The great revisions of Horkheimer and Adorno built a Critical Theory of Reason in the wake of Kant and Hegel, which they opposed over the years to the rise of industrial capitalism. The critique of Freudism and the posthumous 'analyses' of Hitler or Himmler by Eric Fromm were far from articulating political facts with Freudian categories, which he suspected of disregarding social determinations. The applications of psychoanalysis to the examination of capitalist oppression seemed more determined in Otto Gross and his theory of matriarchy, and above all in the dramatic adventure of Wilhelm Reich with his hypotheses concerning the links between fascism and sexual repression. Later, not without success, Herbert Marcuse would fuel the themes of the '68 movement' with 'repressive desublimation' and unidimensionality.

But, essentially, questions of politics and madness were for a long time dealt with at a distance from the concrete historical situations that could have associated them. These syncretic events – veritable mass traumas of the European twentieth century – occurred during and after the civil war in Spain, the Second World War and the Holocaust, in stages during which the institutional approach to psychotic patients underwent an upheaval.[4]

No one is a prophet in his own country

After the defeat of the republicans in 1939, François Tosquelles, a psychiatrist and psychoanalyst in Barcelona and doctor/commanding officer of the military region of Valencia, took refuge in France and underwent the ordeal of being confined in the Sept Fons internment camp. Doctors who knew and admired him obtained his release and welcomed him in 1940 at the Saint Alban's psychiatric hospital in Lozère. France was living under the Occupation and the Vichy government. Far from the powers of the State, the department, poor and fairly inaccessible, sheltered many members of the Resistance. The hospital, which was partly run by nuns, took them in and protected them. Tosquelles, arriving at the asylum where his friends gave him full powers, began by establishing the principle of an inalienable right to wander around freely. The walls were knocked down and the bars and the keys removed; the doors remained open and the asylum communicated naturally with the village and the surrounding countryside. The conquest of space was this freedom to go out, to work on neighbouring farms and to bring back something to eat in the evening. To survive.[5] The civic autonomy of the patients was acknowledged in the right to form an independent association – a legally declared club with its elected bureau and its own *treasury*, a journal and daily meetings. The psychoanalytic approach, which concerned both the carers and those cared for, gradually gained ground in the hospital.

Tosquelles set himself the task, as a matter of principle, of treating the institution and its pathoplasty, of shaping day after day the regulations, habits and rituals of the members of the personnel, of questioning the 'desire' of each one: 'What are we doing here?' This 'revolution within the revolution', in which clinical practice and politics are always intertwined, was the act of birth of the discipline of institutional psychotherapy.

Jean Oury, as an assistant doctor, and Félix Guattari, as a 'patient', met Tosquelles at Saint Alban at the end of the war. They had spent their adolescence in the same Paris suburb, united by militant activities. In 1953, Félix joined Oury who had just founded the La Borde psychiatric clinic, near Blois. They tried out a new approach to psychoses, integrating Tosquelles's teaching and the theory of Jacques Lacan, who became their analyst.

Lacan's science

The Ecole Freudienne, created in 1964, confirmed Lacan's rupture with the *International Psychoanalytic Association* (IPA) (1953), where the dominant influence was that of a deliberately adaptive Ego psychology. Lacan developed a linguistic theory of the Unconscious hailed by Louis Althusser, a Marxist and professor of philosophy at L'Ecole Normale Supérieur (E.N.S.), who found in the Lacanian approach all the characteristic elements of a 'science'. This was the beginning, in post-war France, of a structuralist era, rooted in the linguistics of Saussure, Benveniste and Jakobson, the anthropology of Lévi-Strauss, and the semiology of Barthes. For Althusser, the practice of 'reading' the foundational texts (*Reading Capital* (*Lire le Capital*) appeared in 1965) convinced him that there was an analogy between Lacan's innovating enterprise and his own hypothesis of the epistemological 'break' of 1844 in Marx's work. In his famous *Seminar* (rue d'Ulm), the prestigious psychoanalyst, who posed as a faithful reader of Freud, examined dreams and fantasies as rebuses or palimpsests, a matter of divided or overdetermined discourses. These materials, he believed, must be analysed with linguistic procedures; the identification of tropes (metonymies and metaphors) marks the condensations and displacements that make it possible to turn back from a ciphered speech towards the truth of the Desire of the Subject.[6]

Lacan deployed his first announcement: 'The Unconscious is structured like a language' in order to finish once and for all with medical, physicist, biological or psychological temptations which, in his view, distort its specificity. Althusser, for his part, espoused the schema of discursive levels, where the obvious nature of the first statements hides deep layers that he, like the psychoanalyst, will be able to bring into broad daylight, including in the political domain of the State's ideological apparatuses.

One or two alienations

The creation of La Borde, and the relative margin of freedom that a private clinic can enjoy, was to pose a multitude of problems for the exercise of psychoanalysis, which is necessarily dependent on its economic, legal and sociocultural context. Historical reality, as conceived by Freud, must surpass the individual and buried memory of each patient in order to take into account the collective history that envelops it in an unapparent way. The first attempts to draw up an inventory in the clinic may seem close to structuralist monographs, to their way of studying the exchange of women, material goods and speech in distant tribes or villages of 'stateless societies'. But in this domain Guattari was already particularly interested in the work of Pierre Clastres, whose research challenged both classical Marxism and the temptation of an 'African Oedipus'. Beyond a reference to the human sciences, the critical description of the treatment setting was matched by a will to analyse and transform the social context, in a constant to-and-fro between the political economy and the libidinal economy, thus without dissociating them. Jean Oury did not hesitate to take up the term 'alienation' which he divided into two distinct forms, 'mental' and 'social'. The first, perhaps genetic, is that which the dominant mode of psychiatry seeks to formulate in a universalizing code of 'mental disorders'[7]. The other form of alienation, social, is so common that much effort is needed to avoid confusing it with habits, with the 'psychopathology of everyday life'. La Boétie and Machiavelli had remarked, one in a spirit of exhortation and the other in a spirit of ruse, on its power of deception and confusion, its capacity to make men turn against their own interests. Marx revealed its subterranean existence, thereby outlining a reflection on the immaterial productions of our capitalistic societies, the continuous fabrication of subjugated 'subjects'. The essential thing, for Guattari, was to bring these two dimensions into confrontation by arranging practices in such a way that the clinic was not the only one in question. And Oury readily entrusted him with the responsibility for the concrete mutations aimed at bringing about a progressive 'de-alienation'.

Clinical

At La Borde, during the first years of work it was necessary to assess an institutional subjection that could not easily be circumvented. The changes, reforms and inventions constantly came up against this obstacle:

> In a clinic, a common feature of the medical and administrative domains is that they are at the junction point between the establishment and the State. It is precisely at this junction point, a point of interpenetration through which the whole of the dominant code infiltrates all the material cogs of the establishment, that the circumscription of the totalities as well as their subordinations are delimited. As a registered (subject to Social Security) health establishment (subject to medical, prefectorial and ministerial tutelage), and a private establishment (subject to a commercial system), the clinic is a totality permeated by the multitude of social and administrative constraints organised by the State … While we can accept the idea of a relative principle of freedom within the establishment, we know that at the junction point between the establishment and the state, the margins of freedom are almost zero. (Rostain et al. 1976)

Social alienation showed its face here.

Oury and Félix shared the tasks. Medicine and psychoanalysis belonged to the regal domain of Oury, who continued to teach and 'work-through' Lacanian themes, comparing the Seminar with the philosophical ideas of the scholastics, Nicolas of Cusa, Kierkegaard, Marx and the German phenomenologists.[8]

Guattari took charge of the 'institutionalization', the organization of daily life, the work and management of what was not yet called 'human resources'. The unusual nature of his interventions can be illustrated quite well with the following anecdote. In the 1970s, the club of the ('paying') patients of La Borde clinic, an independent and legal association, was in constant dialogue with those that Jean Oury liked to refer to as the 'paid'. The custom was to replace monitors during their holidays by groups of residents who acquitted the tasks of stewardship, cleaning, cooking or transport between the clinic and the city of Blois. The clinic paid the club for the work done, according to salary scales close to those of the usual employees. The club managed this money according to the wishes and agreements of the residents present at the meetings.

Marcel, a 'resident' for the last eight years, was silent, immobile and solitary. He rarely responded to questions, except sometimes to ask for a bicycle that would enable him to go to the village 'to get some cigarettes and a glass of white wine'. At Guattari's request, the elected officials of the club took this request into consideration during an assembly. They were not in favour of incurring the expense on the grounds that Marcel did nothing and did not even attend meetings. Félix pleaded for Marcel's cause. The club, he said, was paid by the clinic according to the normal model of capitalistic exploitation – that is to say, money in exchange for effort and time. It had the duties and rights of a collective proletariat, but its main function, beyond its social debt, was the project of care and treatment. Marcel was not improving with medication. The bicycle might be a beneficial replacement for pills and neuroleptic injections. There was no reason, moreover, to imprison him in the constricting dynamic of labour and salary. Values of use against values of exchange, 'from each according to his ability, to each according to his needs'. After a long discussion, the club's agreement was obtained. Marcel went into the town, accompanied by those he accepted, and bought his bicycle. In a few days his character had changed, he started speaking with half a dozen residents or monitors whom he had seemed to ignore up until then. A small group of cyclists organized outings in Sologne, prepared lunch bags and repaired the bikes. Alcohol and tobacco seemed secondary. All in all, a few grains of utopia, between Marx and Mauss, seemed to be a good prescription.

This analogy is only meaningful if we include it in the body of critiques and transformations that affected the structure of the institution and that prevented the crystallization of an 'ideal place of treatment', accredited once and for all. To return now to the gift. The effects of a decision by a small group of people, some of whom suffered from serious mental disorders, was obviously not of a nature to modify the psychiatric apparatus of the country and the 'liberal' rules that characterize the relations between work and salaried workers, unemployment, borrowing or credit. But in this specific case, the experiment took account simultaneously of what seemed to be the consequence of an individual disorder – of a 'mental alienation' – and of the modes of exchange and values that manifested the 'social alienation' of a whole community. The decision not to remunerate work according to the canonical rules gave money other possible functions, and in particular that of serving as a means of exchange for symptoms within the context of an economy of desire.

On complicity

Félix, compared with Oury, who was relatively sedentary, was an agent of the 'outside world'. He took care of foreign affairs, embassies, political strategies, whether regional or national. His reputation became, more or less everywhere, that of an unclassifiable leftist. During the Algerian War, although he was a member of the Communist Party, he was close to several Trotskyist groups that supported the FLN (*Front de Libération Nationale,* [National Liberation Front]). He created, under a pseudonym, *La Voie Communiste,* a fractional newspaper which printed more than 15,000 copies, and then small independent political formations. He played an important role in the revolt of 1968, many of the acting figures of which he knew. Extending the range of his work at La Borde, he created a Federation of study groups and institutional research groups (FGERI), then a Centre of Research and Training (CERFI). He travelled to Italy and Germany during the period of violent political activism of the 'Years of Lead' (1966–86), and later on to Brazil (where he met Lula), to Japan and to the United States in the wake of the successes of the French theory. He also frequented various ecologist movements, which he tried to bring together into an ecosophical ensemble coupling natural ecology with social ecology and mental ecology (Guattari 1989).

In all his creative activities, Félix conveyed his refusal to direct, to take on power, to last at any cost, thereby sketching out an ethics of precarity and finiteness that is already present in the last pages of *Anti-Oedipus*. His friends were often astonished at his capacity to interrupt a militant activity that he felt was too bureaucratic or ritualized, at his taste for risk and experimentation.

Up until 1968, Lacan's theoretical principles, taken up and honed by Oury, served as armature for the strategies that sought to transform the team of carers into a collective, a demanding set-up that Félix compared to the 'group-subject' defined by Sartre. The permutation of the tasks of the carers – the 'grid' – elaborated by the monitors themselves, put the roles, statuses and functions of the personnel in perspective. The Structure, the Subject and the Signifier provided a structure for mapping and local reforms. The Symbolic, the Imaginary, and the Real delineated symptoms, dreams, fantasies and *passages à l'acte*.

Oury created the GTPSI (Groupe de travail de Psychotherapîe et de Sociotherapie Instutionnelles [Work Group for Institutional Psychotherapy and Sociotherapy]) with ten or so friends, public hospital psychiatrists: a committee sometimes comparable, in its practice of 'free association', to certain rituals of the Freudian group of the 'Wednesday Society' in Vienna. His brother, Fernand, a primary school teacher, founded Institutional Pedagogy. Both of them separated themselves clearly from the current of institutional analyses which, in France, as in the United States (including Erving Goffman), excluded psychoanalysis from their sociological research (April 2009).

Whatever their divergences, Oury and Guattari shared a total militant complicity on the ground. They helped Algerian separatists and supported the struggle for the legalization of abortion. Only the anti-psychiatric wave, which culminated around 'May 1968', divided them; for tactical reasons, Félix remained close to Laing and Cooper in England, Basaglia and Jervis in Italy, and Mony El Khaim in Belgium, while Oury energetically opposed those who seemed to detest the psychiatric discipline or to be ignorant of the richness of psychoanalysis.

The rift

The turning-point that occurred in 1969 was not only linked to Guattari's encounter with Deleuze. One should not forget that, at the heart of the group of communist philosophy students at the Sorbonne – the 'cell' – Félix had been the first to take a passionate interest, beyond Sartre's ideas, in Lacan's teaching. His enthusiasm coincided with Oury's and they were in total agreement for several years concerning the primordial situation, clinical and political, of language (see Dosse 2007).

Later, after a period of a few years, when Félix no longer felt he had a place in the Ecole Freudienne, it seemed to him that the linguistics of reference of the *Seminar* and the *Ecrits* (Saussure, Benveniste, Jakobson) should make way for Hjelmslev and Peirce, and be refuted as the sole armature of a theory of the Subject.

For Félix, the Normalian students of the group of the *Cahiers pour l'analyse*, who had tried to marry Althusserism and Lacanism during the period 1966–8, had undermined the basis of the relationship he had had with Lacan, alongside Oury, a few years earlier. According to him, their approach prohibited the historical factors of subjectivation from being taken into account; 'in reality', he argued, 'the Lacanians themselves have not yet grasped the intrinsic relation between the Lacanian theory of subjectivity and history' (see, Kerslake 2008).

This judgement coincides with what those close to Lacan themselves consider as his apolitism. Jacques-Alain Miller, dubbed as Lacan's heir, has expressed the substance of this:

> What would a reader think who was browsing through Lacan's writings and sayings in the hope of being able to characterize Lacan's relation to politics? It seems to me that what would strike the reader most would be Lacan's mistrust of the ideals, systems and utopias which fill the field of politics. He does not believe in the laws of history. He rejects Bossuet along with Toynbee, Comte with Marx. No word of his suggests that he upheld the idea of a perfect city, be it in the past or projected into the future. There is no nostalgia, and no hope either. As for the present, for modernity, like Freud he has a very sharp sense of its impasses. Tomorrow only sings the song of discontent. What one finds on the contrary, and in abundance, are comments on politics ranging from irony to cynicism, punctuated by sarcasm and mockery. Politics is both comical and murderous. He recalls from Cardinal de Retz's *Memoirs* that it is 'always the people who pay the price for political events'. He depicts the conqueror always arriving with these words in his mouth: 'Get to work!' For Lacan, the alienation of work is a fact, but a structural fact, so that the class struggle merely encourages the exploited to compete to become in turn the exploiters, a situation the exploiters strive to perpetuate. (Miller 2003)

In 1969, Lacan was clearly contested. Machine against Structure. Guattari's text, which was proposed for a working session of the *Ecole,* introduces machinism as the materialistic basis for a description of the desiring psyche. He was offered the possibility of publishing it in *Scilicet* on the condition of anonymity, since the review was placed entirely under Lacan's name. Félix refused the transaction and the rupture was effective.

The question of Foucault

At the moment of the meeting between Deleuze and Guattari, Michel Foucault, whom I long considered as the virtual 'third man' of their conceptual machine, had already devoted himself at length to the theme of what History and Politics do with madness, and the discourses and mechanisms that the latter oppose to it; that is to say, to the question – an insistent one since Georges Canguilhem – of the norm and of the powers that set it up, of the pathological and its exclusion (Foucault 1961). But his work as an archivist, including in his *History of Sexuality,* never takes into account the powers of the Unconscious to which he opposes the discursive, and not necessarily repressive, productions of power. Thus, concerning the reproaches of 'pansexualism' directed at Freud, he says that their authors are mistaken regarding the nature of the process:

> They believed that Freud had at last, through a sudden reversal, restored to sex the rightful share which it had been denied for so long; they had not seen how the good genius of Freud had placed it at one of the critical points marked out for it since the eighteenth century by the strategies of knowledge and power; how wonderfully effective he was – worthy of the greatest spiritual fathers and directors of the classical age – in giving new impetus to the secular injunction of having to study sex and transform it into discourse. (Foucault 1976: 159)

It was Foucault's painstaking work with his collaborators, *Moi, Pierre Rivière, ayant égorgé ma mère, ma soeur et mon frère…,* which best attests to a polyphonic attempt to understand, and sometimes to 'defend' madness. In this collective book the historian, the psychoanalyst, the specialist of the Norman peasantry in the nineteenth century, the sociologist and the man of law each speak in turn. He tries to identify what, in Pierre, who killed his sister, his brother and his mother, has its roots in his singular biography and what comes from 'outside', from the relations of power, from class confrontation or from voluntary servitude, that is, from the history of a society that was still despotic in the first third of the nineteenth century. It was an 'ecosophic' essay ahead of its time (Foucault 1994).

Deleuze with Lacan and Freud

Deleuze had already taken the measure of Freudian concepts. For example, in the case of the 'death drive', he distanced himself from Lacan in 1967 in order to return to Freud's first terms and to re-establish the notion of instinct which, notwithstanding its indiscriminate use in Anglo-Saxon translations, seemed to him more exact:

> In *Beyond the Pleasure Principle* (1920g), Freud distinguishes the life instincts from the death instincts, Eros and Thanatos. But this distinction can only be understood in the light of another, deeper one, between the death instincts (or the instincts of destruction) themselves, and the death instinct. For the death instincts (and instincts of destruction) are given or presented in the unconscious, but always mingled with the life instincts ... When we speak of death instinct, on the other hand, we are referring to Thanatos in the pure state. To refer to it, we should in French keep the term instinct, which alone is capable of suggesting such transcendence, of designating such a 'transcendent' principle. (Deleuze 1967)

In doing so, he attributed to Freud's thought the title of philosophy and often returned to *Beyond the Pleasure Principle* which he regarded as a masterpiece. Deleuze also took up afresh the question of perversions and, with them, the place of 'negation' and 'denial' – to which he adds 'suspense', in the construction of their symptoms and literary creations. The *Presentation of Sacher Masoch* also became, with the eleven arguments aimed at differentiating sadism and masochism, and the analysis of the contract linking Severin to Wanda of *Venus in Furs*, a laudatory addition to a number of Freudian principles (Deleuze 1967: 27–8).

Deleuze also maintained a silent, but profound philosophical dialogue with Lacan. In *Diffférence et répetition* (1968) he constantly works on Lacan's interpretations, which he corrects or translates into philosophy, thereby pursuing the Lacanian theorization of Freud. At any rate, he does not oppose the statements of the *Seminar,* but seems to want to make them compatible with his own approach to the Unconscious, repression and the virtual.

His dissection of the corpse of structuralism seems to come to a standstill. Lacan congratulated himself on an adhesion – which he considered evident – to his thought in the last chapters of the *Logic of Sense* (Deleuze 1969), where Deleuze insists on the place and function of the sexual in the organization of the psychic apparatus. He revisits the ideas of Melanie Klein, which help us to understand the transition from a machinic existence of the body to the progressive armature of the 'immaterial aspects' of language and thought, against the uncertain backcloth of an oedipal structure. A precarious accord still seems possible.

A long time after the period of their virtual conversation, Slavoj Zizek attempted an acrobatic demonstration of the 'Becoming-Lacanian of Deleuze', in spite of the misunderstanding opposing their discourses: 'In Deleuze's conceptual edifice, there is an oscillation between two contrary logics, that of the generative power of the flow of "becoming", and that of the sterility of this flow. The second logic, more "repressed" in the reception of Deleuze, allows us to establish an unexpected link between the Deleuzian notion of "dark precursor" and the Lacanian concept of "symbolic castration"'.[9]

This sleight of hand was right on an essential point. The *Logic of Sense* is supplementary proof of Deleuze's deep interest in psychoanalysis, particularly when it discovers the incessant and 'aberrant' movements of desire, the fragmentation and multiplicity of the intensive montages that mark the depressive and schizoid moments of early childhood. His book may be read as the measured logical and critical inventory of a number of Lacan's theses, possibly reprocessed by Serge Leclaire, Jean Laplanche and Jean Bertrand Pontalis. To define, for example, the nature of phantasy as an event, the castration conveyed by speech or the effects of meaning that separate the penis from the symbolic symbol, Deleuze freely uses once again the categories and graphs that arm Lacanian *lalangue* (Deleuze 1969).

The radical anti-familialist critique towards which Guattari led and accompanied him, would have, three years later, the lustre of an unexpected destructive jubilation, to which the verve and fury of Anti-Oedipus would mischievously draw attention.

The patients, the militants, the madmen

Deleuze received from Guattari the account and commentaries pertaining to two experiences. Félix was living and working every day with psychotic patients, but at the same time he was pursuing intense political activity, increasingly foreign to the pseudo- or post-Marxist dogmas and modes of organization. The writing machine that was elaborated between them on the rapprochement of a philosophical way of thinking and a concrete existential experience was a 'disjointed conjunction' in certain respects, for it was not based on any symmetry of forms of learning. In 1969, Félix had little knowledge of Deleuze's work; nor had he devoted much of his time to Spinoza, Hume, Nietszche, Leibniz or Bergson.

The best way to understand the profound seduction exerted by Guattari over Deleuze is by reading the philosopher's preface to *Psychanalyse et transversalité*, a collection of texts concerning madness and psychiatry on the one hand and militantism on the other, two issues united by the approach to 'groups' and the 'institution' (Guattari 2003).

The introduction hails the discovery and the overturning of priorities, a displacement of the questions that would be discussed globally in the theses and critiques of *Anti-Oedipus*, and then in the fields and domains of *A Thousand Plateaus*.

Underlining in passing the duality of Pierre and Félix, first names and characters that he distinguishes in the militant psychoanalyst, Deleuze identifies in the essays three kinds of problems: (1) In what form should politics be introduced into psychoanalytic practice and theory (once it has been said that, in any case, politics is in the unconscious itself)? (2) Are there grounds, and if so, how, of introducing psychoanalysis into revolutionary militant groups? (3) How are we to conceive of specific therapeutic groups, whose influence would have repercussions for political groups, and also for psychiatric and psychoanalytic structures?

Deleuze clarifies Guattari's answers to these introductory questions. They may be summed up as follows: (1) The unconscious is directly related to a whole social, economic and political field rather than to the mythical and familial coordinates traditionally invoked by psychoanalysis. (2) Political groups must be separated into subject-groups and subjugated groups: the first, which are rare, are defined by coefficients of transversality, which ward off totalities and hierarchies; they are agents of enunciation, supports of desire, elements of institutional creation. The second, which are numerous, accept a hierarchy set up to ward off a possible inscription of non-meaning, death or breaking apart to prevent creative cuts. (3) A transformation of psychoanalysis into schizoanalysis implies an evaluation of the specificity of madness. One has to agree with Foucault when he announces that 'it is not madness that will disappear in favour of mental illnesses that are positively determined, treated and asepticized but, on the contrary, mental illnesses, in favour of something that we have not yet understood about madness. For the real problems are on the side of psychosis'[10] (see preface to Guattari 2003).

In spite of the numerous expressions of tribute, it is the divergences with the Lacanian reinterpretation of Freud – the critiques directed at the notion of *signifiance*, the universality of lack, 'familialism', phallic symbolism and castration – that draw the authors of *Anti-Oedipus* closer together. Both agree on accommodating the philosopher clinician and making the disciples carry the weight of psittacism and the idiocies pronounced in his name. A necessary strategic detour makes them distinguish Anti-Oedipus from anti-Lacan.

An attentive reading nonetheless confirms the way in which Stephane Nadaud, in his meticulous study of their work, emphasizes the clarity of a rupture:

> Though Deleuze-Guattari do not generally mince their words and are often very acerbic in their critiques, Lacan remains miraculously spared. And yet one would have to be blind not to see that some of the essential principles of his theory are criticized in depth: even it is only on the back cover of the book which sets out one of the theses of *Anti-Oedipus,* namely, that the unconscious is not structured like a language, that 'it is neither figural nor structural but machinic'. (Guattari 2004)

The schizoanalytic cut occurred a short while after the end of the 'GTPSI moment', in the noisy context of 'anti-psychiatries', when Félix gave up any hopes of making himself heard by the Lacanian Areopagus and engaged with Deuleuze in the philosophical and political critique of a structural Unconscious.

The unusual twinning of schizophrenia and capitalism seemed like a surrealist, almost delusional idea, a monstrous hybridization. The minimal intention of the authors of *Anti- Oedipus* is, however, not to articulate or make madness and Revolution similar, but to lead this conceptual assemblage towards the concrete terrains of their 'analysis'. Contestations and struggles must be understood as a part of a pragmatic process of constant reorganizations of militant groups or collectives. Conversely, clinical practices (diagnoses and treatments) concerning the extended field of mental troubles will be examined, invented and modified in the light of the daily work that psychosis and the institution requires. Both of these experiences are dealt with simultaneously. Irrespective of the places of engagement and action – prison, hospital, asylum, school, street – the objective is to take account of madness in the political field and, conversely, the social violence in psychotic suffering.

In spite of Marx and Freud, the indivisible economy

The important and final chapter of *Anti-Oedipus,* an 'Introduction to Schizoanalysis', notwithstanding its profoundly rebellious tone, is a materialist critique of the Freudian or Lacanian Unconscious and presupposes a common productive force to the clinical approach to psychoses and the follies of History.

The fusion into a single nature of the two regimes of the libidinal economy and the political economy underlies, irrespective of the historical evolution of their definition, the propositions of *Anti-Oedipus*, and then of *A Thousand Plateaus*.

Having identified a first reason to be suspicious of Marxism and psychoanalysis – their tendency to speak in the name of a 'memory' and a 'development' – Gilles Deleuze specifies his critique:

> The second reason that distinguishes us from any Freudo-Marxist venture is that such ventures set out first and foremost to reconcile two economies: a political economy and a libidinal or desiring economy. In Wilhelm Reich, too, we find the maintenance of this duality and this attempt at conciliation. Our point of view, on the contrary, is that there is only one economy and that the problem of a veritable anti-psychoanalytic analysis is to show how unconscious desire invests the forms of this economy. It is the economy itself that is a political economy or a desiring economy. (Deleuze 2002: 385)

The materialist affirmation of a production, turning its back deliberately on the function of lack, would thus be particularized in the concepts of machine and desiring machine. At the beginning of another analysis, of a different analysis, an act of liberation frees itself from the restrictions, forcing and eidetic reductions that claim to approach the Unconscious by means of representations. This abrasion, this 'curettage', must rid psychoanalysis of the anthropological pivot of the Oedipus complex, of its allegedly universal presence confirmed by the imaginaries of tragedy and myth. The factory against the theatre.

But despite the innumerable critiques directed at psychoanalysis, Deleuze and Guattari nonetheless recognize an essential foundational act which they take over and whose consequences they infer:

> Freud founds the desiring economy by discovering the quantitative libido as the principle of every representation of the objects and aims of desire … He is the first to disengage desire itself, just as Ricardo disengages 'labor itself' (*travail tout court*), and thereby the sphere of production that effectively eclipses representation. And subjective abstract desire, like subjective abstract labour, is inseparable from a movement of deterritorialization that discovers the interplay of machines and their agents underneath all the specific determinations that still linked desire or labor to a given person, to a given object in the framework of representation. (Deleuze and Guattari 1972: 300)

The two friends see themselves as part of the phylum of an analysis of psychoanalysis. But their work has neither the characteristics of a hermeneutic nor the procedures of a Derridian 'deconstruction'. It is no longer a matter for them of interpreting or criticizing a partial and closed system, but of pushing the 'decoding' of psychoanalysis (that of Freud and of Lacan) beyond the limits of the discursive or textual formations that have too long sustained a politics of the castrating Father and an ethics of guilt. Their *oeuvre* refuses myth and claims to be 'differential', turned towards an incessant and dispersed becoming:

> The negative or destructive task of schizoanalysis is in no way separable from its positive tasks (all these tasks are necessarily undertaken at the same time). The first positive task consists in discovering in a subject the nature, the formation or the functioning of his desiring machines, independently of any interpretation … The schizoanalyst is a mechanic because schizoanalysis is solely functional. (*AO* 322/385)

The first volume of *Capitalism and Schizophrenia* turns away from lack, from negation and from pleasure to give desire its full potency of eruption. Even the 'royal road' of the dream, close to phantasy and narration, is not above suspicion. The essay claims to be an incitement, a risk of delusion and poetry, an invention of forms and an exploration of affects. There is no reason to be surprised, then, by the provocative literary form – a manifest or pamphlet opposing oedipal classicism, this new regiosity when 'God is dead'.

The reader of *Anti-Oedipus* notices that writing, its words and rhythms, espouses the climate of industrial machines, those of Chaplin's *Modern Times*. It heats up, emits and captures. It breaks down, and it starts again.

> There is, as it were, a profound sense of revolt in the war declared by schizoanalysis on the denomination of language. The heterogeneous world of semantic and material arrangement does not follow, for them, any intrinsic logic of organization or mathematical law of development. In *The Machinic Unconscious*, published between *Anti-Oedipus* and *A Thousand Plateaus*, Guattari sets out alone to work on a semiotics, with new tools and vocabulary. He makes use of a first lever that he finds in Hjelmslev, in his choice of demembering the false relationship between the content and the expression, and to search, further upstream, the materials and substances that 'formalize' these two entities and multiply their links. He sets out, then, to elaborate a machinic economy of components and signs which lie outside the semantic and syntactic facts of language. A multiplicity of collective arrangements of enunciation (CAE), combining economic, institutional, biological, physical, gestual, sensorial, mimicking, iconic or musical elements, follow fruitful vanishing lines. But Félix insists: by affirming its own axiomatics, its mode of subjectivation – that of profit and private property – Capitalism is constantly confiscating this productivity, limiting it and channelling it through the dynamic of reterritorializations. (Guattari 1979)[11]

From part-objects to desiring machines

The first pages of *Anti-Oedipus* evoke irremediably Melanie Klein's partial objects. Like the fragments of a body condemned to the uncertainties of their difficult relations, these desiring machines appear under aspects that the British psychoanalyst clearly anticipated. It is a question of flows emitted, cut off or picked up by machines which multiply their functions, and are linked together by proliferating segments in interwoven arrangements; the mouth cuts, takes in or rejects food, proffers words, closes in anorexia, empties itself when vomiting, cries out, breathes in and out. It is a machinic knot, a privileged crossroads of the first moments of extra-uterine life. Deleuze and Guattari hailed these inventions and were familiar with the precise nature of the research into psychotic or autistic children that followed on from them (Donald Meltzer, Wilfred Bion, Donald Winnicott, Frances Tustin, John Bowlby, Esther Bick, Genevieve Haag, Didier Houzel, Jacques Hochmann…). Their critique is directed nonetheless at the persistence of its oedipal catechism, which is so evident in Klein's interpretations during the play sessions with children. Something holds her back in her 'machinic' approach to the instincts: 'It is very curious that Melanie Klein, whose discovery of partial objects was so far-reaching, neglects to study flows from this point of view and declares that they are of no importance; she thus short-circuits all the connections' (*AO*: 40).

Schizoanalysis abolishes any sort of precedence between the critical analysis of the powers of Capital and the clinical experience of 'madness'. Hence the choice of a concept that concerns both of them – deterritorialization or schizophrenic process, and the material bases that underlie them – desiring machines: 'The schizoanalytic argument is simple. Desire is a machine, a synthesis of machines, a machinic arrangement – desiring-machines. The order of desire is the order of *production*: all desire is at once desiring production and social production' (*AO*: 325, emphasis in the original).

The primary physiology of desire, at first restricted to the zones of the mouth, fingers and skin, is already comparable with the principles of the social economy; it involves modes of production, recording and consumption. A theoretical gamble treats the multitude of machines as many agents of a process of which they are not only the result, but also integral parts. We are far, of course, from the thermodynamics or hydraulics imagined by Freud on the basis of Fechner's theories. But we are close, on the other hand, to his very materialistic, and sometimes physical manner, of speaking of Desire and of the drives, acts and words of a somato-psychic articulation.

Numbers, molecules and moles

From the very first lines of *Anti-Oedipus*, the authors' remarks evoke scientific references, sometimes only named, but which are always identifiable by the biological, physical or chemical terms that are new descriptive metaphors of the Unconscious. That moles and molecules can characterize psychic forms of investment of desire shows quite clearly the concern for scientific backing, which Freud, in his time, never disdained.

> What is the meaning of this distinction between two regions: one molecular, and the other molar; one micropsychic or micrological, the other statistical and gregarious? Is this anything more than a metaphor lending the unconscious a distinction grounded in physics, when we speak of an opposition between intra-atomic phenomena and the mass phenomena that operate through statistical accumulation, obeying the laws of aggregates? But in reality the unconscious belongs to the realm of physics; the body without organs and its intensities are not metaphors, but matter itself. (*AO*: 311).

The significance of these hypotheses is immense. They attempt to resolve the ancestral opposition between vitalism and mechanism, to overcome the difficulty of the passage between the somatic and the psychic, and to undo the usual forms of their associations illustrated in particular in clinical psychiatry by the theories of hysteria or depression. In the pages that draw on Samuel Butler's *Erewhon,* or the arguments of Jacques Monod and Raymond Ruyer in the biological field, we should see the hypothesis of a continuous evolving diagram between the inert and the living, machines and organs, the 'body' and the 'mind' (Ruyer 1958; Monod 1970).

In so doing, we find the reasons for an essential distinction at the heart of the arrangements of desire: the effects of number oppose the nomadic multiplicity of the molecular regimes and the structural gregariousness of the molar aggregates. But between the two modes, it is stressed, the and ... and always prevails over the either ... or.

A particular moment in the analysis clarifies the relations between the elements that arm the functioning of desire:

> At bottom, the partial organs and the body without organs are a single and same thing, a single and same multiplicity which must be thought as such by schizoanalysis. Partial objects are the direct powers of the body without organs, and the body without organs is the raw material of the partial objects. ... The body without organs is the matter that always fills space to given degrees of intensity,

> and the partial objects are these degrees, these intensive parts that produce the real in space starting from matter as intensity, = O. The body without organs is the immanent substance, in the most Spinozist sense of the word. (AO 390; 326–7)

The schema recapitulates: matter and the intensities are consubstantial; unicity and multiplicity are never contradictory; desiring-machines comprise two elements (partial objects, body without organs) which together resist the stimulations of the organism.

Schizophrenic process and deterritorialization

The term 'schizophrenic' expresses this functioning of flows and dispersive, multiple vanishing lines, not ordered by a code. It is important, therefore, to understand the choice of 'schizo', this word or part of a word derived from clinical 'schizophrenia' and projected – as cut, splintering, fragmentation and mobility at all the levels of a logic of the living. The psychosis that carries this name reveals the arrest of the process, whatever the causes may be. The most audacious conceptual gamble is that of the rapprochement between the schizophrenic process and capitalistic deterritorialization, two ways of decoding flows that are comparable in their respective fields, the psyche and society.

Deleuze and Guattari make no judgement about this ineluctable tendency of the political economy and of the mind, which are closely associated. They insist on the interplay of certain reterritorializations, these 'catastrophes' that are sometimes useful when they oppose, for example, the deadly destiny of the institutional treatment of schizophrenia in an asylum. But an opposition seems essential to them: 'Psychoanalysis settles on the imaginary and structural representatives of reterritorialization, whereas schizoanalysis follows the machinic indices of deterritorialization' (*AO*: 316).

We are thus moving, step by step, towards the level of political economy, passing through the defile of sexuality and the false biological determinism of reproduction. The machines of desire subordinate those which, by means of familial structuring, attempt to organize its flows, determine genders, ways of loving, erotic norms or the shameful universe of the 'perversions'. Deleuze and Guattari take up an essential distinction of Marx between human sex and non-human sex (Marx 1843: 970–1). And a large part of their Introduction could be understood as the development and illustration of this foundational intuition:

Desire (power of nature, non-human, non-anthropomorphic sex) precedes and produces Need, sex (too?) human, with which it gratifies the Subject: 'Sexuality is not a means in the service of generation; rather, it is the generation of bodies that is in the service of sexuality as auto-production of the Unconscious' (*AO*: 116).

The same logic must displace the vicissitudes of the Libido towards the mutations of the political economy. Keynes, an admirer of Freud, undoubtedly preceded him in this domain when he linked the 'death drive' to the expected misdeeds of Capitalism (see Dostaler and Maris 2009).[12] Schizoanalysis takes up directly a troubling question, expanding on the remarks of La Boetie on 'voluntary servitude'. What is it that surreptitiously opposes the revolt or desire for revolution? Which unconscious metabolisms divide the same subjects or groups between the revolutionary project and fascist violence?

The molar and the molecular are treated once again as dispositions that are never opposed to each other or that never annul each other definitively, thereby challenging in politics the useless concept of 'contradiction'.

Under the cover of destruction or anti-production, we now have a redefinition of the death drive which Deleuze, for a long time, had wanted to remove from the Freudian duality of Eros and Thanatos.[13] It is undoubtedly the most arid part of the Introduction, perhaps also the boldest. Thanatos is not a principle or a determination that can be opposed to sexuality, but an omnipresent and virtual power of desexualization, involution or narcissistic withdrawal, differential but not different from Eros. *Anti-Oedipus* regards death as a continuous unconscious experience, foreign to the I ('One dies', 'One never stops dying'), elaborated or integrated and made profitable by capitalistic anti-production and the industry of weapons of war.

By way of conclusion, a topographical question, which directly concerns the political economy, emerges in the wake of the modifications of the structure of the Unconscious put forward by Freud in 1920. The three terms, Unconscious, Preconscious and Conscious, were replaced by the Id, the Ego and the Superego. Deleuze and Guattari give them, curiously enough, a certain priority again, with regard to the question of revolutionary engagement. How are we to think about the opposition between need or interest (in the indecisive zone of the preconscious) and desire (unconscious), between molar repression and the creative power of the molecular?

What we see emerging, then, beyond a profound transformation of psychoanalytic clinical practice, is the questionnaire and the programme of applications of *A Thousand Plateaus* throughout the various stages of capitalistic globalization.

On the future of psychoanalysis

The ambition of the two volumes of *Schizophrenia and Capitalism* – which are situated partially within the perspective of a 'veritable materialistic psychiatry' – is not to combat or invalidate psychoanalysis but, on the contrary, to extend its range to the critical understanding of our world and to find the means of defusing its charges of destruction. For a long time already, a large number of theoreticians had, in the name of psychoanalysis, been taking paths that deviated from Freudian principles. Jung, who forged a long posterity for himself, is the best known of these thinkers. Adler, who became political too swiftly, was not convincing. But among those who were faithful, friendship and sedition were intermingled: Otto Rank, Sandor Ferenczi, Ernest Jones, Karl Abraham, Wilhelm Stekel or Otto Fenichel were much more than mere adepts.

The expansion of psychoanalysis in the Western world hardened positions and confirmed the 'schools'. Lacan, the most famous of the successors of Freudism, wanted to erect this system of thought into a body of knowledge with philosophical ambitions, whereas Alain Badiou regarded his discourse as an 'anti-philosophy'.

The psychoanalytic doctrine, recasted many times, was raised by Freud to the rank of a Metapsychology capable of organizing its hypotheses over and beyond a clinical and therapeutic approach. In the context of psychosis and the massive political aberrations of our time, it must now become a permanent object of analysis in its turn. It has partly abandoned the confined territory of the dual relationship and the transference and deployed itself in a multitude of institutional, therapeutic, intellectual, artistic and militant practices for which neurosis, that famous 'normopathy', has ceased to be the principal concern. But those who continue to receive patients in their consulting room can also profoundly modify their way of working, whenever they prefer to interest themselves in the investments of desire of their 'analysands' – however bizarre they may be – rather than interpreting the 'message' of a delusion or the symbolic fissure of a 'foreclosure'.

Schizoanalysis acknowledges a new ambition. Beyond an active psychotherapy of the psychoses, it undertakes an analysis of psychoanalysis and the study of the productions subjectivity conveyed by globalization. It is thus both extension and process; and, by taking up the intention of the prefix chosen by Freud, a metapsychoanalysis.

Notes

1 Translated by Andrew Weller.

2 I am thinking, among others, of Eric Alliez, Franco Berardi, Jean Philippe Cazier, Gary Genosko, Peter Pal Pelbart, Anne Querrien, Anne Sauvagnargues, and of François Dosse's (2007) remarkable biographical work, *Gilles Deleuze Felix Guattari. Biographie croisée.*

3 From now on the name 'Félix' will often appear in my text.

4 The extermination of the mentally ill and the handicapped, and the first gas chambers of the Nazi regime, preceded, as early as 1939, the genocide of the Jews.

5 The deadly famine that led to the deaths of 40,000 mentally ill in France during the war caused no victims at Saint Alban.

6 In *Althusser et la psychanalyse,* Pascale Gillot (2009) dismantles with precision the speculative machine that emerged from the encounter between Althusser and Lacan, or virtually from that between Marx and Freud.

7 The Diagnostic and Statistical Manual of Mental Disorders (DSM), published by the American Association of Psychiatry since 1952, has been revised several times or frankly contested. The fifth edition was published in 2013.

8 The spirit of this can be found in Jean Oury's (2012) *Préalables à toute clinique des psychoses, in dialogue* with Patrick Faugeras.

9 Deleuze gives the name of 'disparate' (*dispars*) to the 'dark precursor', 'this difference in itself, to the second degree, which brings into relationship the series that are heterogeneous ou disparate'. *D.R.* (page 157).

10 The terms of the argument extend and clarify Erasmus's *Praise of Folly.*

11 The recent essay by Maurizio Lazzarato (2011) illustrates perfectly the deep connivance between economic alienation and the productions of subjectivity.

12 Bernard Maris was killed in the attack against Charlie-Hebdo in January 2015.

13 See in particular the citation from Maurice Blanchot and Deleuze's commentary (page 148) in *Différence et Repetition* (Deleuze 1968).

References

Althusser, L. and Balibar, E. [1965] (1970), *Reading Capital.* Translated by Brewster. London: New Let Books.

Apprill, O. (2009), *Une avant-garde psychiatrique Le moment GTPSI* (1960-1966). Paris: Epel.

Deleuze, G. (1967), *Présentation de Sacher Masoch.* Paris: Minuit.

Deleuze, G. (1968), *Différence et répetition.* Paris: PUF.

Deleuze, G. and Guattari, F. (1972), *Anti-Oedipus: Capitalism and Schizophrenia*, translated by R. Hurley, M. Seem and H. R. Lane. Minneapolis: University of Minnesota Press.

Deleuze, G. (2002), *Cinq propositions sur la psychanalyse*. Remarks made at a conference in Milan, May 1973, reproduced in Gilles Deleuze: *L'île déserte et autres textes*, 1953-1974. Paris: Editions de Minuit.

Deleuze, G. and Guattari, F. (1980), *A Thousand Plateaus: Capitalism and Schizophrenia*. Translated by B. Massumi. Minneapolis: University of Minnesota Press.

Dosse, F. (2007), *Gilles Deleuze, Félix Guattari. Biographie croisée*. Paris: La Decouverte.

Dostaler, G. and Maris, B. (2009), *Capitalisme et pulsion de mort*. Paris: Albin.

Ellenberger, H. (1970), *The Discovery of the Unconscious: The History and Evolution of Dynamic Psychiatry*. Washington: Library of Congress.

Foucault, M. [1961](2000), *History of Madness*, Khalifa. Editor and Translator by J. Murphy. New York: Routledge.

Foucault. M. (1976), *The History of Sexuality, Vol. 1, The Will to Knowledge*. New York: Pantheon, 1978. Gallimard. Paris. 1976.

Foucault. M. (1994), *Moi, Pierre Riviere* (1835). Presented by M. Foucault. (J. P. Peter, Jeanne Favret., Patricia Moulin, Blandine Barret Kriegel. P Riot, Robert Castel, Alexandre Fontana). Paris: Gallimard (Folio histoire).

Freud, S. (1915b), Thoughts for the times on war and death. *S.E.* 14: 273–300.

Freud, S. (1927c), *The Future of an Illusion. S.E.*, 21: 1–56.

Freud, S. (1920g), *Beyond the Pleasure Principle. S.E.*, 18: 1–64.

Freud, S. (1921c), *Group Psychology and the Analysis of the Ego. S.E.* 18: 65–143.

Freud, S. (1930a), *Civilization and its Discontents. S.E.*, 21: 59–145.

Freud, S. (1933b), *Why war? S.E.*, 22:195–215.

Guattari, F. (1989), *Les trois écologies*. Paris: Galilée.

Guattari, F. (2003), *Psychanalyse et transversalité. Essais d'analyse institutionnelle*. Préface de Gilles Deleuze Paris: La Découverte.

Guattari, F. (2004), *Ecrits pour l'Anti-Oedipe*. Textes agencés par Stephane Nadaud. Paris: Lignes-Manifeste.

Guattari, F. [1979] (2010), *The Machinic Unconscious. Essays in Schizoanalysis*. Translated by Taylor Adkins. Cambridge, MA: MIT Press.

Gillot, P. (2009), *Althusser et la psychanalyse*. Paris: Presses Universitaires de France.

Kerslake, C. (2008), Les machines désirantes de Félix Guattari. *Multitudes*, 34 (3).

Lazzarato, M. (2011), *La fabrique de l'homme endetté* (Ed. Amsterdam).

Marx, K. (1843), *Critique de la philosophie politique de Hegel*. In: *Oeuvres. III. Philosophie*. Paris: Gallimard, Bibliothèque de la Pléiade, nrf, I982.

McGuire, W., ed. (1994), *The Freud-Jung Letters*. Translated by R. Manheim and R. F. C. Hull. Princeton: Princeton University Press.

Miller, J.-A. (2003), Lacan et la Politique Propos recueillis. *Cités*, 2003/4. No 16. P.U.F Paris.

Monod. J. (1970), *Le hasard et la nécessité.* Paris: Seuil.

Oury, J. (2012), *Préalables à toute clinique des psychoses, in dialogue* dialoguant with Patrick Faugeras. Paris: Erès.

Rostain, M., et al. (1976), *Histoires de la Borde. Dix ans de Psychothérapie institutionelle à la clinique de Cour-Cheverny. Revue Recherches,* 21 (March to April, 1976.)

Ruyer, R. (1958), La genèse des formes vivantes. Paris: Flammarion.

4

What is Ecosophy?

Manola Antonioli

Relationism

The term 'ecosophy' appears almost at the same time (without precise knowledge of the influence between the two schools of thought) in the work of the Norwegian philosopher Arne Naess and that of Félix Guattari:[1]

> 'Ecosophie' est composé du préfixe 'éco-'que l'on trouve dans 'économie' et dans 'écologie,' et du suffixe '-sophie' que l'on trouve dans 'philosophie ... La sophia n'a aucune prétention scientifique spécifique, contrairement aux mots composés de logos ('biologie,' 'anthropologie,' 'géologie,' etc.), mais toute vue de l'esprit dite 'sophique' doit être directement pertinente pour l'action ... La sophia signifie le savoir intuitif (acquaintance) et la compréhension, plutôt que la connaissance impersonnelle et abstraite.[2]
>
> ['Ecosophy' is composed of the prefix 'eco-'that is found in 'economy' and 'ecology', and of the suffix '-sophy' that is found in 'philosophy' ... The *sophia* has no particular scientific claim, unlike *logos* compound words ('biology', 'anthropology', 'geology', etc.), but any 'sophic' standpoint must be *directly relevant to action ... Sophia* indicates intuitive knowledge (*acquaintance*) and understanding, rather than impersonal and abstract knowledge.]

The prefix 'eco' also refers to the Greek *oïkos*, which stands for house, household, habitat and, by extension, our environments. Based on the suffix *sophia*, Guattari then described ecosophy as a complex ethico-political articulation (one might add, as we will see, aesthetico-philosophical) 'between the three ecological registers (the environment, social relations and human subjectivity)'.[3] In a recent book, entitled *Pour une écologie de l'attention*, the Swiss intellectual Yves Citton deserves credit for drawing attention to the common fundamental orientation of these two approaches to ecosophy: 'the necessary concatenation of several primarily interdependent levels' and the 'core understanding that individuals do not pre-exist the relations that shape them[4]', which is also a fundamental statement of the Deleuze–Guattari philosophy:

> Relationism has an ecosophical value because it dispels the belief that entities or people can be isolated from their environment. Talking about interaction between entities and their environment leads to misconceptions, because *an entity is an interaction.*[5]

In opposition to the standardized discourse about 'sustainable development', which emphasizes (often in a sanctimonious and guilt-inducing manner) the relations between 'individuals' and their environment, ecosophy (especially in its Guattarian variant, which I specifically refer to here) draws our attention to the plurality of ecologies, environments, habitats, that do not 'surround' us as a container would envelop its contents, but that define us and that we constantly define and reconfigure in a network of relations.

First of all, we need to emphasize the plurality of ecologies. On the one hand, there is a 'managerial[6]' ecology that aims to save our resources and reduce the environmental impact of our modes of production and consumption. Its purpose is to extend (in a supposedly more 'durable' and 'sustainable' way) the same lifestyles and modes of production adopted by the Western world since the successive industrial revolutions, with the goal of spreading them to so-called emerging countries. In this 'green capitalism' or 'eco-business' we can see no questioning of the purpose and need for the market production of material or immaterial goods (such as knowledge and culture), no real environmental *wisdom* (*sophia*), but rather a last attempt (that we now know is inevitably doomed to failure) to save the economic system and the values associated with the ideals of 'development' (regardless of whether they are sustainable or not), 'growth', 'consumption'.

Another ecology, more radical, from which ecosophy stems, considers that 'the ecological crisis refers to a more generalized social, political and existential crisis' and that it cannot be solved by ad hoc measures to safeguard natural environments. According to Guattari, the political, social and economic issues today, elude more and more 'party politics' and require the reforming of social practices that are better suited to local-based and global planetary problems. This perspective is not only about transforming the context of traditional capitalist economy in a 'sustainable' way, but also about developing alternative 'life conditions' that allow us to escape the 'not only unsustainable, but also unwanted nature of a development system that encourages the "fabrique de l'infélicité" [manufacture of infelicity]'. This project, on a global scale, implies promoting any new practices (slowing down, short cycles, pooling knowledge and creativity, downsizing, new production and consumption paradigms) that allow us to 'enhance the links to each other and to our environment[8]'.

Minor science and aesthetic paradigm

Ecosophy (as we have seen) does not aim to be recognized as a 'science', but as a form of 'wisdom' that we could liken to nomad, itinerant, minor sciences, as described by Deleuze and Guattari in the 'Treatise on nomadology' in *A Thousand Plateaus*.[9] It is, according to Deleuze and Guattari, a kind of science (or more accurately, an alternative approach to science and knowledge) characterized by affect, singularity, variation which cannot be reduced to a set of 'techniques' and does not operate through 'theorems' either. It is deployed through singular projects always centred on 'problems-events'.

Nomad sciences are spread out (like war machines) in an open space occupied by 'objects-flux' or 'objects-events', whereas major or Royal sciences envision enclosed spaces for objects and linear knowledge, which are structured and inflexible. Yet, the most interesting cases (in science, as in philosophy, art and politics) are always on the borderlands, where organization and nomad knowledge patterns are pressurizing knowledge or state power that strive to ward them off without success and end up (all too often) appropriating and transforming them.

Minor, itinerant or nomad sciences do not seek to take power, but subject their operations to the sensitive nature of intuition and construction, where they follow the singularities of matter, outline and link actions in a smooth space-time. Forms of '*connaissance approchée*' continuously guided by considered evaluations rather than by rational laws always generate more problems than they can solve: ecosophy could be interpreted as one of these sciences, techniques, fringe knowledges that are not in opposition but in constant exchange with the institutional or 'major' sciences (in this context, known as 'scientific' ecology or approaches labelled 'sustainable development').

In this combined thought and action project, what Guattari calls a new 'aesthetic paradigm' plays a key role. In this case, 'aesthetic' should not be understood as the specific field of art, reserved to a select few, but more generally in the etymological sense of *aesthesis*, sensitivity, sensitive dimension, operating by affects and singularities, a basis for any 'minor' science. In an article published in the review *Terminal*[10] in 1992, shortly before his death, Guattari writes that art has always been an essential part of the structure of any society, but that its gradual transformation into a separate and specific field, reserved to specialized corporations (think of the sad future reserved to 'specialized corporations' in the field of 'contemporary art'), has turned it into a 'soul supplement, a fragile superstructure, that we regularly predict will end'[11], whereas (since the caves of Lascaux) it has always had a crucial role in the expression of individual and collective subjectivities.

The interest of art according to Guattari lies in its ability to produce a de-framing, a breakdown of the serialized and standardized meaning ('homologized' according to Pasolini) which allows those who have access to it to reinvent and resingularize themselves. This meeting may impact irreversibly on the course of an existence and generate fields of possible 'far from equilibria' of everyday life.[12]

Wishing for a change of aesthetic paradigm, to which art can firstly contribute, means recognizing that our societies (now 'back against the wall', already written about by Guattari over twenty years ago) will need, in order to survive, to develop research, innovation, creation – dimensions which, in every field and area of existence, stem from aesthetics. Therefore, the aesthetic paradigm does not solely derive from artistic creation, even if renewed artistic creation can fundamentally contribute to its change and the emergence of a new trend in diverse fields such as science, economy, urban life, school, the psychiatric establishment, forms of sociability, and (as a result) each level of ecology (including, of course, preservation and reinvention of natural environments).

Guattari raises a very good point when he claims that 'art is the field that resists[13]': against the decline of subjectivities and environments produced by advanced capitalism, the artist is some sort of 'wandering knight' who aims towards heterogenesis (in opposition to capitalistic homogeny); against the simplification of money as a universal equivalent, art can ensure diversity and singularity. Art can work with painting, colour, sounds, but also with concepts, with spatial, urban or natural environment: its strength is the ability to constantly change material.

Ecology of the virtual and 'post-media' era

As Stéphane Nadaud rightly stressed in his preface to Guattari's writings, which he recently collected in *Qu'est-ce que l'écosophie?*[14], ecosophy as 'manufactured' by Guattari (as always, assembled from his readings, encounters and activist commitments) cannot be reduced to *ecology* as is usually proposed: *eco-sophy* is closer to philo-*sophy* than *eco*-logy, to the extent that there are at least three environments that we must be concerned about (that is why Guattari speaks of mental, social and environmental ecology in the literal sense), but in reality much more numerous (economic, media, technological, urban environment, all involved in a questioning around the preservation of natural and psychological balance that are both individual and collective, and in any case, according to him, necessarily global).

The first element of ecosophy is the need for a new 'mental ecology', to which Guattari devoted a large part of his life while working at the La Borde clinic run by Jean Oury, where institutional psychotherapy was practised. Using criticism of the Freudian and Lacanian subconscious as a starting point, Guattari has developed the concept of a *schizo-analytic* or *machinic* unconscious, open to social and economic interactions, to historical and political events and not focused exclusively on childhood and family background. This approach to the unconscious allows us to better understand that the former territories of the self, family, occupation, religion, culture and social or ethnic group affiliation are degraded under the impact of mass media of communication and information, of new technologies that cannot be considered only as extra-psychological factors but as an essential component to what Deleuze and Guattari call a 'production of subjectivity', which cannot be broken down into component parts:

> L'inconscient, j'y insiste, n'est pas quelque chose que l'on rencontre uniquement en soi, une sorte d'univers secret. C'est un nœud d'interactions machiniques, à travers lequel nous sommes articulés à tous les systèmes de puissance et à toutes les formations de pouvoir qui nous entourent.[15] [The unconscious, I insist, is not something that one finds only within, some sort of secret universe. It is a node of machinic interactions, through which we are linked to all power systems and all power formations that surround us].

Ecosophy must therefore include a reflexion on communication and media ecology and (more generally) the ecology of the virtual. Standardized, reassuring, condescending speeches in the media only 'smooth' and render the acceleration of history we are witnessing less and less comprehensible; new computer tools could produce a collective intelligence, new means of political dialogue, but they remain ineffective if not combined with new existential virtualities, new sensibilities.

The perspective Guattari has on traditional media is thus extremely critical. For example, television exercises, in his opinion, an influence on the viewers' unconscious that is akin to suggestion or hypnosis, by producing an 'avoidance behaviour', and depreciates their perception of the outside world and its complexity. Even so-called serious topics are handled in increasingly shorter segments, following the dynamics of widespread acceleration in a post-industrial society;[16] as the advertising or music video model is applied to the news, memory fades in an ever faster succession of 'current' events.

At the end of the 1980s, Guattari already foresaw the extremely rapid rise of today's digitization and the gradual convergence of screens (television screens are also becoming computers screens, proliferation of images and information transmission channels), which gave him hope for an evolution towards a 'post-media era' where the almost hypnotic dimension of television and the viewer's passive attitude would eventually lead to a re-appropriation of the 'information, communication, intelligence, art and culture machines'.

Unlike Baudrillard, who cast a disillusioned and almost desperate look on the transformation of reality into a world of disconnected simulacra, Guattari tends to rejoice in this loss of referent: the digital photo is not limited to 'reproducing' a reality, but it produces 'a reality, among other possibles'; the information disseminated by the media is technologically engineered by editing processes that happen even in so-called live events broadcasts. Moreover, there is no 'good old time' where things, before the advent of technology, would have been what they were, since, from the outset, myths, rituals, all forms of 'fabulation' have fabricated reality and beliefs. As an atypical ecologist, always driven by a real 'passion for machines', Guattari is aware of the dangers – in the society of control we live in today – caused by the multiplication of security laws but he considers (in the perspective that combines 'capitalism and schizophrenia') that 'new technologies produce, at the same time, efficiency and madness[17]' and that Big Brother's power shows countless cracks that bring about flexibility for new media alternative uses.

> La question de l'éthique des médias et de l'orientation prospective des nouvelles technologies de communication, d'intelligence artificielle et de commande continue est, avec la problématique écologique, un des deux axes de recomposition d'une pensée de progrès pour la planète aujourd'hui.[18] [The issue of media ethics and prospective approaches to new communication technologies, artificial intelligence and continuous control is, with the ecological question, one of the two axes reconstructing the concept of progress for the planet today].

In an ecosophic perspective, new 'media ethics' is therefore as essential as new 'environmental ethics'.

Urban practices and ecosophy

According to Guattari, environmental awareness does not only concern natural environments, built areas or physical territories, but also the reinvention of individual or collective 'existential territories', in accordance with the intrinsic link between humanity and the biosphere, both depending on the increasingly more complex 'technosphere' which surrounds them. This global shift in the purposes of human activities largely depends on the evolution of cities (where a large percentage of the global population is living), as Guattari tries to demonstrate in his essay entitled 'Pratiques écosophiques et restauration de la cité subjective [Ecosophic Practices and Restoration of the Subjective City'].[19]

Around the world, urban areas look more and more like an 'archipelago of cities', whose components are connected by all kinds of flows and networks, a scattering of deterritorialized world-cities. This global networking of urban areas has, on the one hand, homogenized the equipment, communication and transportation means, lifestyles and mindsets of globalized elites; on the other hand, it has exacerbated differences between habitat areas. The old centre–suburb structure has been deeply transformed and given rise to a three-way segmentation between over-equipped and over-connected urban areas, lacklustre middle-class residential areas, and increasingly more prevalent poverty belts all over the world (major European cities' suburbs, slums or favelas in South America and Asia, homeless people found in the streets and parks all over cities in so-called rich countries). Deterritorialization of advanced capitalism has produced, at the urban level, a generalized reterritorialization based on polarization: rich/poor, integration/disintegration.

According to Guattari, the answer to these problems goes far beyond the fields traditionally assigned to architecture, urban planning, economy, to engage a large number of sociopolitical, ecological, ethical and aesthetical practices and reflexions. Therefore we cannot separate the problems related to physical infrastructure, communication, transportation and services provided by 'existential' functions in urban environments. The urban phenomenon is at the heart of economic, social, ecological and cultural issues, and, as such, cannot be reduced to the matter (though still essential) of new construction techniques and the introduction of new materials that help combat all forms of pollution and nuisances.

Guattari then suggests that future urban renovation programmes systematically involve, for the purposes of research contracts and social experimentation, not only architects, urban planners, politicians, but also social sciences researchers and more importantly future inhabitants and site users. The goal is then to anticipate, by a collective approach, the evolution of the built framework, but also new lifestyles (neighbourhood practices, education, culture, sports activities, transportation, children or elderly care, etc.):

> Ce n'est que dans un climat de liberté et d'émulation que pourront être expérimentées les voies nouvelles de l'habitat, et pas à coups de lois et de circulaires technocratiques[20] [Only in a climate of freedom and emulation can new habitat approaches be experimented, and not through laws and technocratic bulletins].

Architects and urban planners are thus asked to become 'polysemic and polyphonic artists', not working in universal contexts, intended to be reconfigured in response to so-called basic needs that are defined once and for all (as in urbanism and modernist architecture), even if these needs are now expanded to integrate the requirements for environment preservation/comfort', 'well-being' or inhabitants' health. Projects that wish to initiate an ecosophical reconversion will have to push for the development of new aesthetical, ecological and social living paradigms, based on singularities defined by collective procedures of analysis and dialogue.

Still within the framework of French political and philosophical ecology, André Gorz repeatedly uses the adjective 'ecosophical', in his book *Misère du présent. Richesse du possible*,[21] referring explicitly to Félix Guattari in a chapter devoted to the necessary mutations of the city of the future and by mentioning the Guattarian proposal of 'Cité subjective [subjective City]'. According to Gorz[22] a new urban policy is also necessary for an alternative society project to take hold: through the organization of social space and activities, landscaping, equipment, sites that can be made available to the inhabitants, la politique de la ville appelle les auto-activités à se développer, leur en donne les moyens, les reflète à elles-mêmes comme étant non pas des improvisations éphémères ni des palliatifs subalternes adoptés faute de mieux, mais bien ce qu'une société qui demande à naître attend de tous et de chacun: projet commun proposé à tous, porteur de liens sociaux nouveaux[23] [city policy calls for auto-activities to grow, gives them the means to do so, reflects them back not as ephemeral improvizations or sub-par palliatives used for lack of a better solution, but as what an emerging society expects from each and every one: a common project for all, ready to create new social connections.].

Strangely enough, most current urban conversion projects seem to ignore or underestimate the importance of the collective demand for a new 'urban nature' which is expressed in practices as diverse as the proliferation of public parks and shared vegetable gardens, *guerrilla gardening*, permaculture or urban culture, the function of landscape, artistry, research on urban biodiversity.[24] The introduction of living organisms is generally limited to plants, more for their aesthetical function than for their ethical, social and political importance, whereas the presence of animals in the city[25] is rarely taken into account.

In many works, the geographer Nathalie Blanc emphasized on several occasions the need to rethink urban and rural, city and nature categories with regard to their role in the built and non-built environment, in our social and political performances and to renounce the ingrained environmental notion of 'rural', 'virgin' or 'untamed' nature, when our lives are ever more rooted in cities:

> C'est là qu'il y a besoin d'un réaménagement des catégories. [this is where categories need to be redesigned]. Ce qui ne veut pas dire faire l'impasse sur la 'nature rurale' ou la 'nature sauvage', bien sûr, mais repenser leur place en l'articulant avec celle de 'nature urbaine' … Et c'est là un vrai enjeu intellectuel. Il faut l'affirmer avec force.[26] [Which, of course, does not mean overlooking 'rural nature' or 'untamed nature', but to rethink their place together with 'urban nature' … That is the true intellectual issue. It needs to be strongly stated].

Public spaces and common spaces[27]

The notion of public space is a recent concept, used more and more in very diverse fields (philosophy, geography, urban planning, sociology, politics, economy or anthropology). Its two-sided nature makes it delicate to apprehend. This plurality of perspectives, categories of perception and action makes it both a rich and complex concept. Urban and architecture philosopher Thierry Paquot then concluded that 'l'espace public est un singulier dont le pluriel – les espaces publics – ne lui correspond pas[28] [public space is a singular whose plural – public spaces – has no correlation]'. Public space and public spaces cannot indeed be simply equated to one another, mainly because of the a-territoriality of the former, in contrast to and in complementarity with the geographically determined aspect of the latter. Public spaces are supposed to be areas open to all and therefore common to all; this openness and common use is being systematically jeopardized by the growing privatization and 'franchising' of urban spaces.

Beyond the opposition of *private* and *public* inherited from political philosophy, the philosopher and anthropologist Marcel Hénaff[29] reminds us of the need to envision *common spaces* in the city, which allow for a *common world* to persist in the fragmentation and dislocation of urban areas and lifestyles. According to Hénaff, this 'common world' is primarily built on inter-relational practices (neighbourhood links, random or organized encounters, but also mores, civilities, traditions of all kinds: expression of emotions, relationships between men and women, between young and old, signs and language usage, etc.). It is also a *vernacular order*, which preserves signatures and local styles in a globalized world:

> Ces pratiques du monde commun font depuis toujours la chair de la vie citadine. Elles confèrent coloration et particularité à tout ce que l'on entend par monde social. Elles forment l'*atmosphère* dans laquelle est ressentie et comprise la relation à l'espace public.[30] [These shared world practices have always been the core of city life. They give colour and individuality to the social world as we understand it. They form the atmosphere in which the relationship to public space is felt and understood.]

Common space areas are the street and square, prime places of body movement in an urban environment which seem to work towards their disappearance in a progressive 'dematerialization' of exchanges, areas of 'vicinality' produced by a sense of belonging (even if temporary) to shared spaces, areas of passage and visibility but more specifically areas that allow encounters ('la rue est sans doute le seul espace urbain où *tous* les individus d'une société ont des chances de se croiser[31]' ['the street is without a doubt the only urban area where *all* individuals in a society are likely to meet'). The street remains close to private space (both being separated by houses' doorsteps and buildings' façades) but it can, at any time, turn into a public space during political, sporting or religious events. To deny its access means denying access to the city.

As a result, preserving access to streets and squares becomes a priority for all urban space users. In order to guarantee this form of accessibility, said space must have greater legibility, based on signs, codes, invitations or messages that are not reduced to (ubiquitous) prohibiting and are not lost in blatant commercial overload, and allow city dwellers to use all senses to orient themselves and grasp their territory's growing complexity. The search for a new 'urban quality' is also emphasized in the multiplication of participation, dialogue and ownership efforts that link inhabitants to new housing designs as well as public spaces transformation.[32] Public space creation now requires a debate in the public sphere, with the objective to expand its democratic dimension. However, these generalized approaches always raise many questions with regard to the scale on which they happen, the range of communities involved, their actual influence on project design and implementation.

Beyond institutionalized procedures and difficulties in implementing them effectively, there is a generalized requirement for 'appropriation', a term that has a much more significant historical and philosophical scope and now encompasses all aspects of existence, including urban planning and architecture.

In a recent book, the philosopher Gaëtane Lamarche-Vadel[33] has demonstrated the deep ambiguity of such omnipresent 'appropriation': on the one hand, appropriation seems to have become a 'guideline of existence', an injunction to assimilate the other and the foreign, to 'make the world your own' to assert one's power, property, autonomy, in a context of generalized 'egocracy'; on the other hand, an idea of collective resistance and struggle against alienating lifestyles persists in this concept, aiming towards 'le recouvrement de l'intelligence collective et des usages démocratiques des espaces sociaux[34] [the recovery of collective intelligence and democratic uses of social spaces]'.

As with the daily life strategies outlined by Michel de Certeau, and beyond (or alongside) strategies for institutional consultation, there is a multiplication of collective appropriation efforts that are organized according to 'minor' logic and facilitate countless 'machines de guerre urbaines [urban war machines]' operated by inhabitants, architects, artists.[35] Despite the issues they raise, all these approaches (institutionalized or spontaneous) clearly demand the substitution of an 'urban order' imposed from the outside with an increased commitment from the inhabitants within their environment and a wider participation in the design of public spaces, paving the way for an expanded democracy and 'urban quality' that cannot be reduced to quantity.

Calls for 'urban nature' and real 'landscaping projects', a search for new common spaces, participatory approaches, based on dialogue and appropriation (not reducible to the concept of 'property') now emerge as some of many leads to an 'ecosophical' city and the assertion of the need for a sharing of the sensitive, where environmental criteria are taken into account as part of a political and wider aesthetical project.

Translated from French by Stephanie Daneels

Notes

1 Arne Naess, *Ecology, community and lifestyle* (1989), Paris, Dehors, 2008; Félix Guattari, *Les Trois écologies*, Paris, Galilée, 1989 and *Qu'est-ce que l'écosophie?*, texts

gathered by Stéphane Nadaud, Paris, Lignes/IMEC, 2013 (Available in English: Félix Guattari, *The Three Ecologies*, London and New Brunswick, NJ: The Athalone Press, 2000).

2 Arne Naess, *Ecologie, communauté et style de vie* (1989), *op. cit.*, p. 72 (quotes translated from the French edition).

3 Félix Guattari, *Les Trois écologies*, *op. cit.*, pp. 12–13./Félix Guattari, *The Three Ecologies* (London and New Brunswick, NJ: The Athalone Press, 2000), *op. cit.*, p. 28.

4 Yves Citton, *Pour une écologie de l'attention* (Paris : Seuil, 2014), p. 45 (quotes translated from the French edition).

5 Félix Guattari, *Qu'est-ce que l'écosophie?*, *op. cit.*, p. 33 and p. 66. (quotes translated from the French edition).

6 Yves Citton, *Pour une écologie de l'attention*, *op. cit.*, p. 156 (quotes translated from the French edition).

7 Ibid., p. 157. Yves Citton borrows the expression 'fabrique de l'infélicité' from an article bearing this title by Franco Berardi (Bifo) published in issue 8 of the *Multitudes* periodical (March to April 2002).

8 Ibid., p. 156.

9 Gilles Deleuze and Félix Guattari, *Mille plateaux*, Paris, Minuit, 1980, 'plateau' 12, '1227 – Traité de nomadologie: la machine de guerre', pp. 434–527 (Available in English: Gilles Deleuze and Félix Guattari, *A Thousand Plateaus: Capitalism and Schizophrenia* (Minneapolis and London: University of Minnesota Press, 1987). 'Plateau' 12, '1227 – Treatise on Nomadology: – The War Machine', pp. 351–423.)

10 Félix Guattari, 'Vers une écosophie', in *Qu'est-ce que l'écosophie?*, *op. cit.*, pp. 59–70. (quotes translated from the French edition).

11 Ibid., p. 66.

12 Ibid., p. 67.

13 Ibid., p. 152.

14 Félix Guattari, *Qu'est-ce que l'écosophie?*, texts presented and arranged by Stéphane Nadaud, Paris, Lines/IMEC, 2013 (quotes translated from the French edition).

15 Ibid., p. 195.

16 Cf. Hartmut Rosa, *Acceleration: Towards a Critical Theory of Late-Modern Temporality*, Paris, La Découverte, 2013. (English edition: Hartmut Rosa, *Acceleration: Towards a Critical Theory of Late-Modern Temporality*, NSU Press, 2010).

17 Félix Guattari, *Qu'est-ce que l'écosophie?*, *op. cit.*, p. 430. (quotes translated from the French edition).

18 Ibid., p. 439.

19 Ibid., pp. 31–58.

20 Ibid., p. 52.

21 André Gorz, *Misères du présent. Richesse du possible*, Paris, Galilée, 1996.

22 Ibid., pp. 161–5.

23 Ibid., p. 162.

24 Cf. Manola Antonioli (dir.), *Machines de guerre urbaines*, Paris, Editions Loco, 2015.

25 Cf. Nathalie Blanc, *Les animaux et la ville* (Paris : Odile Jacob, 2000) (quotes translated from the French edition).

26 Nathalie Blanc, 'Environnements naturels et construits: une liaison durable', in Afeissa, H.S. (Dir.), *Ecosophies, la philosophie à l'épreuve de l'écologie*, Editions MF Dehors, 2009, p. 229 (quotes translated from the French edition).

27 In this paragraph, I took the liberty to partially incorporate Manola Antonioli's (Dir.) conclusions, *Machines de guerre urbaines*, Paris, Editions Loco, 2015.

28 Thierry Paquot, *L'espace public*, Paris, La Découverte, 2009, p. 3. (quotes translated from the French edition).

29 Marcel Hénaff, *La ville qui vient*, Paris, L'Herne, 2008. (quotes translated from the French edition).

30 Ibid., p. 200.

31 Ibid., p. 211.

32 In this regard, I refer to the reading of the file 'Espaces publics et concertation', *Métropolitiques*, made available online on 09/19/2012 and searchable at http://www.metropolitiques.eu/Espaces-publics-urbains-et.html.

33 Gaëtane Lamarche-Vadel, *Politiques de l'appropriation*, Paris, L'Harmattan, 2014.

34 Ibid., p. 10.

35 Cf. Manola Antonioli, *Machines de guerre urbaines*, *op. cit.*

5

Schizoanalysis and Ecosophy: Scales of History and Action

Anne Querrien and Andrew Goffey

In 1972, in *Anti-Oedipus,* Gilles Deleuze and Félix Guattari set out to replace psychoanalysis with schizoanalysis. When they did so, women's liberation[1] and the affirmation of homosexual desire[2] were beginning to magnetically attract political activities and reflection. The love of women for other women catalysed a rebellion and a demand for single-sex political meetings, in which the problems of everyday life in their entirety were addressed, rather than discussions being limited to the vindication of a right to abortion and to contraception, as had frequently been the case earlier. The male militants who were still dominant in May 1968 found themselves disorientated. This new subjective situation had nothing to do with the situation that had prevailed in the beginnings of psychoanalysis, when young women from well-bred families, finding themselves hesitating between marriage and motherhood on the one hand, and paid literary or scientific work on the other, called – like Virginia Woolf – for a 'room of one's own' for the purposes of creative endeavour. The problem of desire – and this was something Deleuze and Guattari were tapping into – was no longer one of its channelling via castration, its repression through bourgeois decorum and manners, but its bolstering by ongoing social transformation, in the political emergence of affirmative minorities fleeing domination.

Schizoanalysis has both practical and theoretical origins, having been invented as much in the organization of a collective milieu, in the framework of CERFI, as in the clinical setting of the La Borde clinic and institutional psychotherapy. Above all it happened through the elaboration of an ensemble of concepts, which were to constitute so many tools for the concrete analysis of immediate dual or collective situations, and in analyses of a more prospective kind, the establishing of historical and political points of view on and for individual and collective action.

The operational core of schizoanalysis is formed by a handful of concepts: collective assemblage of enunciation; rhizome, faciality, refrain and cartography. With these, schizoanalysis aims not only at untangling individual difficulties in everyday life but equally at fomenting the collective adoption of attitudes able to generate development in the directions indicated by new social movements: ecology, the taking back of a creative relation to the earth destroyed by capitalism, with its belief that with its ever more frenzied deterritorialization it could always produce more value. Schizoanalysis operates across and challenges the segmenting of life into the registers of the individual and the collective, the therapeutic and the political, the mental, social and natural. Moreover, it also challenges a traditional separation of thinking and action, theory and practice, for as Guattari puts it 'the very form of the division of labour between militancy, the analysis of the unconscious and intellectual activity should wither away'.[3]

After setting out some reminders about the way in which Guattari and Deleuze defined and sought to use these concepts, we will try to apply the main concepts[4] of schizoanalysis to the significant optional matter which Guattari for his part discovered in the ecological movement, the militant movement that followed immediately after those of women's and homosexual liberation, and which took from these predecessors their respect for diversity and their attention to minoritarian options. Guattari not only took part in the ecological movement as a grassroots militant but also, in a much more original way, by proposing the elaboration of transversal connections between the different branches of its fragmented movement, with a paper – *Le fil vert* – and through his belonging to several of its different currents. While the ecological movement in France had limited the scope of its reflections to technical problems, Guattari attempted to construct ecological problems as directly philosophical and political issues, as problems that were immediately ethical in nature because of lacking any technical, or technocratic, solution. To do this he drew on the work of Hans Jonas,[5] a student of Heidegger's, whose position was nonetheless in many respects diametrically opposed to his own philosophical coordinates. Out of these reflections came a point of view that was both extremely acute and calming in its analyses, culminating in the publication of *Chaosmosis*, which appeared shortly before his death in 1992. So, we will try here to make the concepts of schizoanalysis function within the situations created by the ecological problematic and highlight the three dimensions of *ecosophy*, another of Guattari's later concepts. In ecosophy, environmental ecology, social ecology and mental ecology form three plateaus criss-crossed by movements on the different scales at which schizoanalysis was already playing out: the individual scale, which is already a molar scale in relation to the molecular scale at which different interpenetrating flows meet in both the human body and in ecological situations, which are at a different scale yet again to that of synaptic encounters inside the brain. Guattari's thinking as a whole is subtended by the hypothesis of a sort of holographic functioning that would give a similar image at every scale, a hypothesis which he seems to contradict with the inverse hypothesis of difference at every level, which ensures the change and renewal of images. It is this complexity – that of a system which is always moving, with multiple points of entry – that we would like to make comprehensible to our reader, in order that s/he might have at his or her disposal a polyvalent toolkit, a set of concepts that can be used to understand the situations in which she is involved.

The collective assemblage of enunciation

Involved since his adolescence in the political struggles engaged in by the French Communist Party in its cultural organizations and taking a particularly active role in the publication *La Voie communiste*, Guattari had many opportunities to observe how enunciation in a group is not the datum of an individual but is influenced by the collective that gives the individual an assertive strength. Likewise, in the psychiatric clinic, the psychoanalytic approach to patients is compromised by the difficulty patients have of speaking in a duel relation, with assuming the stance of the 'personologically' individuated subject of enunciation. Speech is expressive in collective situations generated by diverse activities, in a context where the presence of carers is sufficient for such speech to be welcomed and something to be made of it. Expression also occurs through gestures, movements and objects introduced into conversations. Life in proximity to psychotic patients teaches us that one another's utterances in fact arise from collective arrangements, without which nothing would be uttered. On reflection we can see that the collective assemblages of enunciation of militants or citizens obey the same 'laws', linking utterance to the dimension of transversality present in institutions of all kinds as well as in everyday life. In order to transform, say, what someone talks about incessantly so as to get beyond it, blocking them or cutting them off is pointless; what's needed is to introduce an object or some new kind of behaviour into their immediate environment, something they can apprehend, which will reconfigure their assemblage of enunciation and enable them to utter something new. This is how the prospect of passing one's driving test often opened up new outlooks for numerous people in analysis in the 1960s, and it is how Guattari learnt to treat the psychiatric institution as a kind of modelling clay, offering 'transferential grafts', potentialities for transformation and change, to its (im)patients.

Hence, as Guattari put it in *The Anti-Oedipus Writings,* schizoanalysis consists of inventing a language that replaces the (personological) subject of the statement/subject of the enunciation couplet, current in linguistics, which gives us subject understood as largely dominated by social conditioning, with a collective assemblage of enunciation, an articulation of desiring machines specific to the person in question and not (implicitly) contrasted with the social. In *Anti-Oedipus* Deleuze and Guattari ask: what are your desiring machines? If one sets out from the psychological subject and his or her social and economic determinants, for example, one will lose the dynamic proper to each of the strata that these determining factors form, and end up sticking them together in a static fashion, missing the movement that cuts across them. Envisaging enunciation as the subject in question's representation, this is a representation that can't help but be erroneous, because it inevitably lacks knowledge of all of the determinants that need to be taken into account. By contrast, if one constructs a diagram of the dynamic linking together the different forces in question, one can find a centre of gravity and of mobility into which the person can be invited to slip themselves so as to be better able to act in the situation that is bothering them. This analytic work can evidently be carried out on oneself, through an awareness of the singularity of one's position within a collective grouping, and doesn't necessarily require the expertise and privilege of an analyst against whom to counterpose oneself; hence the importance and necessity of looking for transversality, and the coefficients of transversality, in the different social situations within which one moves.

Such coefficients enable one to essay the construction of a diagram of the forces in relation to which one has to situate oneself and to address the way in which they animate the universe in which one is interested, keeping one's room for manoeuvre by taking up an oblique position in relation to these forces. Although Guattari had a lot of time for theory, in militant movements this more practical option means that the ideological differences by which people usually tear themselves to pieces are not given too much importance. What the transversal connections across a collective assemblage facilitate is an experimentation with a disjunctive synthesizing of the different orientations towards action that are proposed within and across militant movements. Such a synthesis makes it possible to find a point at which heterogeneous forces (which under other circumstances might destroy each other) come into equilibrium – this is how he managed to keep going in the French Green movement. Fighting for an ecological transformation of society through government and the ballot box is not enough, given the extent to which the transformations that are needed depend on everybody's everyday conduct. The assemblages of enunciation within the ecological movement in France would, for Guattari, have to be formed transversally to the different currents that made it up. The relevant statement or utterance would be one that would enable a transversal unity to be achieved, that would have some prospect of application to the movement as a whole. But it's important to note that collective assemblages of enunciation can only appear in experiences and experiments on the ground that aim to make ecology itself live as a heterogeneous assemblage, mobilizing different levels of power, producing new technologies, setting out images of the new life to come. As Cyril Dion and Melanie Laurent's film *Demain* (*Tomorrow*) and the now innumerable *guerrilla gardening* initiatives show, such assemblages are not going to appear in the parliamentary, party political, arena.

Schizoanalysis set itself up following Guattari's theoretical undertaking with Deleuze to critique Freudian and Lacanian psychoanalysis, as a decidedly collective – and collectively singular – undertaking. Guattari practised schizoanalysis by himself, in his consulting room, as well as with numerous militants, artists and intellectuals who were close to him in terms of their creative aims or political viewpoints. Biographical materials formed for them a kind of commons, which were worked on together and individually, in relation to specific time-scales and commitments. This sharing out of a social and collective concern, of a preoccupation with creation, made practice risky. A desire to work together that was left unsatisfied for example, might generate resentment that could be as violent as the transference that preceded it. The tendency of schizoanalysis was one of becoming a mutual practice that was generalized so as to allow for both a collective elucidation of the stakes of action – what should be done – and the procedures to be followed in order to achieve collectively elaborated goals – how should we do it. This was what the institutional organization of the clinic at La Borde – with its complex play of group institutions and the 'grille' – aimed to realize. It's also what the experiment with CERFI, in the late 1960s and early 1970s, was aiming at.

However, in CERFI's case, the precariousness of the public funding thanks to which it had developed (and the organization's dependence on it), entailed the constitution of a mixed collective assemblage, which was in contradiction with what the funding system imposed, a kind of social-science-researcher-becoming. Other new collective assemblages were subsequently created on the basis of this professionalization, assemblages which for their part were somewhat distanced from the experimenting with schizoanalytic concepts in which CERFI had engaged in its beginnings. Similarly, at La Borde, the tendency that Guattarian schizoanalysis had of exceeding the limits of the institution posed a problem for Jean Oury, who was the director of the clinic and had a responsibility for it vis-à-vis the authorities. The difficulties that Guattari himself encountered testify to the fact that revolutionary collective assemblages of enunciation, generating events, are always unstable and need to be protected as much as possible. The concept of the rhizome offers a way to explore a logic of relations within and through which collective assemblages of enunciation can be extended and flourish, and hence it forms the second concept in the schizoanalytic toolbox that we want to consider.

Rhizome

The rhizome is a modality of relation that is opposed to the modality of relation that we most frequently encounter in the major sciences, in newspapers and in commentary of all sorts: the tree that starts out from an individual, the CEO of a business or the leader of some organization, a person who forms a reference point for a genealogical tree and orders other people present within the field into a hierarchy. The rhizome, as Guattari (and Deleuze) tell us, connects any point whatsoever in a field with any other, through relations that aren't necessarily identical. Beings linked together by a rhizome are not necessarily of the same nature: a non-human, an animal, plant or object, can form part of a rhizome, just as they form part of a collective assemblage. The rhizome extends collective assemblages into a much vaster space, where the question of relation rather than enunciation dominates: what or who am I connected with, and do I – in fact – *want* to be connected?

Free association in psychoanalysis or schizoanalysis is one way of bringing to light a rhizome, of sharing with an analyst the knowledge of what or whom one is associated.[6] Rhizomes are also fabricated through writing, minor writing à la Kafka in particular (who had always fascinated Guattari) which moves through the diary form, short stories, experimenting with different kinds of writing to give desiring machines and the difficulties in functioning with which they are connected, a capacity for movement to get beyond obstacles. Rhizomes are formed bit by bit, associating people and things as they encounter each other in a singular assemblage. A rhizome forms a multiplicity, a movement across an assemblage with an ever increasing number of dimensions, a production of lines that proliferate incessantly. Sooner or later, of course, a signifier, an invariant point, will take power, facilitating the attribution of the rhizome to, for example, an author, whom it will be taken as representing (as with the 'oeuvre'). But at the moment that it takes off, at the moment that the heterogeneous materials of the rhizome are constituted (with their subterranean and invisible workings), the notion of the rhizome is a good tool with which to authorize the constitution of a heterogeneous material to work on, to get past the injunction to unify, to focus or fixate, and (thereby) abandon the seductions of the multiple.

Rhizomes make it possible to go a very long way in research, because they invite us to stretch out, to prolong and to relay the line or lines of flight that can be discovered in them. 'Always follow the rhizome by rupture; lengthen, prolong and relay the line of flight; make it vary until you have produced the most abstract and tortuous of lines of *n* dimensions and broken directions.'[7] Rhizomes are constructed gradually, without following any model or repeating a deep structure: they are fabricated, enacted, following the desire of each and every one, each group, and change their form as connections accumulate and reconnect to one another. But rhizomes offer no assurance: there's no guarantee that a rhizome won't be transformed into a tree, taking a fixed form that dictates the relations between the points which, until then, it had connected. If this happens, the rhizome is dead or dying, that desire can do nothing but replicate well-worn paths and conform to a normal – and normalized – structure, which channels the multiplicity of movement from point to point. And yet rhizomes can nonetheless be remobilized – albeit with some difficulties – as productive outgrowths on dead trees. This is the kind of work that schizoanalysis tackles.

The multiple rhizome which each of us constitutes, through our writings, paintings, myriad creations, which weds the movement of desire in its connections with everything that surrounds us, Deleuze and Guattari tell us, has neither beginning nor end but rather 'it grows and overflows from the middle/milieu'.[8] This is a piece of very practical advice that is often repeated in Deleuze and Guattari's common work: take things by the middle, in their milieu, don't try to make them depend on origins. Things quickly escape their origins, and the search for origins doesn't tell us all that much about the actual factors through which they are currently being determined. It is in the middle, in a milieu, that things happen, that desire flourishes, growing in all sorts of directions via the lines of the rhizome. Do a drawing of your rhizome, write it, put it together gradually, as the movements of your desire evolve, and you will find these different movements gaining strength. This is the contrary of what happens when such movements are traced back to the fiction of a common origin, which forces you to put to one side everything that you can't link back in that way. There will be more to your desire as you become a free, shifting, mobile subject, even if you move in very minimal ways. Making a rhizome is the basic tool for doing schizoanalysis.

Faciality

The expression of affect, the displacements brought about by desire, bud and flower on the face, but they can only be detected here because the face has been the object of a long-term modelling over hundreds and hundreds of years that has endowed it with axes, coordinates and transformed it into a flat surface for inscription. Judaeo-Christian history has imposed the face of Jesus Christ as the ultimate reference point for this placid, platitudinous common-place, a point of fusion between suffering and jouissance. As an object for the relentless work of painters and sculptors over twenty centuries, expression and its potentialities, as they come to light in the face, have been confiscated by representation and its possibilities, in a process by which the body is made submissive to the mind and accorded a representational signification. For Guattari in *The Machinic Unconscious*[9] faciality forms the coordinates of the face that intervene so as to define what is and what isn't licit, what is and isn't similar, what does and doesn't resemble, so as to reterritorialize what escapes when rhizomes are produced. The face – a bit like space itself – is referred here to a planar geometry, one that is formed by the eyes, the forehead and the nose, 'which gathers together, formalises, neutralises and crushes the specific traits of the other semiotic components'[10] that attract the gaze, to which it opposes its immobility, relative to the mobility of other elements of the body. The planar geometry of the face is what you look at in a portrait and it's what you see when looking at someone you are listening or talking to, guiding your responses. The movement of attraction through which the faciality machine operates transforms the eyes of the other into veritable black holes, into tensors for the destruction of alterity. Any movement beyond this tension can only risk social exclusion. As Guattari often emphasizes, there is an 'optional matter' as regards one's conduct in this field of faciality: either one submits to dominant capitalist facialitarian forms, integrating oneself with the forces of repression of desire – both for oneself and for others – or one develops singular faciality traits, picking up the thread of the rhizome again, by avoiding black holes and allowing oneself to be carried off by the machinic connections of lines of desire. Schizoanalysis cannot in and of itself make this choice on behalf of the analysand – but it can help the analysand to clarify the terms on which such a choice is made. Thinking faciality allows the analysand to follow the ways in which it is effectuated in the concrete faces that surround him or her, without having to pass via forms of expression – in language – that entail even more subjection to convention and crushing self-evidence than those of the face. Teasing out the face and the limits of its codification of desire in turn facilitates an apprenticeship to the signs by which we are surrounded in everyday life, the myriad blinking, winking eyes, black holes and – hopefully – a-signifying faciality traits that look out at us from screens, walls, billboards, surfaces of all kinds.

But faciality does not start and end with the human face. It extends to the face of the earth, to landscapes that are only fixed and 'natural' for those whose profession it is to obey their destiny, even while desire is constantly fabricating mobile images, dynamic and fugitive differences. All civilizations have endeavoured to produce rules for the representation of the landscape, and as with the cases of the face and the portrait, they have played on the duplicitous posture of freedom and creation for the clerics and subjugation for the population at large, who are subjected to obligatory users guides and models of vision. The invention of the perspective and of chiaroscuro, for example, led to the landscape art of classical times. Chinese *fen shui* equally drives the art of the painter and the gaze of the spectator. And within modernity it is the photographic apparatus which frames the way in which the landscape, or the face in the portrait, must be seen. One might equally refer to the demand made by Jesuit priests on the faithful – to compose in their mind's eye a landscape for the life of Christ in order to prepare them to receive God. If this resulted in the Jesuits finally being obliged to catalogue such landscapes in picture catechisms, this was because the faithful clearly struggled to do their spiritual exercises correctly. The contemporary landscape, of course, is marked by war, desolation and waste: from coal tar sands and despoliated rain forests through refuse dumps and industrial wastelands. As Guattari puts it: 'We are now in the presence of a double movement, that of:

- the constitution of a face-landscape which is deterritorialized from the inside and focuses on a microscopic black hole which is at one and the same time a vanishing point and central point, a point of arborescence and of closure, the translation of which generates the illusion of a homogeneous world of signification; and
- the setting up of facialitarian syntaxes that generate the illusion that the universe of abstract machines also arises from centralizing structures, from a monosubjectivism, a monotheism, which is correlative to the degeneration and decline of the polycentrism of animal and animist cosmologies.'[11]

This faciality-landscaping[12] tends to dissolve the territorial limits of traditional societies even while – through its central, guilt-inducing eye, on which all the coordinates of representation are based – maintaining its hold on the social in its entirety. Whether it is in the service of domination or forms part of a militant and artistic search for deterritorialization, the media work at modifying faciality traits, so as to pull them back in to the centre or, on the contrary, to distance themselves. The latter, centrifugal, tendency is of course all the more difficult to accede to, given the multiplicity of directions to explore. With its claims to universality, it is thus attraction by the centralizing force of faciality that makes itself felt the most, particularly given that it founds the individuation of enunciation on the tangent between the libido and capital, in the feeling of emptiness which is at the origin of the existential anxiety characteristic of capitalism in its declining years. It's no longer the case that modern faciality traits are articulated with local components, as in deterritorialized collective assemblages: faciality traits have become abstract, binary characteristics that classify individuals according to typifiable distances from a statistical norm. Guattari gives a systematic cast to the damaging effects of this oppressive capitalist faciality, which smoothes out the world in one direction only, that of abolition in the black hole of the superego. 'Capitalist faciality teaches us *to not see*, to abstract out from the richness of things, to adopt a limited point of view, from this side of which identification becomes impossible… . At the end of the day it is this faciality that masks the subjugating functions of the dominant semiologies by presenting its operations as being grounded on invariable logical procedures rather than on concrete apparatuses of power.'[13]

But at the same time, Guattari also insists on the other possible option, the option that schizoanalysis will seek to develop, through the marking out of lines of flight and the production of a machinic rhizome susceptible of carrying faciality traits away from the tolerable deviations from superegoic redundancy. The invention of new machines and of practices with them, as in the case of computers, is what will allow for the proliferation of experiments with new faciality traits or new landscaping traits. However – and here a little schizoanalytic pessimism is necessary – semiotic treatment through information technology is still very poorly adapted to the analysis of deterritorialized processes, because it too rests on the binarity of the signifier, predisposing it to the poor treatment of inclusive disjunctions, and to a preference for trees. Let's not forget here how much structuralist thinkers such as Jakobson, Lévi-Strauss and Lacan were attracted to cybernetico-informatic concepts.

Faciality and its landscapes form very particular territories of expression, and rather than simply criticizing them or trying to ground them in universals, schizoanalysis seeks out and follows carefully any of the artful, artificial attempts at modifying them that might enable the desiring capacities of machines to develop.

The transformation of the face of the earth through the landscaping traits that sustain binary machines is the principal focus of attention of ecology and so it offers one way of branching across into Guattari's later thinking. It is through the transformations of the landscape that one starts to realize to what extent the entire surface of the earth has been littered with the harmful toxins of a demented system of proprietary production, or just how much the capacities for renewal of the earth have been compromised. Ecology seeks to intervene on the surface of the earth through new practices that are more respectful of natural cycles. Ecosophy develops three levels or dimensions of apprehension of relations to the earth. *Mental ecology* works on rebuilding the link of each and every one to the earth, wrecked as it is by the extreme deterritorialization of capitalism gone astray by a concentrating of all attention on private property or by State-led identitarian fixation on what region someone comes from or belongs to. *Social ecology* develops new relations of production between humans, or between humans and non-humans, and works towards a situation in which respect for the latter, for the landscape, the quality of the earth, provides the opportunity for a transformation of relations of production, in a more gentle direction, towards greater respect among humans. *Environmental ecology* provides the knowledges that will allow for these new relations to be explored and developed. The concrete contents of these ecologies will differ according to place, and the landscape traits in play will thus also be just as diverse as the new assemblages of jouissance and territoriality put into play by ecosophic praxis. Guattari nonetheless envisaged a fundamental shift in his ecosophical apprehension of the transformation of the face of the earth, which was that the assemblages of the three ecologies would be decentralized, unlike the centralization that capitalist faces and landscapes aimed at, and which technocratic tendencies in traditional ecological thinking did little to question. Everything is up for reinvention and reassembling with the breaking up of capitalist faciality.

Refrains

Faciality and its landscapes are visions, powerful images capable of animating collective behaviour and of triggering the seduction of individuals. In the domain of sound, the role of capitalist encoding and of the shifters of singularization are assumed by refrains. For both, Guattari provides an exploratory formulation in *The Machinic Unconscious*, which he reprises – repeating with deterritorializing variation – with Deleuze in a quasi-pedagogic fashion in *A Thousand Plateaus*. However, refrains have for the most part been studied much more as signalling the emergence of a particular territory, as the product of an action that aims at making this territory emerge, rather than from the point of view of their role in capitalist encoding. Numerous musicians, for example, have taken up the concept of the refrain as an inspiration for the way they work the relations between repetition and creation, as in Pascale Criton's 1995 composition 'La ritournelle et le galop' in homage to Deleuze. Or in the work of the Brazilian musician and professor of musical theory, Silvio Ferraz, for whom the refrain is a machine for the production of differences, for connecting lines of flight, codes, milieu and rhythms. For both of these musicians it is a matter of assembling a plurality of components and of constituting a territory in which such components enter into modulation and then leave, freeing up autonomous microfragments which will constitute new knots of assemblages, and so on. Every model of composition is like the entrance point into a territory whose rules have not yet become stratified. The deterritorializing refrain allows for the passage from one milieu to another. A new persona-component is borne from the modulation between the components of associated milieus. Heterogeneous sounds combine in a 'new refrain into which unforeseen modulations enter, in a free play of connections to bring about other refrains and unforeseen modulations'.[14] The musicologist Maël Guesdon has emphasized the importance of Guattari's preoccupation, since his very earliest writings, with the material and psychic effects of repetition on subjectivity. Right from the outset he was seeking to construct what Guesdon calls a sensory ecology of expressive speeds (*allures expressives*), questioning how the living appropriate the forms that surround them and compose the milieus in which they live, so as to make of them territories inhabitable by all. Guattari equally looked to history to discover how groups of humans constituted sounds as signals to affirm their identity, to group their members together and to defend themselves from their enemies. He looked to biology for similar examples of the use of signalling by sound in the relations within or between groups of animals. This was a question that had already been explored by Eibl Eibesfeldt and Paul Géroudet in relation to birds: from a common base their songs differ slightly so as to signal circumstances to be indicated to partners or strangers. Like birds and animals more generally, in the everyday humans express a constant stream of refrains, which detach themselves on the margin of capacities to knot together new relations, freedoms that are subject to choices oriented towards openness, and therefore also to micropolitical conflicts. Inversely, an event, an encounter, can only be effective if it composes itself with the characteristic refrain of the individual or group concerned. The refrain plays the role of a component of passage between the world before and the world after, and one notes here once more that in Guattarian vocabulary, this doesn't occur through words or signification so much as through a tonality, an air, an ambience which speaks volumes about the sense of the operation.

In *A Thousand Plateaus*, the way that Deleuze and Guattari reprise the latter's intuitions about refrains articulates a question about artistic creation, whereas in *The Machinic Unconscious* it was only a question of biology and sociology, of the modulation of human and animal sounds. The plateau 'Of The Refrain' opens with a reproduction of Paul Klee's *Twitter Machine* (which students of Deleuze have a habit of sending to each other to show their expressive, desiring capacities – regrettably, with the development of social media, twittering has become much more attenuated as an image of desire). The plateau defines the refrain in the same way as Silvio Ferraz: movement from chaos to the territorial assemblage, organization of the territorial assemblage, leaving the territorial assemblage for other assemblages, the formation of a process producing life. Deleuze and Guattari set out here a veritable user's guide for the concepts of territory, milieu and rhythm:

> There is a territory when rhythm has expressiveness. What defines the territory is the emergence of matters of expression (qualities). Take the example of colour in birds or fish: colour is a membrane state associated with interior hormonal states, but it remains functional and transitory as long as it is tied to a type of action (sexuality, aggressiveness, flight). It becomes expressive, on the other

> hand, when it acquires a temporal constancy and a spatial range that make it a territorial, or rather territorialising, mark: a signature.'[15]

And they continue by affirming that it is the artist who is the first human to set out the limit or make the mark that defines a territory. Romulus and Remus – and all the other founders of cities – would doubtless disagree with them, united as they are in the culpabilizing belief that the foundation of a city necessitates, in the first place, a sacrifice. Deleuze and Guattari apply themselves to describing the nomadic space in which the signature has value as a temporary possession, in which in the long term, property has no meaning, something of a model, then, in our epoch, in search of the common. The refrain expresses this temporary territory: 'matters of expression enter shifting relations with one another that "express" the relation of the territory they draw to the interior milieu of impulses and exterior milieu of circumstances'.[16]

The rest of the plateau makes these expressive refrains into faces or rhythmic personae, counterpoints to the melodic or harmonic faces and landscapes produced by the fashioning of transcendents. This reprise testifies to the emancipatory character of the refrain signalled by Ferraz. The analysis of the refrain is founded on that of the territory, and territories are far from being containers or belongings. As we have seen in the case when Guattari writes about this alone, the territory is a component of passage, a condition for the formation of a creative process.

However, Deleuze and Guattari together add to this a concern for 'consistency', making the refrain of central importance to a question that had concerned Guattari since the mid-1960s.[17] To make a set of heterogeneous elements hold together, rhythm synchronisers are needed, just as machines are needed to make an assemblage hold together. Indeed, this is a hypothesis that, in different ways, individually or together, Deleuze and Guattari everywhere maintained: it is the cutting edges of deterritorialization, the most deterritorialized element of the assemblage which, in carrying off the other elements of the assemblage, makes the assemblage hold together. Deterritorialized, heterogeneous consistence always has primacy over reterritorialized, homogenized, substance. Except, as they themselves point out, the consistency of the assemblage comes up against the stratification of the milieus.[18] A fascinating analysis of the oeuvre of Paul Klee and of the comparative merits of painting and music in leading us into the cosmos follows their discussion of consistency, and it stresses the ways in which these two arts achieve a molecularization of their respective matters of expression, to the point of facilitating complete deterritorialization. We then come back again to the refrain – to its sticky, territorial attachment on its fascist side, and on the other, to the way in which its inventiveness gets madder and madder (to the extent that machines capable of accompanying it can develop).

> So just what is a refrain? Glass harmonica: the refrain is a prism, a crystal of space–time. It acts upon that which surrounds it, sound or light, extracting from it various vibrations, or decompositions, projections or transformations. The refrain also has a catalytic function: not only to increase the speed of the exchanges and reactions in that which surrounds it, but also to assure indirect interactions between elements devoid of so-called natural affinity, and thereby to form organised masses. … It is of the nature of the refrain to become concentrated by elimination in a very short moment, as though moving from the extremes to a centre, or on the contrary, to develop by additions, moving from a centre to the extremes, and also to travel these routes in both directions.[19]

From the middle of the 1980s onwards, Guattari moved closer to the ecological movement, a relative newcomer to the political scene. The ecologists were – and still are – radically opposed to any of the kind of major works that are likely to accelerate the flows of humans and commodities, the growing speed of which they consider to be the principal cause of the ruining of the planet and the potential cause of new armed conflicts in the struggle for access to raw materials. Guattari seems, little by little, to have felt the need to abandon an affirmation of the benefits of the infinite processuality that forms the basis of the transformation of the refrain into a crystal of time, a crystal that is perhaps capable of operating at a molecular level without any human intervention, in favour instead of a new configuring of the world to be defined. Although his appraisal of refrains will undergo further developments (in *Chaosmosis*), it is his sense that the ecological problem cannot be reduced to the harmful effects of a way of life and an economy which would only need changing quantitatively – and thus in a reactionary manner in relation to the social practices in effect – that starts to matter. What is needed is to succeed in following experiments with new ways of living that are being tried out by people most sensitive to these kinds of questions and, in particular, to understand how they articulate a transformation of the interests and attention of militant subjectivity, with a modification of social relations in the workplace, in the ways in which public spaces are occupied, in practices of aid and of solidarity, with the re-composition of geopolitical relations. It is not a matter of falling back on convivial little territories and humming little ecological ditties in familial relations but of opening up a welcome to migrants, of participating in struggles to end the dependence of the economy on oil, the end of exploitation in the Global South. To see such a programme through, a personal and collective development is needed for everyone, for which Guattari's *Schizoanalytic Cartographies* offers some means for orienting oneself.

Schizoanalytic Cartographies

Throughout his life as a researcher, whenever discussing rhizomes, faces, landscape or even viewing the diversity of refrains in space, Guattari evoked the *cartographies* of desire. In his critical combat with the institutions of psychoanalysis, his ambition was to give everyone the means to orient themselves in the trajectories of their lives, to enable others to get a vision of this to facilitate a collective apprenticeship to the transformation of existing social coordinates. Guattari's cartographies form part of his challenge to the presumptive authority of 'psy' expertise. Criss-crossing the history of the world, *A Thousand Plateaus* situates concepts in particular social, linguistic and political configurations but only admits this singularization of the trajectories of desire at the risk of their reductive analogization, even their falling back on historical configurations that are simply not adequate to bear them. In this regard, what Guattari, continuing to think schizoanalytically, felt the need for was a method of visualization, one that would allow for a radical analysis of the equation that is proper to a given individual as well as the grasping of the history of the world in all its dimensions.

For Lacan, of course, grasping the trajectories of desire entailed the Borromean schematization of the real, the imaginary and the symbolic, a tripartite division and articulation that has the advantage of being able to cope with every situation, in a manner that is universalizing (a requisite for the basic coordinates of a cartography) even as it posits the impossibility of universalizing formalism. Its disadvantage, however, is that it doesn't really offer any way of making reference to the world as it is made within human history, other than as it can be apprehended through 'batteries of signifiers'. Guattari's *Schizoanalytic Cartographies* by contrast thus has four dimensions, enabling it to incorporate a reference to time, to the accumulation of experience within human history, and to the world and its movements independent of the human.[20]

Always grasped through their articulation within the dynamic cycle of assemblages, the four dimensions (marked recurrently using the FTUΦ abbreviation) in relation to which Guattari thus situates the history of the world and individual history are the following:

1. The dimension of material *flows* (F), which in many respects approximates Lacan's real, but with Guattari's heavy insistence on the fact that matter

at the molecular level is made of particles. The most numerous of such particles – electrons – are in motion, a motion that can and does produce unforeseen encounters, events, out of which new configurations of flows can be formed, such that there is nothing definitive about any flow at all. At every possible scale, it is the fluid multiplicity of matter – and not the reassuring figure of nature – which through its unforeseen twists and turns has the capacity to modify our environment in a manner that is, crucially, independent both of our will and our apprehension.

2. The existential *territories* (T) which form the milieus in which humans and animals, even plants (according to the most recent of research) evolve, in which the living being transforms its environment through its actions, conserving it for itself, while destroying it for other species. In short, existential territories are also to be understood in terms of irreversible transformations which aim at permanence.
3. Incorporeal *universes* (U), which are formed through the transformation of existential territories and their impetus to form operators of conservation and transformation, through the abstraction of qualities that are present in those territories and the actions that lead to them. It is on the basis of existential territories that surplus values of code are constructed, driven by the deterritorializing and deterritorialized flows that define common tools, disciplines, theories, musics. These surplus values of code are apt to push the deterritorialization of existential territories further, extending the possibilities for opening up inherent in incorporeal universes.
4. The machinic *phylum* (Φ) to which the territorialization of flows gives birth throughout human history, via their intersection with the operations that the conceptualization of incorporeal universes, and the production of more or less powerful collective assemblages of enunciation allow. The philosopher Gilbert Simondon has outlined the principle of this machinic phylum and its production, most notably through the hybridization of disciplinary fields that previously developed separately from one another. Unlike Simondon though, Deleuze and Guattari together, and Guattari by himself (in both *Schizoanalytic Cartographies* and *Chaosmosis*) offer a much more extensive definition of the machine than the more obviously classical one offered by Simondon. Any cutting into a flow forms a machine, as far as they are concerned: the baby's mouth when it is drinking breast milk, for example. In this respect and following this more extensive definition, the machinic phylum is both historical, for everyone, and specific, depending

> on how the flows in question are cut (into) in each case. Where someone is situated cartographically will be defined by searching for the flows that animate them, by the flows one cuts into as a way to fuel – rather than fetter – one's own dynamics.

In very practical terms, knowing about the flows (F) one is animated by makes it possible to deduce what existential territory (T) one belongs to and how one can intervene in and modify it. But with what political theories or ideologies? What practices of abstraction? In relation to what disciplinary references? (U) And perhaps, even, through the invention of what new machines (Φ)? And how, through further deterritorializing cycles of the assemblages through which these four 'functives' are articulated, can one extend and prolong the potentialities thereby made available.

Every action, every project, in fact requires the invention – the instituting – of a specific apparatus, one that is adapted to one's projects, conditions, to the collective assemblage that will put it to work. Likewise, everyone should, with the help of the diagrammatic tools of schizoanalysis, be able to detect the principal flows that force the movement of his or her situation, the existential territory with/in which one operates, what additional universes of reference will be needed to act and which incorporeal domains to turn to, so as to articulate flows and knowledges in a new machinic production.

A more intent and careful consideration of Guattari's revised proposals for machinic analysis make some of the limitations of recent protests more evident: proposing the occupation of public spaces as their principal political means, they seem happy simply to broaden out or relink existential territories, without considering how to transform the incorporeal universes that serve as their reference points or how to produce the new machinic operators that are indispensable for transforming the global situation. As such they are at risk of falling back onto identitarian and/or compensatory demands and of missing the broader ecological dimensions of the impasses of contemporary capitalism. The diagrammatic mapping processes that Guattari develops require a more radical transformation of our relations to the earth.

The relatively complex language that Guattari uses to set out his analysis registers this difficulty of transforming a schizoanalytic cartography into an operative short-term cartography. It seems that in the ecological domain, the possibility of existential territories evolving in the direction of a veritable experimentation with new territorial inscriptions is being affirmed with increasing insistence, to the extent that traditional configurations of environmental exploitation have turned out to be dangerous impasses. 'Cheap nature', as some are calling the ultra-exploitative capitalist regime of extraction, is coming to an end. But strangely, in his ecosophy, Guattari adopts a tripartite representation, even though – as he had very clearly explained with Deleuze (in *Anti-Oedipus*) – such a representation would only ever result in the dimensions of time and history being evacuated. If we try to hybridize schizoanalytic cartographies with ecosophy, we might hypothesize that the dimension of flows, of the real which sustains the myriad transformations of energy around which the *Cartographies* are organized, forms the environmental ecology addressed to the transformation of the planet at the very different scales of elements and territories. Social ecology would be dealt with by existential territories, in the sphere of what Lacan calls the imaginary, social representations of life in common, and endeavours to transform them as a function of new principles, such as those of equality – of gender or of humans more broadly, or, in a more Deleuzoguattarian manner, animal–vegetable or imperceptible becomings. Mental ecology, for its part, would be produced through the incorporation into such becomings of new scientific knowledges, and through the incorporation into everyday awareness of new ethical reflections. Guattari's psychiatric practice in turn rendered him sensitive to a dimension of this ecology that few specialists think about, that of existential anguish faced with the negative promises of the future. The sentiment of the 'end of the world' that other psychiatrists (particularly Tosquelles) had picked up on in relation to psychosis here acquires a peculiarly world-historical dimension. However, the possible transposition of the four-headed thinking of cartographic thinking into ecosophy leaves some tasks still to be worked through. The machinic phylum, the material, rather than imaginary, production of new modes of life, the processes of putting becomings to work, remains to be integrated into ecosophic reflection, in an ecology of machines or an ecology of images, such as that proposed by Anne Sauvagnargues,[21] without which the ongoing production of subjectivity that both schizoanalysis and ecosophic praxis demand risk missing a vital resource.

Chaosmosis

Guattari's *Chaosmosis*[22] registers a state of total disillusionment in relation to the methods that have been employed hitherto for the conduct both of individual subjectivity and for the relations between social groups or human societies.

Chaosmosis is the registering of a state of confusion and of the weakening of the markers necessary in the face of the current state of the world, an obligatory passage for whoever wants to reshuffle cards and create. Chaosmosis is not the old revolutionary tabula rasa but registers a breakdown of previous relations which pushes towards a new articulation of resources, across all dimensions of existence. Planetary problems linked to climate change and the dwindling of raw materials will only be resolved through violence and bloodshed, as we are seeing in the multiplication of wars today, unless social relations, international relations, but also the mental resources that are employed to tackle these problems, both individually and collectively, are not profoundly transformed. While the creativity of desire in *A Thousand Plateaus* generated infinite openings, Guattari's ecological research, in particular following his reading of Hans Jonas, had led him to rethink his perception of the development of the world, in a more intensive, microscopic direction, that of an infinity tending towards the infinitely small. Becoming imperceptible, which had already been evoked as the 'destiny' of all becomings in *A Thousand Plateaus*,[23] entails an ethical positioning, the search for a transformation of the world on the basis of where one finds oneself in it: a 'micropolitics'[24] of interactions that is animated by a search for the common. Communism in this sense ceases to be what it was in Guattari's youth – a space to be conquered, gun in hand – but something to be created at every moment, wherever one might happen to be, with whatever means one has at one's disposal. Everywhere that subjectivity is liberated, freed up from what conditions it, what keeps it on a leash and obliges it to participate in maintaining domination, it can become invested in tangible projects that can offer a means of orientation for this molecular revolution. Chaosmotic in its modes of propagation, this revolution from below will not be victorious straightaway, but it will disturb the powers that be sufficiently to make them produce, somewhat reluctantly no doubt, fissures and cracks into which the desire for change that already exists will rush.

Perhaps the tools described above will not be sufficient to enlarge these fissures and cracks and develop ecosophical spaces. But they do indicate the direction in which to look for the new modes of existence on the way to being created. Schizoanalysis and ecosophy conjoin their efforts in detecting the emergent, and in sorting through all the propositions that strengthen the living creature, the animal, the human and the cosmic. By building bridges, transversal (disciplinary, professional, militant) connections between these efforts, schizoanalysis and ecosophy form together forces in a position to undermine the mental, social or environmental rocks that hinder the flourishing of desire and its transformative potentialities. Whether this is at the individual scale of an analysis tackling the relationship with others and the world, or at the collective scale of an organization that sets out to be a force for life and transformation, or, indeed, at the planetary scale, indispensable to the analysis of changes underway, schizoanalysis and ecosophy come together to arm us in our desire for a 'new softness', as Guattari put it in *Chaosmosis.*

Notes

1 Cathy Bernheim *Perturbation, ma soeur* (Paris: Seuil, 1983) and *L'amour était presque parfait* (Paris: Editions de Félin, 1991).
2 Guy Hocquenghem *Le désir homosexuel* (Paris: Seuil, 1972).
3 Félix Guattari *Lines of Flight. For another world of possibilities* (London: Bloomsbury, 2016), p. 98.
4 Our selection is largely pragmatic – there are of course other concepts that are important in the development and operative functioning of schizoanalysis. We do not claim to be making definitive statements here.
5 Hans Jonas *The Imperative of Responsibility: In Search of Ethics for the Technological Age* (Chicago, IL: University of Chicago Press, 1979).
6 Max Dorra 'Pour une révolution des l'entendement' *Chimères*. Special issue on 'Les paradoxes du rêve' No. 86 (Paris: ERES, 2015).
7 Gilles Deleuze and Félix Guattari *A Thousand Plateaus* (Minnesota, MN: Minnesota University Press, 1987), p. 11.
8 Ibid., p. 21 (translation modified).
9 Cf Anne Sauvagnargues *Artmachines* (Edinburgh: Edinburgh University Press, 2015), pp. 218–31.
10 Félix Guattari *L'inconscient machinique. Essais de schizo-analyse* (Paris: Editions Recherches, 1979), p. 79.
11 Guattari, *L'inconscient machinique* op. cit. p. 92.
12 We have preferred here to render the neologism 'visagéité-paysagéité' as 'faciality-landscaping' so as to avoid the ugliness of 'faciality-landscapity'.
13 Guattari, *L'inconscient machinique* op. cit. p. 107.
14 Silvio Ferraz, 'La formule de la ritournelle', in *Gilles Deleuze, La pensée-musique*, ed. Pascale Criton and Jean March Chouvel (Paris, Centre de documentation de la musique contemporaine, 2015)
15 Gilles Deleuze and Félix Guattari, *A Thousand Plateaus* (Minnesota: Minnesota University Press, 1987), p. 315.

16 Ibid., p. 317.
17 The question of consistency becomes a concern in the later essays of his *Psychoanalysis and Transversality* as well as in his *Anti-Oedipus Writings*. The link between the former and the refrain have been commented on extensively by Gusdon.
18 Deleuze and Guattari, *A Thousand Plateaus* op. cit. p. 336.
19 Ibid., pp. 348–9 (translation slightly modified).
20 The formalizations of expression and content, which had played a crucial role in both his own work and that with Deleuze, are to be understood here as particular *stases* of the deterritorialized semiotic energies that the four dimensions articulate.
21 In her *Artmachines* op. cit.
22 Félix Guattari *Chaosmosis* (Sydney: Power Institute, 2005).
23 Deleuze and Guattari, *A Thousand Plateaus* op. cit.
24 Suely Rolnik and Félix Guattari. *Molecular Revolution in Brazil* (New York and Los Angeles: Semiotext(e), 2008).

6

Heterogenesis, Ecosophy and Dissent

Jean-Sebastien Laberge

> *The major problems in the world are the result of the difference between how nature works and the way people think.*[1]
>
> Gregory Bateson

This chapter supports the idea that it is Félix Guattari's ecosophy that exposes and establishes the political aspects of Gilles Deleuze's philosophy of difference, something they developed in their collaborative works, and that it is in ecosophy that the philosophy of multiplicity reveals its links and directly confronts political pluralism. This chapter therefore proposes to build the link between Deleuzian metaphysics and Guattarian political ecosophy. From a Spinozist perspective, it is evident that the link between metaphysics and practical philosophy is primordial: it must be founded on an understanding of Nature. In other words, it would be pertinent to try and understand Nature in order to edify a coherent lifestyle, just as Spinoza begins his *Ethics* with God in order to culminate with human liberty. From this angle, heterogenesis allows us to go from Deleuzian metaphysics to Guattarian practice. In a similar way, Deleuze's re-actualization of Spinozist univocal metaphysics finds its practical formulation in the aesthetical–ethical–political pluralist choice promoted by Guattarian ecosophy. Finally, I put forth that an ecosophical democracy, one that is coherent with the pluralism implied by heterogenesis as articulated in a dissensual manner, can only flourish within a federalist framework. In this sense, federalism is the politics of multiplicities.

Introduction

The main aim of this chapter is of a programmatic nature. That is to say that the goal is to open up a research perspective and put certain issues in the spotlight.

Nevertheless, this text engages in a well-known debate, that of the existence of a Deleuzian (or Deleuzian–Guattarian) politics. Following on from Alain Badiou, it is worth noting that we do not find 'practical considerations about political orientations'[2] but rather 'a Deleuzian ethics under the name of "politics"'.[3] It is a well-known fact that ontological anarchism and Deleuzian vitalism lead directly to an ethics of experimentation which is the framework for (revolutionary) political activism. In considering that all forms of politics necessarily crush the constitutive singularities of reality by muzzling the complex power of pluralism in the power of the inevitably simplistic and reductive monism, leaving perpetual revolution as the only perspective, it is as if the creator of the idea of multiplicities was simply allergic to the molar.

However, this perspective, as right as it may be (it is not my intention to enter into debate about this here), is marked by a singular omission: the refusal to take into account the work of Félix Guattari.[4] So, if the question is to understand what Deleuzian politics entails, I believe that the answer is to be found in the work of Guattari. This seems all the more obvious when we take into account the fact that Deleuze defined himself as a pure metaphysician, and that Guattari was a veritable activist and practitioner, as well as an aspiring politician and thinker of the institution.[5] This chapter seeks, therefore, to demonstrate the match between Deleuzian metaphysics and the political thought that Guattari called ecosophy. In this sense, I believe that the political implication of Deleuzian heterogenesis is best articulated by a dissensual democracy as outlined in ecosophy. In other words, the full formulation of the co-extensive pluralism of the philosophy of multiplicities is to be found in ecosophy. It is in this context that I put forth a perspective which I believe Guattari was advocating for, namely, federalism. In truth he only touches briefly upon federalism and never delves into how it could eventually articulate the magic formula of 'pluralism = monism'.[6] This is precisely the reason why I believe this chapter to be programmatic, simply because such a form of federalism still needs to be invented. Federalism: the politics of multiplicities?

Before addressing my subject matter directly, I would like to underline the fact that it is not a bold statement to say that demands for a greater pluralism in our democracies are today few and far between. That being said, it is worth mentioning that the 2001 UNESCO Universal Declaration on Cultural Diversity clearly stipulates that 'cultural diversity is as necessary for humankind as biodiversity is for nature'.[7] Furthermore, the 2001 Cotonou Declaration declares that 'the States' and Governments' adoption of cultural policies promoting cultural diversity is now, more than ever, legitimate and necessary'.[8] Despite this, fifteen years later, not only has the promotion of cultural diversity remained a litigious element, but on top of that it would seem that our era is marked by a return to identity politics and an undeniable rise of xenophobia. Guattari had already noted that these resurgences are signs of an absence of viable political alternatives.[9] In this manner, it is essential today to establish the theoretical foundations of an ethical–political paradigm that recognizes the value of diversity in all its forms and, most importantly, proposes concrete perspectives.

To begin with, I would like to recall that Deleuze is very clear when defining his work as follows: 'I believe in philosophy as a system. … For me, the system must not only be in perpetual heterogeneity, it must also be a heterogenesis, which as far as I can tell, has never been tried.'[10] To illustrate my point, special note should be taken of two elements in this affirmation. The first is that he explicitly recognizes that his body of work constitutes a system, a point I will return to later. Secondly, it is the Guattarian concept of heterogenesis that he employs to define his own philosophy, thus giving a clear metaphysical meaning to this central concept of Guattari's thought. Heterogenesis is particularly central to ecosophy where it has an aesthetical–ethical–political meaning as when Guattari concludes *The Three Ecologies* in defining it as 'processes of continuous resingularization. Individuals must become both more united and increasingly different'.[11] Heterogenesis is therefore presented as a crossroads between their two bodies of work: between Deleuze as a metaphysician and Guattari as a practitioner. However, have we not jumped too rapidly from ontology to ethics?

From metaphysics to practical philosophy

In his lecture of 17 March 1981, Deleuze mentions that the link between ontology and ethics 'was founded and developed by Spinoza … . [The project to create] a type of ethics that would act as the correlate of an ontology, which is to say a theory of being, … is a Spinozist path to take, it is a path signed Spinoza'.[12] We can argue that Deleuze follows this path because, in covering Spinoza's problem of expression for his complementary thesis, a metaphysical problem that 'contains within it all the difficulties relating to the unity of substance and the diversity of its attributes',[13] he takes on a perspective that permits him to identify a new logic in this problem: the logic of expression.[14] From this logic is born the road to expression, which is, to quote Pierre Macherey, 'an ethics, in the strict sense of a way of living, a true *ethos*'.[15] Is this not, in fact, what Guattari proposes: an art of living in which a new ethical–aesthetical paradigm is imperative?

In his work prior to meeting Guattari, not only does Deleuze complete Spinoza's quest for univocity by appropriating his expressionism and, in so doing, laying the foundations for what he will later resume with Guattari in the formula 'pluralism = monism',[16] but he also pursues his Kantian critiques and transforms the transcendental which becomes the Natura naturata.[17] In this way Deleuze provides us with a real standpoint that leads to an art of living, an ethics in which the praxis attains its full scope. 'Thus, to be in the middle of Spinoza is to be on this modal plane, or rather to install oneself on this plane – which implies a mode of living, a way of life.'[18] It is well known that this leads to an art of good encounters, a true art of Ethics according to him, intimately linked to the common and indissociable notion of perpetual experimentation.[19] This ethical imperative of experimentation aimed at creation is a vitalism, a joie de vivre, a liberation movement for life against sorrowful nihilism.

This system, which I referred to earlier and that takes form in the three Deleuzian works published in 1968–9, offers the theoretical framework in which Deleuze and Guattari will eventually develop their work. Indeed it was this factor that grabbed the latter's attention and led to their meeting. In this sense, I consider that it is not only the philosophy that Deleuze develops by himself and with Guattari that can be qualified as expressionism, but the rest of the Guattarian corpus too. The machines (a fundamental concept for Guattari and central to the *Anti-Oedipus*) are intrinsically expressive.[20] In an interview,[21] Deleuze puts forth that the notion of assemblage, which takes over from the idea of a desiring machine, could constitute the unity of *A Thousand Plateaus* seeing as he and Guattari attempted to substitute it with the notion of behaviour, highlighting the importance of ethology.[22] He adds that the latter opens a general logic to us that they have but outlined, a logic, he specifies, that Guattari calls diagrammatism. This logic is further elaborated on in the ecology of the virtual, meaning the *metamodelling* that Guattari develops in his ecosophic cartography.[23] However, Guattari does not stop at developing its theoretical aspects, which constitute the essence of the complex *Schizoanalytical Cartographies*, he also touches on the practical aspect, the ethical and political implications of this machinic conception of nature and, in particular, subjectivity. In this sense, the works Guattari produced between 1988 and 1992 follow on from the schizoanalytical research that he undertook with Deleuze.

From the Spinozist art of living which follows from the metaphysics of univocal difference (and correspondingly to the vital involvement in perpetual heterogenesis) comes a responsibility. In expressionism, the power naturally found in all singularities enables a veritable grasp on reality which in turn implies not only a responsibility towards our own singularization, but also, most importantly, a respect for otherness, a commitment towards the pluralism that is inherent in heterogenesis. It is this responsibility, this commitment – ethical, aesthetical and political – that Guattari expresses with great clarity in his ecosophy.

Ecosophy

In literal terms, ecosophy is a wisdom of the home, *oikos-sophia*, an art of living in Nature, to dwell in Nature or even life – a veritable art of living. It is a position that directly links the axiology and the praxis and, by this fact, institutes a responsibility.

It is pertinent to note that the term ecosophy was first employed at the beginning of the 1970s by the Norwegian philosopher Arne Næss.[24] Næss was attempting to put an end to the primacy of humans over nature in order to restore the entirety of the latter's rights. He thus considered that a profound change in mentality was needed due to our relationship with nature being so deeply rooted in our culture. His works were later picked up and used as a base for Deep Ecology, something with which he did not identify. Indeed, Guattari classified these ecologists as Green Khmers! In order to put an end to the eminence of humans over Nature, these activists simply flip the pyramid and place humans under Nature, failing, in the process, to place the human *in* Nature as Næss was actually suggesting. While the latter placed the emphasis largely on environmental ecology, and in particular its preservation, Guattari – who was unaware of Næss's body of work – prioritized mental and social ecology, placing the emphasis largely on subjectivity. I would like to emphasize the point that beyond the significant differences between their conception of subjectivity and the role it plays in their respective ecosophy, they both agree that a profound cultural change is needed in the way that we conceive Nature, in our relationships, and even in the reasoning behind our actions.

Guattari considered it necessary to 'put the emphasis on subjectivity as the product of individuals, groups and institutions'.[25] The reason, as he states elsewhere, is that '[w]e are here to forge life, to produce subjectivity'.[26] According to Guatarri, we produce subjectivity in much the same way as a plastician moulds his raw materials,[27] only the work is never complete and, furthermore, we must always start over again. In considering the production of real subjectivity to be at an impasse, he calls for a new aesthetical paradigm and thus also profound changes to our ways of thinking and acting, or, in other words, to our art of living. As artisans of life, we engineer subjectivity.

We should recall that subjectivity is 'pre-personal, polyphonic, collective and machinic'[28] and that the concept of machinic assemblage 'implies that the *being* differenciates itself qualitatively and leads to an ontological plurality, … *universes of reference*, heterogeneous ontological universes'.[29] We must therefore 'admit that every individual and social group conveys its own system of modelising subjectivity; that is, a certain cartography'.[30] This pluralism is of course a perspectivism. In this manner a plurality of singular perspectives exists, each one qualitatively different and, as for Deleuze,[31] in perpetual heterogenesis. It is precisely this heterogenesis that is the guarantor of human activity and by which means the praxis has a hold on the real.

> The 'aesthetic posture' resides in the fact that the ontological plurality 'in question' does not fall within a Being with a capital b, but within an 'optional matter' with incessant mutations. In their procedural statements, the assemblages of enunciations are producers of irreducibly heterogeneous and singularizing ontological components.[32]

In such a way that 'the reality is no longer one and indivisible. It is multiple, and marked by lines of possibility that human praxis can catch in flight'.[33] Following on from this affirmation of the fundamentally plural aspect of reality, Guattari exhorts us to abandon the sterile and reductionist consensus indisputably put forth by our modern democracies and therefore supported by the homogenizing Integrated Global Capitalism. In other words, these two regimes favour consensuses with the dominant value-systems, thereby encouraging homogenous production; the dictatorship of the majority and the axiological capitalist equivalences lead to an impoverishment.

According to Guattari, we should instead value the dissensus, 'we must demand a redefinition of democracy that goes, not towards a generalized consensus, but towards the singularization of its components'.[34] Instead of the impoverishing consensual democracy encouraged by homogenesis, we must dare to reach for the enriching dissensual democracy that heterogenesis calls for.

On this point, Guattari admittedly falls in line with Lyotard's position, namely that of the inevitable political dissensus.

> Where my opinion differs is in the idea that, for me, the disensus [*sic*] is not absolutely not antagonistic to the organization of a social struggle at all other levels. And with this in mind, new pragmatics must be forged and social practices implemented that will help hold these contradictions together.[35]

The meaning here is that, according to him, it does not lead to a political aporia, just like for Lyotard who considers the incommensurability of differences to be insuperable. Then, why isn't dissensus an aporia and in which type of politics can it fit?

First, because reality and subjectivity are always transindividual (or even transworld), which leads to an immediate political design. The human being does not need to be socialized, he always is, there is no partitioning.[36] Guattari therefore believes that the fact 'that there is a communication between these different territories and these different value systems, that there are transactions, exchanges, is something that is part of the constitution of our ontological horizon'.[37] He notes, in addition, that 'if the ultimate stage of praxis does indeed come down to an ontological production, then its various "machinations" are called to conjoin precisely because of their heterogeneity'.[38] Here, Guattari is referencing the real distinction which Deleuze puts forth in *Expressionism in Philosophy. Spinoza* and which leads to the conceptualization of disjunctive synthesis.[39] It is essential to highlight the fact that expressionism allows us to consider the consistency of immeasurable expressions, singularities that Deleuze called multiplicities.[40] Nevertheless, Guattari realizes that 'it's about living the antagonism, the dissensus, without claiming to magically or transcendentally resolve it'.[41] Let's not forget that at a virtual level, contradiction does not exist. It only presents itself at an actual level.[42] We must therefore face this fact. 'The world of values is thus fundamentally contradictory, antagonistic, confrontational; democracy consists in managing this world with its contradictions, its risks, its embarrassments.'[43] Ecosophic democracy is not aimed towards a simplified consensus, instead it values the vitality and richness of the dissensus, and, in this sense, lives up to the complexity of the real, that is, of Nature.

Secondly, the dissensus is not an aporia since each individual vision of the world 'always harbor[s] an element of uncertainty at its heart. That is, in truth, its most precious capital; on its basis, an authentic hearing of the other could be established'.[44] This is because, lest we forget, subjectivity is always partial. We could also bring to the table Mikhaïl Bakhtine's notion of incompleteness of self, from whom Guattari took the notion of polyphony. From this perspective, 'rather than relations of opposition, it is a matter of forging polyphonic interlacings between the individual and the social. Thus, a subjective music remains to be thereby composed'.[45] It is the act of listening to the other, being open to his disparity, to his singularity that 'constitutes an essential preparation, a permanent appeal to this order of uncertainty, a stripping of forces of chaos'.[46] They allow for the reversal and restoration of meaning to dominant structures by 'recharging them with potentiality, by deploying, through them, news of creative flow'.[47] Guattari is insistent: 'Let us leave consensual politics behind, accept the otherness of the other, their differences; from this ethical movement of revival of the other something can happen.'[48] In other words, it is through the dissensus, or through seeking the rupture of meaning that it provokes, that a perspective for social creativity can emerge. The most heterogenetical components can lead to innovative modalizations and constitute autopoetic creative hotbeds which will allow other things to be built. From dissensus, therefore, a new solidarity can emerge. One which articulates at different levels in a fragmentary and polyphonic manner. 'Ecosophic democracy would not give itself up to the facility for consensual agreement: it will invest itself in a dissensuel metamodelization.'[49]

A choice and a responsibility

Ecosophy is therefore 'the prospect of an ethical-political choice of diversity, of a creative dissensus, of a responsibility regarding difference and otherness'.[50] I would like to insist upon this point: ecosophy is a choice. For Guattari, singularity is 'comme un carrefour praxique et, donc, un choix, – like a praxic crossroads and, this, like a choice. This ethical choice of re-plunging is always possible[51] in the line of questioning linked to the process of singularization. It is due to the collective aspect, among others, of all assemblages that we remain in some sense stuck with the values that are offered or left to us, and which are usually dominant. Guattari talks about 'a pitch by which meanings and denotations of use get under our skin and, more often than not, prohibit access to the sharp edges of these existential functions of pragmatic recovery'[52] that can be qualified as ontological and that allow for resingularization. So, to what extent can we speak of choice and responsibility if the individual is indissociable from collective assemblages of expressions?

Guattari believes that 'there is an ethical choice in favor of the richness of the possible, an ethics and politics of the virtual that decorporalises and deterritorialises contingency, linear causality and the pressure of circumstances and significations which besiege us'.[53] From a Spinozist perspective, we can in effect determine the existence of two types of causality. The first type is linear, which leads us to an infinite regression, from effect to effect, and the second ties us directly to the chaosmosis. It is thus possible to make the leap into the chaosmos, to resingularize oneself, to reload oneself with complexity.

> Accessing such a 'given' is already ontologically participating by right. The term 'right' does not appear here by chance, as at this proto-ontological level it is true that it is already necessary to affirm a proto-ethical dimension. The ontological constellation's game of intensity is, in some way, a choice of being not only for yourself but for all the otherness of the cosmos and for the infinity of time.[54]

If for Sartre, choosing oneself was to choose what we hope a human being to be, for Guattari, choosing our 'world', our values, is to assume a perspective, a constitutive otherness of reality. This is what the praxis allows for, and Guattari thus believes that 'praxis precedes the being'[55] as 'human praxis engenders [ontological] heterogeneous universes, engenders practices',[56] in short, 'the process precedes the heterogenesis of being'.[57] Guattari thus deeply roots ethics and politics in stating that 'if there's choice and freedom at certain "superior" anthropological stages, it's because we will also find them at the most elementary strata of machinic concatenations'.[58] Above all, with this liberty comes a responsibility:

> A responsibility towards the being to be taken as creativity, this is what I attempted to present as ecosophy, as wisdom of the *ecos*, not only the wisdom of inter-human relationships, but also those of relationships with the environment, with machinic phyla, with the world of meaning, with the existential territory.[59]

Guattari holds that 'today, individual and collective subjectivity lives under a regime ... of ignorance of difference and otherness in the human domain as much as in the cosmic register'.[60] That is to say that our current practices are largely incoherent with this machinic conception of Nature, and, as put forth by Gregory Bateson in the exergue citation, inconsistent with our current understanding of nature as fundamentally heterogenetic, complex and interlinked.[61] We can then easily comprehend that the central question for Guattari, the one that drove him to developing an ecology of the virtual – an entire piece of theoretical work on the process of subjectivation – is:

> How do we change mentalities, how do we reinvent special practices that would give back to humanity – if it ever had it – a sense of responsibility, not only for its own survival, but equally for the future of all life on the planet, for animal

> and vegetable species, likewise for incorporeal species such as music, the arts, cinema, the relation with time, love and compassion for others, the feeling of fusion at the heart of cosmos?[62]

In short, a mentality or subjectivity on par with the complex wealth of plurality; a singularization that values and feeds off otherness. Above all, one that encompasses *a sense of fusion in the heart of the cosmos*. It is tempting, here, to think of the third type of knowledge of Spinoza that – although linked to an experience of eternity for Spinoza, Guattari puts the focus more on a recognition of our finitude – invites just such a fusion with Nature.[63] In my opinion, this is an invitation to a type of singularization, an art of living that attempts to be more in line with Nature, that seeks to enrich itself, to have a more polyphonic subjectivity.

Guattari affirms that 'the only acceptable finality of human activity is the production of a subjectivity that is auto-enriching its relation to the world in a continuous fashion'.[64] Two elements should be underlined here. First, we find here a strong imperative that brings to mind another aspect of Spinozism. If Spinoza, on the one hand, believes that 'the more reality or being a thing has, the greater the number of its attributes',[65] I would say that the more plans in which we participate, the more becomings in which we take part, the more transversal and polyphonic we are, the richer our experience of reality will be. This enriching undeniably calls for a new progressivist axis as it will 'only take on meaning with a true social experimentation as its guide, leading to a collective evaluation and reappropriation, and enriching individual and collective subjectivity'.[66]

Secondly, this imperative undeniably denotes a form of perfectionism to be found in Guattari. On this topic, suffice it to say that this perfectionism should be linked to the one exhibited by Deleuze (a matter to be investigated further), which in turn should be linked to the perfectionism found in Spinoza and Nietzsche, emphasizing the potential of becoming active and the importance of embracing life. In summary, it is a cooperative and non-elitist democratic perfectionism which implies, as does all perfectionism, a form of politics that not only allows for such experimentation, but also favours it.

Tolerance

But what sort of politics can allow for such experimentation as well as the cohabitation of a dissensual perspective? Let us recall that in *l'Abécédaire*, Deleuze stated that a truly leftist politics is impossible, at best a left-favourable politics is imaginable, in other words one that is fundamentally tolerant towards difference and experimentation.[67] Following on from this perspective, Deleuze states in referring to Spinoza that 'wherever he goes he only asks ... to be tolerated, himself and his uncommon aims, and from this tolerance he judges concerning the degree of democracy, the degree of truth, which a society can bear'.[68] Democracy is thus linked to the capacity to tolerate the truth of heterogeneity. However, Guattari does not stop at this notion of tolerance or of a simple respect of otherness. Rather, he considers dissensus to be a

> Politics that in principle accepts differences. And not only the acceptance of difference, the tolerance, but in addition the love of the difference, of the engine that it represents. *It is because I do not understand you, because you are different, that I am attracted to you. From this difference I want to draw something essential for me.*[69] (italics in the original)

Ecosophic democracy cannot be satisfied solely in tolerating a pluralism out of respect for the liberty of individuals; rather, it sees a fertile soil because 'dissensus is the love of the antagonistic position; to accept that the other's position enriches my position because it is different'.[70] From this love of otherness we can develop praxes that will enrich our relationship with the world; hospitality enriches and pluralizes our existence. Following on from this line of thought, Guattari remarks that 'a "new tenderness", a new ear to the other in their difference and singularity are, here too, still to be invented.'[71] But this task does not rest solely on individuals alone, it is not limited to an ethics of hospitality. Guattari believes in another politics, in other words it is necessary to 'redefine a form of active politics that forces its enunciation and also its audience who recreate feedback phenomena'.[72] In short, not a form of politics that adapts to the people, generally in a consensual or electioneering optic, but instead a form of politics that invents its people, that brings forth the people that are missing, that commits to the becoming of an ecosophical, democratic, dissensual and hospitable people.

Ecosophy is a political aesthetic that looks to invent a people missing from the world. A people that will always be missing, even if they are already here. In other words it is a form of politics that commits to 'the fabulation of the people to come'.[73] In proposing a new ethical–aesthetical paradigm, Guattari invites us to create and, as Deleuze notes, 'there is no work of art that does not call on a people who does not yet exist'.[74] Therefore, if sickness is the halting of the process,[75] in this case of heterogenesis in favour of homogenesis, meaning 'the halting of the subjective production of virtualities',[76] then Guattari proposes 'a veritable clinical analysis of culture',[77] whose goal is to treat 'la vie anormale des gens normaux – the abnormal life of normal people'[78] who have given up on fabulating. In such a manner that Guattari's health is machining the missing people, his ecosophy is a *gaya scienza*. The invention of an ecosophic people is a perfectionism.

Political implications

In addition to pointing out the failure of abstract internationalism and the impoverishment of the media's subjectivity in other places, in *The Three Ecologies* Guattari underlines the failure of political groups and executives to properly understand ecological issues in all their complexity. In the best of cases they are approached from an environmental point of view, although only superficially and usually only attacking industrial pollution from a technocratic perspective. Following on from Guattari, I consider the environmental, social and mental issues to be interrelated and that 'an ethical-political articulation – which [Guattari] call[s] *ecosophy* – between the three ecological registers (the environment, social relations and human subjectivity) would be likely to clarify these questions'.[79] We must acknowledge, however, that we cannot and indeed must not wait for such an articulation to simply come from above.

Guattari is fully aware that solutions can not solely be based on governmental or global actions, they must also come forth through the emergence of a multiplicity of local practices, both individual and collective. Neither should they be 'unified' to a higher level, but rather their uniqueness and divergence should be respected and preserved. The question then becomes what kind of politics can, on the one hand, make room for 'the dimension of existential dissidence (whether individual or collective) and, on the other hand, the collective assemblages?'[80] That is to say a form of politics that allows great freedom to experiment and that can bring out different forms of cohesion for the differences that result from this freedom; a form of politics that forges polyphony in dissonance. The challenge is 'to design a link between these diverse praxes … attempting to articulate them in a relation of dissensus and not in a relation of consensus with the dominant value systems'.[81] That is to say no unification, totalization, simplification, reduction or homogenization, but a complex politics of multiplicities where pluralism = monism. What would such a form of politics resemble? Although he does acknowledge that he has not found the miracle cure, in some places Guattari does evoke the prospect of a solution: federalism.[82]

The path of federalism

I wish here only to sketch out certain elements in order to show the relevance and viability of the federalist perspective. Since Guattari 'consider[s] that progressivist polarisation ought to be reconstituted through more complex schema, according to less Jacobinist modalities, more federalist, more dissensuel',[83] he implicitly acknowledges that federalism permits a complex and dissensual cohesion. By the late 1980s, Guattari perceptively notes that in the absence of new concrete prospects of interlacing between the various modalizations, they tend dangerously to close in on themselves. In such a way that 'nationalistic questions are re-emerging in the worst subjective conditions (nationalism, uniformity, racial hatred ...) since no appropriate federalist response has been advanced as an alternative to an abstract and fictitious internationalism'.[84] A finding that is unfortunately still highly relevant today. The trick is, therefore, to forge such a federalism by gradually experimenting in this direction. 'This implies the promotion of another type of logic, a multivalent logic that allows for both the taking of entrenched positions, or compromise at the molar level, and at the same time, to have an availability, an openness of spirit, a dissensual spirit.'[85] Federalism allows for just such a relationship between different planes.

The intrinsically federalist principal of subsidiarity comes to mind here. The first aspect of subsidiarity is the principle that any action must be performed by the smallest capable entity. That is to say that it holds in highest regard the most immediate autonomy. The second aspect of subsidiarity is that it requires that, when an issue exceeds the capacity of an entity, it becomes the responsibility of more global entities to support it. However, this solidarity always occurs within the limits of the autonomy of each entity and in respect to their precedence. This allows for dissensual molecular assemblage with integral molar assemblage, albeit equally divergent, in such a way that it becomes possible to hold in place dissensual and integral becomings, and to commit to the becoming of an ecosophical population.

By recognizing the power of each singularity, the principle of federalist subsidiarity allows for a genuine ethos of experimentation in view of a new ethical–aesthetical paradigm. Such a form of politics is in a position to encourage the emergence of new practices and values. Moreover, in articulating this principle, federalism does not seek to impose a universal, transcendent and homogenizing solution, but leaves local levels to form their own solution and carry out their own revolution in accordance with their singular reality. In short, federalism does not impose a transcendental guardianship, but rather builds on the authority of a multiplicity of praxes and immanent values.

Conclusion

I therefore consider that when Guattari invites us to forge 'polyphonic interlacings between the individual and the social. Thus, a subjective music remains to be thereby composed',[86] it is towards federalism that our attention must be focused. In this way a polyphonic federalism, meaning an ecosophic, dissensual and hospitable federalism, the fruit of a new ethical-aesthetical-political paradigm, remains to be experienced. Please note, I am not calling for a new regime that should naturally prevail or for the advent of a promised people. Quite the contrary, my interest in federalism lies precisely in its ability to make coexist in a non-hierarchical manner a plurality of regimes and of people. Federalism as the politics of multiplicities. Ecosophical people who are still missing are probably waiting for such a polyphonic federalism.

Notes

1 Bateson, G., cited in Bateson, N., *An Ecology of Mind.*
2 Badiou, *Existe-t-il quelque chose comme une politique deleuzienne?*, p. 16 [Our translation].
3 Ibid., p. 20 [Our translation].
4 Note that the refusal to accord importance to Guattari's contribution and his work are characteristic of the reading performed by Badiou.
5 cf. Deleuze, *Responses to a Series of Questions*, p.41. Guattari worked at the La Borde clinic for over forty years and was an ardent theoretical defender of institutional psychotherapy. In the 1992 regional elections, he was also a candidate for *Les Verts* but did not get elected. He passed away five months later.
6 Deleuze, Guattari, *A Thousand Plateaus*, p. 20.
7 United Nations Educational, Scientific and Cultural Organization, *UNESCO Universal Declaration on Cultural Diversity, art.1.* p. 62.
8 Agence intergouvernementale de la Francophonie, *Cotonou Agreement*, p. 3 [Our translation].
9 cf. Guattari, 'Vers une écosophie', in *Qu'est-ce que l'écosophie?*, p.65; *Supra*, note 76.
10 Deleuze, 'Letter-Preface to Jean-Clet Martin', in *Two Regimes of Madness*, p. 361.

11 Guattari, *The Three Ecologies*, p. 69.

12 Deleuze, *Les cours de Gilles Deleuze. Sur Spinoza. Cours du 17 mars* [Our translation].

13 Deleuze, *Expressionism in Philosophy: Spinoza*, p. 13.

14 cf. Zourabichvili, *Le vocabulaire de Deleuze*, p. 81. Zourabichvili notes that Deleuze 'willingly defined his own work as the elaboration of a "logic"' [Our translation].

15 Macherey, *The Encounter with Spinoza*, p. 147.

16 Deleuze, Guattari, *A Thousand Plateaus*, p. 20.

17 cf. AN, *La transformation spinoziste de l'idée du transcendantal dans la première philosophie de Deleuze.*

18 Deleuze, *Spinoza: Practical Philosophy*, p. 122.

19 cf. Ibid., p. 119: 'The common notions are an Art, the art of the Ethics itself: organizing good encounters, composing actual relations, forming powers, experimenting.'

20 It should not be misunderstood, the devaluation of expression in favour of production in *Anti-Oedipus* is a naturalization of expression that should no longer be understood as a theatrical manifestation, but as a machinic genesis. In short, it is a materialistic reprise of the concept of expression which may have seemed too idealistic. In addition, it offers that the human being is not a mere spectator of Nature, but is involved in its production; the human, as part of Nature, natures Nature; in short, the human machines. cf. Deleuze; Guattari, *Anti-Oedipus*, pp. 6, 55, 133.

21 cf. Deleuze, 'Eight Years Later: 1980 Interview', in *Two Regimes of Madness*, p. 177.

22 It is quite likely that it was due to Guattari's influence that Deleuze became interested in Ethology. This interest culminated in the decisive crossing of Spinoza and Uexküll which led to an innovative concept of cartography.

23 cf. Guattari, *Chaosmosis*, p. 22: 'In these conditions, theoretical activity is reorientated toward a metamodelisation capable of taking into account the diversity of modelising systems.'

24 cf. Næss, *The Shallow and the Deep Ecology Movement.*

25 Guattari, *Chaosmosis*, p. 1.

26 Guattari, 'Praxis éco', in *Qu'est-ce que l'écosophie?*, p. 562. [Our translation].

27 cf. Guattari, *Chaosmosis*, p. 7; Guattari, *The Three Ecologies*, pp. 35, 52.

28 Guattari, *Chaosmosis*, p. 21.

29 Guattari, 'À propos des machines', in *Qu'est-ce que l'écosophie?*, p. 115 [Our translation].

30 Guattari, *Chaosmosis*, p. 11.

31 cf. Deleuze, *The Fold. Leibniz and the Baroque*, p. 20.

32 Guattari, 'Au-delà du retour à zéro', *Qu'est-ce que l'écosophie?*, p. 291 [Our translation].

33 Guattari, *Remaking Social Practices*, p. 271.
34 Butin; Hernot; Guattari, *Entretien avec Félix Guattari*, pp. 54–5 [Our translation]. I thank Aurélien Chastan for bringing this text to my attention.
35 Ibid., p. 55 [Our translation].
36 Idea promoted by Machiaveli, Spinoza and Marx, among others, and that Antonio Negri called Antijuridism. cf. Negri, *The Savage Anomaly*.
37 Guattari, 'Vers une autopoïétique de la communication', in *Qu'est-ce que l'écosophie?*, p. 147 [Our translation].
38 Ibid., p. 148.
39 cf. Deleuze, *Expressionism in Philosophy: Spinoza*, pp. 77–80; Deleuze, *The Logic of Sense*, pp. 174–5; Deleuze; Guattari, *Anti-Oedipus*, p. 309n!. It is worth remembering that *The disjunctive synthesis* is the title of their first collaboration. cf. Deleuze; Guattari, 'La synthèse disjonctive', in *L'Arc* 43, pp. 54–62.
40 cf. Deleuze, *Difference and Repetition*, p. 182 *sq*; Deleuze; Guattari, *A Thousand Plateaus*, p. 482 *sq*.
41 Guattari, '[Subjectivité machinique plutôt que transcendance]', in *Qu'est-ce que l'écosophie?*, p. 340 [Our translation].
42 cf. Deleuze, *The Logic of Sense*, p. 177.
43 Guattari, '[Subjectivité machinique plutôt que transcendance]', in *Qu'est-ce que l'écosophie?*, p. 340 [Our translation].
44 Guattari, *Remaking Social Practices*, p. 271.
45 Ibid., p. 267.
46 Ibid. p. 271.
47 Ibid.
48 Guattari, 'Qu'est-ce que l'écosophie?' in *Qu'est-ce que l'écosophie?*, p. 76 [Our translation].
49 Guattari, *Remaking Social Practices*, p. 272.
50 Guattari, 'Pratique écosophique et restauration de la cité subjective', in *Qu'est-ce que l'écosophie?*, p. 33 [Our translation].
51 Guattari, 'Vertige de l'immanence', in *Qu'est-ce que l'écosophie?*, p. 316 [Our translation].
52 Guattari, 'Au-delà du retour à zéro', in *Qu'est-ce que l'écosophie?*, p. 295 [Our translation].
53 Guattari, *Chaosmosis*, p. 29.
54 Ibid., p. 80.
55 Guattari, 'l'imagination au pouvoir', in *Qu'est-ce que l'écosophie?*, p. 349 [Our translation].
56 Guattari, 'Vertige de l'immanence', in *Qu'est-ce que l'écosophie?*, p. 326 [Our translation].
57 Guattari, *Chaosmosis*, p. 108.

58 Ibid., p. 53.

59 Guattari, 'Vertige de l'immanence', in *Qu'est-ce que l'écosophie?*, pp. 326–7 [Our translation].

60 Guattari, 'Vers une écosophie', in *Qu'est-ce que l'écosophie?*, p. 65 [Our translation].

61 I consider Deleuzoguattarian metaphysics to be the most coherent in view of modern-day sciences. cf. Bonta; Protevi, *Deleuze and géophilosophie*; Capra, *Complexity and life*; Delanda, *Intensive science and virtual philosophy.*

62 Guattari, *Chaosmose*, pp. 119–20.

63 cf. Marange, *La petite machine écosophique*, p. 4. Ecosophy is critical clinical, a joyful knowledge.

64 Guattari, *Chaosmosis*, p. 21.

65 Spinoza, *Ethics*, Part 1, Proposition 9.

66 Guattari, 'Pratique écosophique et restauration de la cité subjective', in *Qu'est-ce que l'écosophie?*, p. 51 [Our translation].

67 cf. Deleuze, 'Left-Wing Politics', in *Gilles Deleuze from A to Z.*

68 Deleuze, *Spinoza: Practical Philosophy*, p. 4.

69 Guattari, 'Subjectivité machinique plutôt que transcendance', in *Qu'est-ce que l'écosophie?*, p. 334 [Our translation].

70 Guattari, 'Praxis éco', in *Qu'est-ce que l'écosophie?*, p. 557 [Our translation].

71 Guattari, 'Pratique écosophique et restauration de la cité subjective', in *Qu'est-ce que l'écosophie?*, p. 53 [Our translation].

72 Butin; Hernot; Guattari, *Entretien avec Félix Guattari*, p. 52 [Our translation].

73 Deleuze, *Cinema 2.The Time-Image*, p.223 [Translation modified ('fabulation' has been preferred to 'story-telling)].

74 Deleuze, "What is the Creative Act?" in *Two Regime of Madness* p.324.

75 cf. Deleuze, *Essay Critical and Clinical*, p. 13.

76 Marange, *Écosophie ou barbarie.* [Our translation].

77 Sauvagnargues, *A Schizoanalytic Knight on the Chessboard of Politics*, p. 173.

78 Marange, *Écosophie ou barbarie.* [Our translation].

79 Guattari, *The Three Ecologies*, p. 28.

80 Butin; Hernot; Guattari, *Entretien avec Félix Guattari*, p. 55 [Our translation].

81 Guattari, 'Vers une autopoïétique de la communication', in *Qu'est-ce que l'écosophie?*, pp. 147–8 [Our translation].

82 cf. *Supra*, notes 83, 84.

83 Guattari, *Chaosmosis*, p. 121. cf. Guattari, 'Vers une écosophie', in *Qu'est-ce que l'écosophie?*, p. 62; Guattari, 'La question de la question', in *Terminal* 57, p. 8.

84 Guattari, *Chaosmosis*, p. 123. cf. Guattari, 'Vers une écosophie', in *Qu'est-ce que l'écosophie?*, p. 65.

85 Guattari, 'Praxis éco', in *Qu'est-ce que l'écosophie?*, p. 561 [Our translation].

86 Guattari, *Remaking Social Practices*, p. 267.

Bibliography

AGENCE INTERGOUVERNEMENTALE DE LA FRANCOPHONIE (2001), 'Déclaration de Cotonou', *Supplément du Journal de l'Agence intergouvernementale de la Francophonie* 23, pp. 3–4.

An, Jing. (2013), *La transformation spinoziste de l'idée du transcendantal dans la première philosophie de Deleuze*. Thèse. Toulouse: Université Toulouse Jean Jaurès. 277p.

Badiou, Alain. (2001), 'Existe-t-il quelque chose comme une politique deleuzienne?' *Cités* 40, [2009], pp. 15–20.

Bateson, Nora. (2010), *An Ecology of Mind*. San Francisco: The Impact Media Group. DVD. 60 min.

Butin, Dominique, Hernot, Yann and Guattari, Félix. (1986), 'Entretien avec Félix Guattari ou ré-appropriation de la subjectivité collective et transformations sociales', *Science-Fiction* 6, pp. 46–55.

Deleuze, Gilles. ([1968]1994), *Difference and Repetition*. Translated by P. Patton. New York: Columbia University Press.

Deleuze, Gilles. ([1968]1990), *Expressionism in Philosophy: Spinoza*. Translated by M. Joughin. New York: Zone Books.

Deleuze, Gilles. ([1969]1990), *The Logic of Sense*. Translated by M. Lester and C. Stivale. Edited by C. Boundas. London: The Athlone Press.

Deleuze, Gilles. (1981), *Les cours de Gilles Deleuze. Sur Spinoza. Cours du 17 mars 1981*. Online, http://www.webdeleuze.com/php/sommaire.html, consulted 23 May 2015.

Deleuze, Gilles. ([1981]1988), *Spinoza: Practical Philosophy*. Translated by R. Hurley. San Francisco: City Lights Books.

Deleuze, Gilles. (1981), 'Responses to a Series of Questions', *Collapse* 3 [2007].

Deleuze, Gilles. ([1985]1989), *Cinema 2. Time-Image*. Translated by H. Tomlinson and R. Galeta. Minneapolis: University of Minnesota Press.

Deleuze, Gilles. ([1988]1993). *The Fold. Leibniz and the Baroque*. Translated by T. Conley. London: The Athlone Press.

Deleuze, Gilles. ([1993]1998), *Essay Critical and Clinical*. Translated by D. W. Smith and M. A. Greco. London and New York: Verso.

Deleuze, Gilles. ([2003]2007), *Two Regime of Madness. Texts and Interviews 1975-1995*. Edited by D. Lapoujade. Translated by A. Hodges and M. Taomina. Cambridge, MA: The MIT Press; coll. Semiotext(e)/Foreign Agents.

Deleuze, Gilles and Guattari, Félix (1970), 'La synthèse disjonctive', *L'Arc* 43, pp. 54–62.

Deleuze, Gilles and Guattari, Félix ([1972, 1983, 2000]1977), *Anti-Oedipus. Capitalism and Schizophrenia*. Translated by R. Hurley, M. Seem, H. R. Lane. Minneapolis: University of Minnesota Press.

Deleuze, Gilles and Guattari, Félix ([1980]1987), *A Thousand Plateaus: Capitalism and Schizophrenia*. Translated by B. Massumi. London and Minneapolis: University of Minnesota Press.

UNITED NATIONS EDUCATIONAL, SCIENTIFIC AND CULTURAL ORGANIZATION (2001), 'UNESCO Universal Declaration on Cultural Diversity', *Records of the General Conference* 31/1, pp. 62–3.

Guattari, Félix ([1989]2000), *The Three Ecologies*. Translated by I. Pindar, P. Sutton. London and New Brunswick (NJ): The Athlone Press, 174p.

Guattari, Félix ([1992]1995), *Chaosmosis, an ethico-aesthetic paradigm*. Translated by P. Bains and J. Pefanis. Bloomington and Indianapolis: Indiana University Press, 136p.

Guattari, Félix ([1992]1996), 'Remaking Social Practices', in G. Genosko (ed.), *The Guattari Reader*. Translated by S. Thomas, pp. 262–72.

Guattari, Félix (1992), 'La question de la question', *Terminal* 57, pp. 8–9.

Guattari, Félix (2014), *Qu'est-ce que l'écosophie?* Edited by S. Nadeau. Paris: Lignes, coll. Archives de la pensée critique. 592p.

Macherey, Pierre (1996), 'The encounter with Spinoza', in P. Patton (ed.), *Deleuze: A Critical Reader*. Translated by M. Joughin. Oxford: Blackwell, pp. 139–61.

Marange, Valérie (1996), 'La petite machine écosophique', *Chimères. Revue des schizoanalyses* 28, pp. 1–11.

Marange, Valérie (2000), 'Écosophie ou barbarie', *Ecorev' Revue critique d'écologie politique* 1. Online. http://ecorev.org/spip.php?article501, consulted 23 May 2015.

Naess, Arne. 1973. 'The shallow and the deep, long-range ecology movement. A summary', *Inquiry: An Interdisciplinary Journal of Philosophy* 16/1–4, pp. 95–100.

Sauvagnargues, Anne ([2008]2011), 'A Schizoanalytic Knight on the Chessboard of Politics', in É. Alliez and A. Goffey (eds), *The Guattari Effect*. Translated by A. Goffey. London and New York: Continuum.

Spinoza, Baruch. ([1677]1901). *Ethics*. Translated by R. H. M. Elwes. London: George Bell and Sons.

Zourabichvili, François. (2003), *Le vocabulaire de Deleuze*. Paris: Ellipses, coll. Vocabulaire de, 95p.

7

'Degrees of Freedom': Félix Guattari's *Schizoanalytic Cartographies*

Hanjo Berressem

Nothing is given in itself
Schizoanalytic Cartographies 211

Introduction

This chapter addresses three related questions: First, what exactly does Félix Guattari mean when he talks, in his book *Schizoanalytic Cartographies*, of 'degrees of freedom'? Second, how exactly are these 'degrees of freedom' related to the notion of the refrain, which, as Guattari maintains,

> constitutes a sort of selector of choices … for the treatment of the bifurcations around which the *degrees of freedom* of a system, the aleatory putting on hold of the enacting of heterogeneous components, will play (SC 147)

Third, how are 'degrees' of freedom related to what Guattari conceptualizes as the 'synaptic moment'? More generally, if the notion of 'schizoanalysis', which provides the framework of Guattari's cartography, concerns 'the capacity of our societies to conquer new *degrees of freedom* in relation to existing economic and social constraints, and recentre the collective and individual purposes of human activity on new objectives' (SC 36), how to bring this collective capacity into play in order to create new 'modes of existence'?

I will develop my argument by way of a commentary on *Schizoanalytic Cartographies*, a book that still awaits the amount of critical interest it deserves as Guattari's magnum opus and legacy. What the book shows is that under his often über abstract writing, his staccato style, his hectic conceptual speeds and rhetorical acrobatics – as many scholars have noted in their communal work, Guattari provides the experimental speed to Deleuze's conceptual slowness – lie a very calm, legato consistence; a deep conceptual rigour; and an insistent question and demand. How can we make life on this planet better? More livable? More in tune *with* or adequate *to* the functioning of the world? How to do this without false romanticism or nostalgia? In the terminology of *Schizoanalytic Cartographies*, what are the diagrammatics we might need for such a project?

To put my argument into rhetorical relief, let me assume, if only for rhetoric's sake, that in the context of most of the scholarly work on Deleuze and Guattari, degrees of freedom are usually measured in degrees of deterritorialization or smoothing. These terms are set against degrees of territorialization or striation, which tend to be measured in degrees of constraint. At the horizon of complete deterritorialization, one can make out the slightly blurred figure of the schizo, who marks the vanishing point of a conceptual perspective centred on total freedom. This vision has led, in parts of the critical community, to what might be called a deep 'Deleuze and Guattarian Romanticism': death to oppressive, striated 'states of order', long live smooth anarchy.

What I want to argue, quite simply and straightforwardly, is that in the light of *Schizoanalytic Cartographies*, the choices are not quite that simple. In terms of the inherent logic of Deleuze and Guattari's collaboration – in cases where Guattari is more present than Deleuze, I will talk of Guattari and Deleuze – this argument concerns in particular the relation between *Schizoanalytic Cartographies* and *A Thousand Plateaus*. In the former, Guattari introduces a fundamental asymmetry into the dynamics that pertain to smoothing and striation. This asymmetry concerns in particular the evaluation of striation, in the sense that it gives a positive value to striation. As such, it 'retroactively striates' *A Thousand Plateaus*. Or at least, it brings out moments in the earlier book that have tended to be, perhaps understandably so, overread.

Diagram

The diagram that makes up the conceptual spine of *Schizoanalytic Cartographies* sections the plane of consistency into four 'radically heterogeneous domains' (SC 18) or 'functors' (SC 26) that are related not so much by one overarching logic – Guattari in fact distinguishes between four causalities that operate in it:

formal, final, efficient and material – as by 'diverse modalities of "transversality" (SC 52), by layerings *of* and movements *between* its four "domains of consistency"' (SC 56). When I call it a fourfold, a long, Heideggerian shadow – Heidegger's fourfold consists of 'earth, sky, mortals and divinities' – falls onto Guattari's diagram. The two fourfolds, however, are 'worlds apart'.

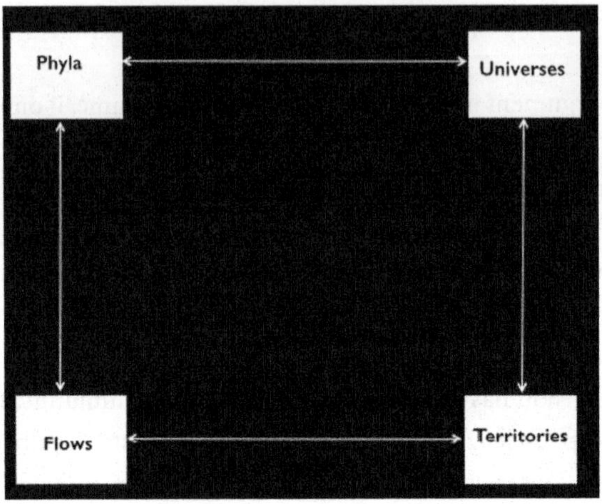

One of the main difficulties of making sense of Guattari's fourfold is that his notion of diagram – which he developed with Deleuze – is quite counter-intuitive. In general, diagrams are 'abstractions' of 'concrete machines', such as the diagram of the network of a subway system, which provides that system's structural blueprint or 'form' from without in the sense that it creates an overview from a position of 'n+1'. Although Deleuze and Guattari sometimes make use of such formal diagrams to visualize certain conceptual constellations, they mostly operate with 'informal' (34) diagrams. These informal diagrams are 'diagrams under the conditions of a given multiplicity'. How, the question is, should a diagram look that 'diagrams' a 'given' world that cannot be reduced to strict laws and stable forms? The informal diagram – which is, paradoxically, a diagram without form – contradicts the 'formalist' uses of diagrams in that it models, or even *is*, the 'given' world seen from *within* this world – from a position of 'n−1' – rather than from without. As such, it is the 'name' for the infinitely many and complex operations in-between the fractal layers, the coagulations, the stratifications and destratification of that world. Ultimately, it is the 'impossible blueprint' of the energetics and intensities of the world and of its changes 'under the condition that there is no dimension outside of this world'. Such a diagram is 'unstable, agitated and shuffled around' (71). Also, it is not only 'descriptive', but also genetic. It is 'fluid, continually churning up matter and [it] functions in a way likely to create change' (30). It is a 'map of intensities' (32) and 'of the relation between forces' (32) that are 'merely virtual, potential, unstable, vanishing and molecular' (32).

As both heuristic device and genetic force, the informal diagram is a 'non-unifying immanent cause' (32) of 'concrete assemblages' (32), with which it shares a logic of 'mutual [reciprocal] presupposition' (32). The most general of these mutual presuppositions is, famously, that of the virtual and the actual. Although these states emerge together, in that genesis, the virtual as informal diagram has a primacy over the actual. This can be seen by the fact that during the inevitable moment and process of actualization, 'the informal diagram is swallowed up and becomes embodied ... in two different directions that are necessarily divergent and irreducible' (33). In other words, in the process of actualization, the informal diagram is split up into two 'aspects': the virtual as actualized, and the actual as virtualized. Or, in a variation of Spinoza, 'virtual and actual *are one and the same thing*, conceived first under the attribute of thought, secondly, under the attribute of extension'.

If the informal diagram is inevitably actualized, one might argue that it makes little sense to retain it as a term. Crucially, however, part of the informal diagram, 'does not stop *not* being actualized'. It remains outside of its own 'actualization' and thus its own 'extensity' as an excess virtuality or 'intensity'. This informal surplus ensures and literally contains the infinite potentiality of change and of becoming. It is 'why and how newness enters the world'. The informal diagram is the dynamic ensemble of virtual, intensive forces in surplus of being actualized, relationalized and formed into extensive matters-of-fact. As Guattari and Deleuze note, 'the diagrammatic or abstract machine does not function to represent, even something real, but rather constructs a real that is yet to come, a new type of reality' (TP 142).

The informal diagram, then, is a diagram as we used to know it, 'turned upside-down and inside-out'. It is:

> an atmospheric element, a 'non-stratified substance' ... The informal outside is a battle, a turbulent, stormy zone where particular points and the relations of forces between these points are tossed about. Strata merely collected and solidified the visual dust and the sonic echo of the battle raging above them ... Each atmospheric state in this zone corresponds to a diagram of forces or particular features which are taken up by relations: a strategy ... But it is the strategy's job to be fulfilled in the stratum, just as it is the diagram's job to become

> stratified. To be realized [better: 'actualized'] in this way means becoming *both integrated and different* (Foucault, 121–2)

There is a difference between relations, which are the results of 'mental' processes, and forces.

> It never functions in order to *represent* a persisting world but *produces* a new kind of reality. … It is neither the subject of history, nor does it survey history. It makes history by unmaking preceding realities and significations, constituting hundreds of points of emergence or creativity, unexpected conjunctions or improbable continuums. It doubles history with a sense of continual evolution" (35, emphases added).

As Deleuze notes, quite beautifully, the informal diagram is 'a machine that is almost blind and mute, even though it makes others see and speak' (30).

Before I deal with how Guattari's fourfold relates to the informal diagram, let me describe it in more detail. The fourfold's conceptual quadrophonics – what is known in acoustics as '4.0 surround sound' – relate the 'domains' of Flows, Phyla, Territories and Universes. In telegrammatic reduction, Flows and Phyla are actual, while Territories and Universes are virtual. On the actual side, which concerns an objective, quantitative, extensive and abstract, field: '1) Flows of matter and energy; 2) the abstract machinic Phyla that preside over *objective* laws and changes' (SC 52, emphasis added). On the virtual side, which concerns a subjective, qualitative, intensive and 'concrete' field, 3) existential Territories, considered from the angle of their self-enjoyment (their 'for itself') and, finally, 4) incorporeal Universes, which *escape* from the energetic, legal, evolutionary and existential coordinates of the three preceding domains (SC 52).

The diagram is not only partitioned into an actual and a virtual side, then, but also into the side of 'the world as such' and the side of 'its' concrete entities, or as Guattari calls them 'consistencies'. 'There is the Given, thus there is the Giving' (SC 58), Guattari notes, modulating Deleuze's differentiation, from *Difference and Repetition*, of 'the given' and 'the given as given'. 'Difference is not diversity' (222), Deleuze had noted. 'Diversity is given, but difference is that by which the given is given, that by which the given is given as diverse' (222).

Together, the given and the giving denote the two complementary planes of the chaotic and the 'chaosmotic' (SC 155) aspects of the world and of subjectivation, or, in Guattari's terms, of the creation of consistencies. In a once more somewhat counter-intuitive logic: there is pure immanence, *thus* there is consistency. 'There is the Given, thus there is the Giving' (SC 58). Immanence is given – it presents itself – as 'the given and the giving'. 'There is the Given, there is the Giving, but neither the one nor the other should be considered as subjected to compartmentalized domains of consistency' (SC 59).

A further difference that pertains to the actual and virtual is that while Flows and Phyla are complex and extensive, Territories and Universes are 'hypercomplex' (SC 104) and intensive. And as if that wasn't complex enough, there is, at the same time, a vertical differentiation. While Flows and Territories have a high degree of consistency and are continuous, Phyla and Universes have a low degree of consistency and are discontinuous. As Guattari notes, 'the Phyla will constitute the "integrals" of Flows, as it were, and the Universes, the "integrals" of Territories' (SC 28). In order to chart a specific 'position' within the diagram, therefore, one always needs at least two 'scanners', one moving along a horizontal and the other along the diagram's vertical axis. It is from within this general frame that the question of freedom and its degrees should be asked. Freedom is distributed in this field. It is 'somewhere' in the movement of the cursors.

Freedom

The notion that 'degrees of freedom' are related to the forces of smoothing and deterritorialization on the one hand, and striation and territorialization on the other comes, mainly, from *A Thousand Plateaus*. In these dynamics, striation is seen, at least tendentially, as negative because it is related to forces of ordering, while smoothing is seen, again tendentially, as positive because it is related to forces of disruption. Specific degrees of freedom seem to lie in the degree of disorder that permeates a system. This seems to be expressed by the slogan '*Deterritorialize the refrain*' (TP 350) that ends the chapter 'Of the Refrain'. At the same time, however, the chapter 'The Smooth and the Striated' ends, more cautiously, with the caveat 'never believe that a smooth space will suffice to save us' (TP 500). Already here, Guattari and Deleuze, it seems, are somewhat ambiguous about the smooth and the striated. Although they stress the complexity and even complementarity of the relations between smoothing and striation, there are few 'champions of striation' in Deleuze Studies, as well as in Guattari Studies, which is what this chapter wants to change.

In *Schizoanalytic Cartographies,* the notions of striation and smoothing are more clearly defined – there are four kinds of smoothing, for instance – and they are less rhetorically loaded than in *A Thousand Plateaus*. More sober. Striation does no longer evoke the 'violent' stratification of consistencies, but rather the degree of their inherent complexity. As Guattari notes, highlighting the *positive* aspect of striation, 'striation reveals itself to be synonymous with processes of *the enrichment of the possible and the virtual*' (SC 98).[1] In analogy, smoothing does no longer pertain only to a liberating, internal de-stratification of consistencies, but rather to changes in the space between consistencies and thus in the relations between them. This general realignment, which relates the terms to different domains, makes the operational theatre of the two terms inherently asymmetric: 'every heterogeneity developed *in an entitarian register* is a striation' (SC 78, emphasis added), while 'every *inter-entitarian transformation* of the neighbourhood between two registers is a smoothing' (SC 78, emphasis added).

This asymmetric distribution was already treated in *A Thousand Plateaus* as the difference between 'intra-assemblage' and 'infra-assemblage'. At that point, however, it didn't have the conceptual power and insistence that it has in *Schizoanalytic Cartographies*, where striation pertains to the amount of the internal complexity of 'consistencies', and thus, in terms of the theory of autopoiesis, to their operational and informational closure, while smoothing pertains to the processes *between* consistencies, and thus a consistency's energetic openness.

My first point, then, is that the degree of freedom is greater the *more* a consistency is striated. In this context, much has been made of Guattari's and Deleuze's machinic ecology in terms of a living consistency's relation to its Umwelt, such as the tick-dog or the wasp-flower machines. What is less seldom noted – perhaps it seems politically incorrect – is that in negotiating its Umwelt, the celebrated 'tick' has less freedom of choice than a whale or a human. As Deleuze notes, 'not having general rules, being held by the instincts to the actual, lacking any stable fancy and reflective procedures, the animal also lacks history' (*Empiricism*, 60). Less individual agency. The tick's 'eigenworld' [*Eigenwelt*] is less complex than that of the dog because it has less parameters of choice and sensibility. Both in terms of relation to the consistency *and* in relation to changes in their respective milieus, it is degrees of complexity that measure degrees of freedom. Less complexity, less freedom. More complexity, more freedom. If this series is projected, infinite complexity, infinite 'freedom'. As Guattari calls it, 'infinite determinability' – which is a term to which I will return.

My first point concerns this new alignment of 'degrees of freedom'. In *Schizoanalytic Cartographies,* deterritorialization and smoothing on the one hand, and reterritorialization and striation on the other, are complementary and asymmetrical operations rather than oppositional, symmetrical ones. They allow for rates of internal complexity – measured in terms of territorialization and striation – to negotiate rates of external, relational change, measured in terms of deterritorialization and smoothing.

Refrain

What about the relation between territorialization and striation? In *Schizoanalytic Cartographies*, this question has to do with the notion of the refrain, which concerns the process of the coming-into-being of singular consistencies by way of the gradual creation of 'virtual territories' – the way sequences are culled from series, or, in other terms, the creation of 'eigenvalues and eigenvectors', which is the mathematical term for the creation of 'habits' within an inherently chaotic, or 'informal' environment. The creation of order not so much *from*, but rather *within* chaos. As Guattari notes, 'under the generic term "refrain", I will group reiterated discursive sequences, *closed on themselves*, having as their function an extrinsic catalysis of existential affects' (SC 207, emphasis added).

In *A Thousand Plateaus*, concrete and bounded machines – consistencies – emerge from within the abstract machine. The difference is that while in *A Thousand Plateaus* the abstract machine is a general, central term – as Deleuze notes in *Foucault*, 'the abstract machine is the informal diagram' (39) – in *Schizoanalytic Cartographies* it holds only one of four positions. What remains similar, however, is that abstract machines operate in-between processes of ordering and disordering. In these dynamics, the decisive question is always whether a 'specific' abstract machine remains in touch with, or 'an attribute of' the overall plane of immanence as a plane of virtual potentiality, or whether it closes itself off from this potentiality. This choice is made possible because the overall abstract machine is, in *A Thousand Plateaus*, often used as 'another term' for the plane of immanence and thus, like that plane, is both generative and disruptive. 'The abstract machine exists enveloped in each stratum, whose Ecumenon or unity of composition it defines, and developed on the plane of consistency, whose destratification it performs (the Planomenon)' (TP 73). It is both Ecumenon and Planomenon, both home and plane. In the 'Nomad Romanticism' that permeates Deleuze Studies, the Planomenon has often been read as the new 'homeless home'. Again, however, it is not that simple. As Deleuze and Guattari note about architecture in *What is Philosophy?*, the plane is simultaneously 'House and Universe, *Heimlich* and *Unheimlich*, territory and deterritorialization' (186).

What is true, however, is that in architectural terms, the wrecking ball is always more 'powerful' than the architecture:

> Sometimes the abstract machine … forces flows into significances and subjectifications, into knots of aborescence and holes of abolition; sometimes … it frees something like *probe-heads* (guidance devices) that dismantle the strata in their wake, break through the walls of signifiance … fell trees in favor of veritable rhizomes, and steer the flows down lines of positive deterritorializaton or creative flight. (TP 190)

Like the informal diagram, the abstract machine defines the 'living diversity and multiplicity' to which every concrete machine is immanent. In fact, as Guattari notes in *The Machinic Unconscious*, 'the most complex combinations are capable of emerging at the level which is believed to be that of "brute matters" or "primary matters"' (158), the challenge being to 'preserv[e] the multiplicity and heterogeneity of all possible entries, all catastrophies, and all emergences of new points of metabolic crystallization' (151).

How do abstract machines create and destroy site- and time-specific 'plane[s] *of consistency*' (11) in *A Thousand Plateaus*? As 'the cutting edges of decoding and deterritorialization' (TP 510), they 'make the territorial assemblage open onto something else, assemblages of another type, the molecular, *the cosmic*; they constitute becomings. Thus they are always singular and immanent' (TP 510, emphasis added). As the 'informal diagram', they define an assembly's 'potential for potentiality'.

One of the more crucial differences between *A Thousand Plateaus* and *Schizoanalytic Cartographies* lies in that in the former, the abstract machine *as* the informal diagram designates the overall, infinitely complex movements of the world's territorializing and deterritorializing operations. Epistemologically, it replaces generalizations such as genus and species, genetically, it 'constructs a singular real': 'the abstract machine is like the cause of the concrete assemblages that execute its relations; and these relations between forces take place "not above" but within the very tissue of the assemblages they produce' (32). In *Schizoanalytic Cartographies*, however, the abstract machine is 'reduced' to being one functor of four. More precisely, it is the 'actual, given rhizome' within which consistencies emerge through operations of 'territorializations', which brings me from Phyla to Territories.

Unlike in Borges's famous tale, in *Schizoanalytic Cartographies*, the territory is not the actual ground onto which a map is projected. Rather, the territory is a virtual, 'more and more formal' diagram that is laid onto a ground – also called, in *A Thousand Plateaus* 'The Earth' – by a concrete consistency, which consists, in fact, and thus literally *is*, nothing but those very operations of territorialization. According to Guattari's diagrammatics, therefore, 'the map *is* the territory'. There are as many territories as there are consistencies within a milieu. At the same time, there are as many consistencies as there are territories.

Fractalization and integration

Although the four domains of the fourfold are ultimately structural rather than chronological, let me treat them, as Guattari himself does, 'in sequence'. From Flows to Universes. To be able to come into existence, territories rely on expressive and diagrammatic movements between Flows and Phyla. By way of an 'irresistible' (145) expressive fractalization – a term Guattari takes from the scientific field of non-linear dynamics – and thus 'heterogeneification' (SC 87), the continuous volume of Flows is broken up into a discontinuous Phylum or Rhizome. It literally explodes from a fluid into a fractal space, like a wave explodes into spray when it hits a rock. In perceptual registers, this fractal explosion creates the field of 'universal variation, total, objective and diffuse perception' (*Cinema 1* 64).

Within the fourfold, this explosion creates a complex rhizome or 'abstract machine'. What Guattari quite beautifully calls the 'irresistible force' of expression brings about 'a deterritorialized and fractal smoothing of the set of *striations of Flows*' (SC 138). This term might raise some eyebrows in Deleuze Studies, because in terms of 'romantic readings' of Deleuze and Guattari, a term such as 'striated flows' does not really make sense, because flows are invariably seen as smooth, while solids are invariably seen as striated. Already *A Thousand Plateaus*, however, contradicts such readings. When Guattari and Deleuze note that 'homogeneous space is in no way a smooth space; on the contrary, it is the form of striated space' (370), this striated space does *not* denote a state of order, such as state order, but an 'originary' state of flow. The conceptual background to this notion is given by the fact that at this point of their argument, the homogeneous space Deleuze and Guattari have in mind is Lucretius's image of a laminar space 'striated by the fall of bodies, the verticals of gravity, the distribution of matter into parallel layers, the lamellar and laminar movement of flows' (370). In opposition to this striated flow, 'smooth space is … the space of the smallest deviation' (371); the space of the 'clinamen'.[2] In terms of *Schizoanalytic Cartographies*, this space is that of 'atomic fractalization'; the fractalization of the 'rain' of atoms that demarcates the birth of the world.

Again, the reason for the many celebrations of the fluid in readings of Deleuze and Guattari is that the relation between the two terms is considered to be symmetrical rather than asymmetrical. Conceptualized without the 'ethical baggage' with which the differentiation between fluid and solid is often encrusted, what are flows? Except for the flow of Lucretius's atomic rain, which is in actual fact not complex at all, flows are extremely complex organizations. What defines them is not so much that they are inherently smooth – in fact, they are prime examples of orientation, eigenvectorization and thus of systematicity as such – but that their striation is curiously indistinct and curiously continuous. What *Schizoanalytic Cartographies* stresses, in fact, is that Flows, which tend to have a positive value in *A Thousand Plateaus* as sites of deterritorialization, are 'in actual fact' highly striated. It is fractalization that breaks up the given volume of continuous flows, creating from it a space that is inherently differential and differentiated. In a genetic register, this moment of fractalization echoes Lucretius's moment of the *clinamen*, which causes the fractalization of the redundant rain of atoms: 'Everything plays out around the springing up of the rupture ..., the point of emergence of expressive fractalization, from which the conversion of certain *material Flows* into *signaletic Flows* will make itself felt' (SC 133, emphasis added). In fractalization, codes are born.

How? The fractalized, differential space of Phyla – a.k.a. the abstract machine – forms the reservoir of differences that allows consistent entities, which in fact come into being *through* and *within* that process of fractalization, to measure and digitalize the world through operations that happen by way of codes as systems of distinctions. Guattari considers the first moment when 'the given', as something for-itself, opens itself up to a giving-in-construction as the 'expressive' moment. Flows become 'signaletic Flows' – and thus 'expressive' – when they 'open themselves up' to a field of differentiation in the shift from continuous flow to differential fractal. In other words, when they become Phyla.

Guattari borrows the terms he uses to conceptualize the passages from Flows to Phyla and, in parallel, from Territories to Universes from Leibniz: 'integration' and 'monad'. The domain of Phyla 'represents the i*ntegral* of possibilities adjacent to F[lows]' (SC 134, emphasis added), 'sensible ex-modules' (SC 182) in Territories 'find themselves *monadized*' (SC 182, emphasis added). In fact, if one were to attempt a visualization of what happens in the process of fractalization, the image would show every drop of liquid within a Flow as a singular consistency *in*, but 'separated from' that Flow. This separation allows it to move in relation to other such singular drops in a complex network in which it has a position in relation to each and all of the other drops. In other words, it is no longer communal but singular. This shift seems to go against another romantic reading of Deleuze and Guattari, which puts the communal ethically before the individual. At this point, however, Guattari is not so much concerned with the individual as with the singular. In this context, fractalization can also be described as a dynamics that frees the singular drop from its 'capture' by the wave. For Guattari, 'expressive fractalization' brings about the creation of the singular from the communal flow, and as such, it brings about the 'possibilities' of an overall machinism and assemblage theory. As Guattari notes, 'Machines of Expression somehow have the function of making the possible ooze out of all the encysted modular forms that harbour it' (SC 138, emphasis added). The striated wave is fractalized into a smooth spray that does no longer have a centre of striation or orientation; a gaseous milieu into which the organization of the flow is 'pulverized'. In this context, Guattari once more takes up the Lucretian image, noting that

> it is this processual option, this refusal of a generalized economy of equivalences, this choice of a 'clinamen' that singularizes repetition, which makes us refuse maps that are fixed and invariant, as of right, in the domain of subjectivity (SC 24).

In mathematical terms, the logic of fractalization is 'analogous' to the logic of differentiation and integration. Deleuze had already used this terminology in describing how part of the informal diagram is integrated into formal assemblages. Its 'realization [better: actualization] is … an integration, a collection of progressive integrations that are initially local and then become or tend to become global' (SC 32).

In semiotic terms, this inherently constructivist expressive fractalization 'produces an added value, it *secretes* a surplus value of code' (SC 134, emphasis added). As a process that opens the world up to 'its' consistencies, 'expressive fractalization' (SC 134) starts 'the double game of being-for-itself … and of being-for-something-else' (SC 134). Through codings, the world 'itself' and *for* itself becomes the world *for* something else that is, at the same time, *of* it and that 'trails the world behind'. As Deleuze had noted in *Difference and Repetition*, 'Instead of something distinguished from something else, imagine something which distinguishes itself – and yet that from which it distinguishes itself does not distinguish itself from it' (28). Deleuze had illustrated this 'unilateral distinction' (28) by way of the phenomenon of a lightning bolt that 'distinguishes itself from the black sky but must also trail it behind, as though it were distinguishing itself from that which does not distinguish itself from it' (28).

This 'something else' are the 'sensible surfaces' of 'germinal' or 'larval' consistencies – mineral, vegetable, animal, human – such as the rock, the plant or the tick. From the 'given' of a fractalized world, the territorialization *of* and *into* these consistencies is

> like the reverse side of the expressive function and I will characterize it as a *diagrammatic function* … This intermediary diagram in some way folds up all the potentialities that expressive fractalization had unfolded except that as a supplement it brings a surplus value of possibility … to the sensible surface. (SC 145, emphasis added)

It is by way of this diagrammatic function that the 'infinite determinability' that was opened up by the irresistible fractalization is folded back, by way of the creation of specific territories, into finite determinabilities. Literally 'anything' can be formed from the spray. This infinite determinability, however, is reduced to a 'finite determinability' in the process of actualization, which changes a logic of 'potentialities' into one of 'possibilities'. 'The status of f(diag) is always precarious, aleatory, problematic, confined, contingenced by the *margin of manoeuvre* that existential refrains allow it [*autorisé*]' (SC 145, emphasis added). In this context, it is important that in Guattari's fourfold, the genetic relation between Flows and Territories goes 'by way of' Phyla. From actual fractalization and diagrammatization, over to immaterial territorialization. Forces of deterritorialization in Phyla and Universes, forces of territorialization in Flows and Territories.

As a recurring pattern (what is called 'rhythm' in *A Thousand Plateaus*), the refrain is the home (what is called 'nomos' in *A Thousand Plateaus*) to which a melody (what is called 'lied' in *A Thousand Plateaus*) persistently returns. It is a characteristic of Guattari's notion of 'meta-modeling' that such refrains can be found in different regimes and on different plateaus: 'Refrains can take rhythmic or plastic form, be prosodic segments, faciality traits, emblems of recognition, leitmotifs, signatures, proper names or their invocational equivalents' (SC 207). As Guattari notes, 'equally they can be established transversally between different substances. … They can be of a sensible order … or a problematic order … just as much as of the order of faciality' (SC 207).

The diagrammatic folding implies a 'contraction' of heterogeneous, singular elements and, what is in actual fact the same, their 'orientation' around what might be conceptualized as a centre, an attractor or a structural nucleus. These foldings create the 'reduced' and 'slowed-down' mode of life of the concrete and 'concreted' sensible entities *in* which the world expresses itself. Once more, the folding is positive. In fact, the joyous acceptance of what were formerly negative terms shows Guattari's truly positive attitude towards the world. How could one not love complex assemblages and consistencies if the world consists of assemblages and consistencies?

In fact, the code-for-itself, in becoming a code-for-something, brings about 'a *striation*, a heterogeneization (or hetero-genesis) of *the sensible world*' (SC 78, emphases added). Guattari calls such 'substantial' (SC 82) entities that denote the realm of 'sensible territorialization' (SC 78) 'modules', as opposed to 'monads', which concern Universes. Modules are related to 'the domain of sensible and signaletic Flows' (SC 171). Their position is that of 'territorialized proto-enunciation' (SC 118). My second point: Refrains function as 'orientations' around which 'more and more striated consistencies' develop.

At the end of this 'toing and froing and after an *enrichment* of their potentialities, the old modular sensible Territories Ts find themselves converted into a new species of existential Territory Te' (SC 143, emphasis added). This is the shift from modules to monads, or: By way of feedback loops, or habits, 'sensible surfaces' at some point – 'at an indeterminate moment and an indeterminate time', one is tempted to say – cross the threshold from 'sensible territories' to 'existential universes' (SC 98). From a world of affect to a world of thought.

As a fully deterritorialized field, the field of Universes is, in analogy to that of Phyla, not only the carrier medium of concepts. More fundamentally, it also de-consistences every concept, and smoothes every thought that emerges in it. It is as such that it is the field of the infinite potentiality of change:

> this smoothing by the incorporeal enunciators U finds its diagrammatic grasp, its root of singularization (the fact that it is not a matter of Platonic Universals cut off from every sensible hook) in the *points of contingencing*, Pc, where the expressive foldings originate and where the diagrammatic foldings-up are snagged. (SC 157, emphasis added)

Within the fourfold, the functor of Universes – which, unlike Plato's Universals, remains tied to the territories of affect – allows for a recuperation of the 'infinite determinability' of the plane of immanence *within the register of a 'concrete, singular virtual'*. Although Universes are invariably tied to the other functors, taken 'for themselves' they show the freedom of the virtual.

Topologically, existential Universes are, like fractal space, infinite. As embodied in consistencies, however, they are infinite *and* bounded. If Rhizomes are actual fractals, Universes are virtual fractals, and as such, they should be understood from within the logic of an assemblage theory. If it is quite unproblematic to visualize, in relation to Phyla, actual objects as assemblages of tiny, interrelated material particles, in order to imagine the logic of Universes, one must entertain a more counter-intuitive image; a thought, broken down into an extremely complicated assemblage of tiny elementary thoughts? One would have to imagine a 'field theory of thought' in which each 'thought' is made up of an infinity of unthinkably small, unconscious thoughts that form aggregates or assemblages that look and feel, from a macroscopic position, like one conscious, solid thought that disperses, from a microscopic position, into tiny movements and complex choreographies. As Guattari stresses, a thought is itself multiplicitous and 'a' thought is 'in actual fact' a complex ensemble of 'pure, elementary thoughts'. These alliances of pure, elementary thoughts form a plane of mental consistency: 'a thought with "*n*" dimensions where everything starts to think at the same time, individuals as well as groups, the "chemical" as well as the "chromosomal" or the biosphere' (*Machinic Unconscious*, 126). Universes, then, consist of a multiplicitous field of pure 'atoms of thought' from which 'consistent thoughts' are composed. As such, Universes share with the informal diagram the function of being genetic machines. Also, they are, like the informal diagram, machines of psychic deterritorialization, in that each change in the landscape of thought functions as a smoothing that changes all of the relations within that landscape.

Synapses

As I noted, the field of thought described by Universes is invariably related to the other functors in the fourfold. In relation to Territories, for instance, they cause 'deterritorialized releases of enunciation and, as such, constitute the incorporeal integrals of sensible refrains' (189), while their relation to Phyla concerns their embodiment. In the fourfold, the convergence of physical and psychic assemblage – of Phyla and Universes – is marked by the 'synaptic moment'. As both 'material objects' *and* 'figures of thought', synapses are the figures of the complementarity of actual brain (material assemblages of 'physical atoms') and virtual mind (immaterial assemblages of 'atoms of thought'). In this complementarity, Universes describe the synaptic landscape from the aspect of intensity, while Phyla describe it from the aspect of extensity: 'electric thought'.

Although they are captured or enfolded in actual architectures of signification, synapses remain fundamentally a-signifying and deterritorializing: 'the synapse … initiates … self-enunciative procedure[s] through its character as a caesura, as a-signifying catalysis' (SC 189). Like rhizomes in *A Thousand Plateaus,* in fact, they are 'operators of "active forgetting", of existentializing eternal return' (SC 178). As Guattari stresses,

> a-signifying synapses, which are simultaneously irreversibilizing, singularizing, heterogenesizing and necessitating, push us from the world of memories of redundancies embedded in extrinsic coordinates, into Universes of pure intensive iteration, which have no discursive memory since their very existence acts as such. (SC 178)

Synapses, then, 'have the double function of delimiting fields of the possible whilst reinforcing their virtual scope' (SC 165).

Guattari relates the moment of 'chaosmic conjunction' of the actual and the virtual not only to the logical range of determinability – finite and infinite – but also to the parameter of speed.

> Existential synapses work as operators for the crossing over of Chronic and Aïonic temporal drives functioning in contrary directions … . They also constitute a bridge, generating components of passage between the molar registers of discursive sets and molecular registers of non-discursive intensity. (SC 177–8)

The spectrum is thus between 'null consistency of infinite speed [+∞] (ϕ. and U)' (107), and 'high consistency of null speed [−∞] (F. and T.)' (107). The infinite speed of deterritorialization in Phyla and Universes, the finite speed of territorialization in Flows and Territories.[3]

These extremes are crystallized at the synaptic moment of the meeting of Phyla and Universes, which is defined by a paradoxical 'coexistence of infinitely fast and infinitely slow speeds' (SC 140). It is a moment that is 'at the same time both infinitely rapid and infinitely slow … d±∞' (SC 152), both stable and chaotic, both continuous and discrete.[4] Universes are defined, then, by the 'irreducible ambivalence d±∞' (SC 172).

Again, what is at issue is the construction of 'ordinary consistencies and temporalities from infinitely slow speeds of separability and infinitely rapid speeds of continuity' (SC 129). In 'slow consistencies', the chaotic speed of infinite determinability is decelerated into the chaosmic speed of finite determinability.

> The whole question consequently becomes one of making the speeds of infinite redundancy of the first hold together with the absolute decelerations of the second, whilst rendering possible discontinuous intensive striations at

> the crossover between the two entitarian dimensions. Once again, one comes back to the paradox of the continuous that envelops the discontinuous and the intensive, the discursive. (SC 112)

Rather than being inherently 'bad' or 'tragic', therefore, which it tends to be read as in a Deleuze and Guattarian romanticism, this deceleration is the prerequisite for the creation of chaosmotic consistency, and thus for the development of the 'durational time' of the virtual Aion, as a complement to actual Chronos. As Guattari and Deleuze had noted in *A Thousand Plateaus*, the refrain, as 'a crystal of space-time' (TP 348) in actual fact 'fabricates time' (TP 349) in the sense of providing a consistent 'field of gathering' of 'memorial' traits of earlier states of existence.

At the synaptic moment, the complementary fields of the given and the giving are fully installed. What still needs to be done, however, is to relate the fourfold to the plane of immanence. One way to do this is through a reference to the formal distinction between the field of quantity, which belongs to the given, and the field of quality, which belongs to the giving. These are once more simultaneously operating but formally distinct parameters. The question is thus not whether the purely quantitative exists 'in itself' – in fact, as 'the given' it is the prerequisite of the qualitative – but how it can be accessed from within the qualitative.

In the fourfold, the quantitative and the qualitative cannot be categorically distinguished because the two registers are 'scanned' cross-wise. While the actual–virtual axis goes from right to left, the axis of rates of integration goes from bottom to top. Flows are actual and analogue, Phyla are actual and digital, Territories are virtual and analogue, Universes are virtual and digital. Within this shifting field, 'Flows of energy are intimately mixed with signaletic Flows is an everyday experience' (SC 89). This dispersed perspective, which defines specific instances within the fourfold's overall dynamics, is what makes the diagram a 'meta-model' or, in other terms, a phase-space defined by processes rather than fixed 'states'. As Guattari notes about this processualization in relation to continuity and discontinuity, 'we will no longer have to consider that the continuous and the discontinuous are passively given, but that they participate in processes of continuation-discontinuation' (SC 156).

Degrees of freedom

As Guattari noted, 'there is the Given, thus there is the Giving' (SC 58). There is the left side of the diagram, thus there is the right side. Freedom, as the result of the differential and complementary function of striation and smoothing (f (s/s)), is never anarchy. At the same time, however, constrained freedom is *based* on anarchy, which defines the plane of immanence, as the most interior outside of Guattari's diagram, and thus constrained freedom 'trails anarchy behind'. True anarchy defines the plane of immanence as the fourfold's 'other side', or as its other *aspect* in the sense that the fourfold is 'the plane of consistencies'. As fully chaotic, the plane of immanence is 'the primary matter of virtuality, the inexhaustible reserve of an *infinite determinability*' (SC 103, emphasis added). It is in an '"originary" state of "Brownian" dispersion … a place in which nothing referred to anything so as to refer to everything, at such a speed that nothing remains of these references. One might say that the memory … of the arrangements of the soup of chaos equals zero' (SC 119). The only characteristic, in fact, is that it has no characteristics. It is without consistency and consistencies, and thus it is without forms. The only and basic principle that defines the plane of immanence is that of constant, infinitely fast change and determinability. It produces, at each moment, infinite and pure change, and as such guarantees an infinite potential for change. It continuously charges the milieu of the planes of consistency and the planes of composition with the potential for change. As such, the principle, or ground of the world is a force of infinite change as a source of infinite potentiality.

> It is worth retaining a certain mistrust of overly static representations of chaos, especially those which would try to illustrate it in the form of a mixture, of holes, caverns, dust, even of fractal objects. What is particular about the chaos of the 'primordial soup' of the Plane of immanence is that it can only exist in and as the process of 'chaotizing' and in such a way that it is impossible to circumscribe a stable configuration in it and to maintain its consistency. Each of the configurations that it can outline has the gift of dissolving, at an infinite, if not absolute, speed. In its essence, chaos is rigourously ungraspable. (SC 103)

The dynamics of the plane of immanence consist of 'chaotic multiplicities composing and decomposing complex arrangements at infinite speeds' (SC 108). As a mathematical phase-space, in the state of chaos every 'state' is equally probable or improbable. It is 'essentially glischroidic, without limit, without contour, without any possible internal displacement or division into subsets' (SC 105).

This turbulent state of white noise, which equals infinite complexity, continuously charges the 'pink'[5] milieu of the plane of consistency with the potential for change. In fact, the plane of consistency, which is the 'other aspect' of the plane of immanence, is already 'within' the plane of immanence, which is why Guattari adds that already the plane of immanence also contains 'existential filters selecting relatively homogeneous sets of arrangements characterized by the iteration of local and localizing decelerations' (109). Drawing on the terminology of dispersion, Guattari describes the mode of presence of the plane of immanence 'in' the plane of composition as that of the presence of the 'powdery diversity' (SC 111) of the 'aerosol of immanence' – a word made up of *aer* (air) und *solutio* (solution) that describes a heterogeneous dispersion of solid or fluid particles in a gas, such as particles of pigment in a spray-can or drops of water in the atmosphere – that runs, at all times, 'through' the plane of consistency and its constructions. Guattari's fourfold, then, charts the plane of consistency as the constructivist 'aspect' of the plane of immanence which 'like an aerosol, ... stays in a state of suspension at the heart of the "chaosmic" Plane of Consistency' (SC, 155).[6] As a fully dispersed field, Guattari and Deleuze consider the plane of immanence as

> a void that is not a nothingness but a *virtual*, containing all possible particles and drawing out all possible forms, which spring up only to disappear immediately, without consistency or reference, without consequence. Chaos is an infinite speed of birth and disappearance. Now philosophy wants to know how to retain infinite speeds while gaining consistency, by *giving the virtual a consistency specific to it.* (WP 118)

Plane of immanence: white noise. Plane of consistency: pink noise. Whether the plane of consistency is seen as the plane of immanence's *other* (formal distinction) or as its attribute (ontological identity), it is *never* and *nowhere* anarchic, or *always* and *everywhere* anarchic. As the two planes are complementary, however, it is *never* and *always*, as well as *nowhere* and *everywhere* anarchic.

As the plane of 'consistencies', however, the plane of consistency is always defined by degrees. There are always only degrees of freedom. Symptomatically, there are no 'degrees of anarchy'. There is no freedom in anarchy. The question is never about complete freedom, but about creating milieus that allow for degrees of freedom: 'How do we produce [the subject], capture it, enrich it, and permanently reinvent it in a way that renders it compatible with Universes of mutant value? How do we work for its liberation, that is, for its resingularization?' (*Chaosmosis*, 135). How to produce new 'modes of existence'?

What 'refrains of freedom' means to me then, is that for a 'refrained consistency' – and we have to understand the tautology of that term – the highest degree of freedom can only be 'purely virtual' and 'Universal'. There is no infinite freedom – a freedom without degrees – except on the plane of immanence *as* the plane of indifference, which means 'without degrees'. As indifferent to freedom, the plane of immanence does not *know* freedom. In fact, it knows nothing. It *is*, however, everything.

Notes

1 Processes of striation and smoothing are not to be confused with processes of molarization and molecularization, which pertain to rates of flexibility and elasticity *within* striated entities, such as the strength of bonding between its elements.

2 See in this context Deleuze's analysis of the clinamen in 'Lucretius and the Simulacrum', as well as Michel Serres's analysis of the clinamen, especially his differentiation between turbulence and vortex, in *The Birth of Physics*.

3 The 'infinite speed of transformation [+∞]' (SC 105) transgresses even 'the sacrosanct principle of contemporary physics based on the speed of light, which consists in fixing a threshold limiting the size of the ensemble of possible speeds' (SC 1505). 'Like' the speed of the plane of immanence as a chaotic multiplicity, it is 'synonymous with the absolute lability of iteration and, as a consequence, with *zero consistency*' (SC 106, emphasis added). The other vector is defined by the finite speeds of 'slow consistencies', 'the deceleration of existential 'grasping' (or self-referential agglutination). … these 'decelerated' speeds are synonymous with an intensification of consistency. When they fall to a quasi-null speed [−∞], the sequences of opening back up can become of a quasi-infinite length' (SC 106).

4 As Guattari notes, 'd+∞ = continuity' (SC 213), 'd−∞ = discontinuity' (SC 213).

5 For the distinction between 'white noise' and 'pink noise', see: Berressem, 'Vibes: Tape-Recording the Acoustic Unconscious'.

6 See also Deleuze in *Cinema 1*: 'In the final analysis, we would have to speak of a perception which was no longer liquid but gaseous. For, if we start from a solid state, where molecules are not free to move about (molar or human perception), we move next to a liquid state, where the molecules move about and merge into one another, but we finally reach a gaseous state, defined by the free movement of each molecule' (84).

Bibliography

Berressem, Hanjo. (2015), 'Vibes: Tape-Recording the Acoustic Unconscious', in Julius Greve and Sascha Pöhlmann (eds), *America and the Musical Unconscious*, 140–86, Atropos and New York.

Deleuze, Gilles. (1990), 'Lucretius and the Clinamen', in *The Logic of Sense*. Translated by M. Lester and C. Stivale. New York: Columbia University Press.

Deleuze, Gilles. (1986), *Cinema I. The Movement-Image*. Translated by H. Tomlinson and B. Habberjam. Minneapolis: University of Minnesota Press.

Deleuze, Gilles. (1991), *Empiricism and Subjectivity: An Essay on Hume's Theory of Human Nature*. Trans. Constantin Boundas. New York: Columbia University Press.

Deleuze, Gilles. (1994), *Difference and Repetition*. Translated by P. Patton. New York: Columbia University Press.

Deleuze, Gilles. (2006), *Foucault*. Translated by Séan Hand. London: Continuum.

Deleuze, Gilles and Guattari, Félix. (1990), 'Lucretius and the Simulacrum,' in *The Logic of Sense*. Translated by Mark Lester with Charles Stivale, 266–79, New York: Columbia University Press.

Deleuze, Gilles and Guattari, Félix. (1994), *What is Philosophy?* Translated by H. Tomlinson and G. Burchell. New York: Columbia University Press.

Deleuze, Gilles and Guattari, Félix. (2005), *A Thousand Plateaus: Capitalism and Schizophrenia 2*. Translated by B. Massumi. Minneapolis: University of Minnesota Press.

Guattari, Félix (1995), *Chaosmosis: An Ethico-Aesthetic Paradigm*. Bloomington and Indianapolis: Indiana University Press.

Guattari, Félix (2011), *The Machinic Unconscious: Essays in Schizoanalysis*. Translated by Taylor Adkins. Los Angeles: Semiotext(e).

Guattari, Félix. (2013), *Schizoanalytic Cartographies*. Translated by Andrew Goffey. London: Bloomsbury [*Cartographies Schizoanalytiques* © Éditions Galilée, 1989].

Serres, Michel. (2000), *The Birth of Physics*. Edited by David Webb. Translated by Jack Hawkes. Manchester: Clinamen Press.

8

The Desiring Machines Do Not Die: Impersonal Death and Feeling of Eternity

Oleg Lebedev

This chapter aims at taking hold of one of the most formidable phrases that punctuate Deleuze's works and which, like an aphorism, demands to be pondered and dwelt on, and requires from us an endless power of meditation. Appearing on page 395 of *Anti-Oedipus*, the phrase says: '*les machines désirantes ne meurent pas*' – 'desiring machines do not die'.[1]

This condensed and laconic utterance would appear mystical and poetic if it did not result from great conceptual work preventing one from presenting it in an immediate and direct way.[2] Thus, what we ought to be interested in is the manner in which, in light of the various meanings taking hold of it, it is possible to slowly unfold the perspective such a thesis holds and to grasp its significance. Fundamentally, this is not a question of quantity, that is, the number of occurrences of the topic of death within Deleuzian work or the number of influences, but one of quality: you can sometimes read only a single paragraph by an author and understand everything, as if you had read all of his works. Are we capable of such a miraculous reading? In this respect, Deleuze's method has always been the following: we need to dwell on authors (or to chew, as Nietzsche would have it) and seek what suits us in their works. Therefore, what we need to take on here is more a sort of pondering on formulae, even if we do not go all the way. Thus, instead of presenting an exhaustive study of the theme of death in Deleuze's work, this will rather be an outline of the Blanchotian and Spinozist touches of said formula, as well as the development of its presupposition from the viewpoint of the theory of the unconscious. This approach in fact is dictated to us by Deleuze's practice for commenting on philosophical texts: proceed by trial and error, being sensitive to the frequency of words, to the sounds these make once you give light hammer strokes on them.[3]

Nevertheless, a preliminary observation immediately imposes itself. Proposing to analyse the Deleuzian conception of death takes us to a series of slippery slopes and to a perilous path. We will quickly get lost either in considerations on the philosopher's personal death – the ultimate nonsense – or in the meditation on the meaning of human existence or even in the idea that to think and reflect upon death has been one of human thinking's core concerns since time immemorial. This is one way to explain things but not the most interesting one. Furthermore, all those trails are deceptive in my opinion: coming back to this image of frequency, the sounds they produce precisely are those made by the *priests*, in the sense Nietzsche gave to that word, as they carry a whole theological train made up of the inadequacy of being, guilt or meaning.[4]

Thus, these considerations are questionable, from an ideological viewpoint, inasmuch as their unavowed goal is to reintroduce the forces of negativity, be it through the psychoanalysts' 'ridiculous death drive',[5] through a religious mentality or even through an obscure premonition of the absurdity of human life. This is the reason why the very notion of death is so conniving with the praise of the order [*ode à la loi*] as a thirst for transcendence, and does easily give rise to becoming the object of a sermon or of an ambiguous humour of a satire. Everywhere do sad affects of a mortified and diminished existence triumph, having already gone through all compromises, which is perfectly in keeping with the desire of those wanting our domination. Therefore, an implicit idea crosses all these approaches of the topic of death: 'hatred against life, against anything free, passing and flowing … depression, guilt used as means of contagion, the kiss of a vampire'.[6]

The first problem emerging consists in questioning the possibility to dissociate the song of death from any kind of statement implying that human nature is miserable. Couldn't we drop those scenarios that fulfil a conservative function by attempting to give a strictly technical answer? More precisely, let us remember that the idea of a body without organs maintains an ambiguous attraction/repulsion relationship with working pieces formed by partial objects and is the starting point of the theory of the unconscious. Two principles, which are only contradictory in appearance, then seem to be ruling over the main philosophical intuition present in *Anti-Oedipus*: (1) the condition of the machinic unconscious is the *desiring death*, the body without organs as a motionless motor forcing us to leave organs behind; (2) but the functioning of that very unconsciousness is the *desiring life*, the re-appropriation of miraculated organs by that very body without organs. The former opposes desire's consumed inner stasis to its arrangement and elaborations. On the contrary, the second principle turns those machines into primal elements organizing themselves by aggregation or layout and whose value emerges from the combinations they allow themselves. The desiring machine's cycle's sound health is that passage, that very conversion of one principle into another, that circulation between condition and functioning, where movements go both ways: sometimes the rise of the catatonic state in which intensity is at its zero level towards the testing of intense becomings and feelings, sometimes the decrease from all intensity towards the death it embraces and which generates it.

For Deleuze and Guattari, the first logical moment in that exchange indeed seems to be the motionless motor, the death drive, the moment of utter dissipation, of non-being or annihilation. 'Antonin Artaud a découvert le corps sans organes, là où il était, sans forme et sans figure. Instinct de mort, tel est son nom, et la mort n'est pas sans modèle. Car le désir désire aussi cela, la mort, parce que le corps plein de la mort est son moteur immobile'.[7] Yet, here too we must carefully keep from detecting any song praising negativity: desiring death, embraced death, death as a primal condition are the many expressions that must be understood in the sense towards which all of Deleuze's philosophy tends, that is, the release of the powers of life. The fact that, as if their own discovery frightened them, the authors immediately added a few lines a bit further down, stating that 'the body without organs is no witness of the original void'[8] comes as no surprise. So, we can see that Deleuze and Guattari set out the problem of death in very simple terms: you cannot have movement – *kinesis* – as a basic principle without integrating stopping or resting forces, those precisely conceptualized in *Anti-Oedipus* in terms of body without organs. Movement and rest, body without organs and partial objects: this is a dissonant agreement between the machine's various pieces, different and coexisting, different in their very coexistence and inseparability. Nothing but this logic, this physics of relationships, this materialistic psychiatry turning desire into pulsating movements and rest, conjunctions and disjunctions, is suitable for seizing the strengths, the very laws and passions of the unconscious.

Since *A Thousand Plateaus* replays the same circulation, this beat between the degree zero on the one hand, the ultimate limit a body without organs actually is, and intensities on the other, and it might be more appropriate and more definite with regard to the danger of desire to repress itself. In a consciously and knowingly paradoxical manner, Deleuze and Guattari state that the body without organs is both terror and ecstasy, non-desire and desire, that we have one anyway but that we never stop accessing it. Everything is decided upon it. It is not 'mine' or 'yours'; rather, we are on it. In the final analysis, the zero intensity is what remains once everything has been removed; in other words, once we reach the point where all strata, namely meanings, subjectivations and organizations, no longer remain. From now on, the body without organs is introduced as pure intensive matter, the unmoved mover whose organs-machines form the working elements with their own power.[9] But we could further say that what still was too ambiguous in *Anti-Oedipus*, in which the body without organs was a condition and this condition for the unconscious to function precisely was that of a desiring death, slightly strengthens. Interpreting that type of statement the fascist way is easy, like the 'stupid and revolting' shout: long live death! So the desert grows, machines come to a standstill and fall silent, shut themselves away on to the body without organs turned into an ally against the nature of the death drive; a bare repression corresponding to the very moment when the positivity of the schizophrenic process is interrupted and eventually produces schizophrenics as clinic entities indeed. This is why in *A Thousand Plateaus* terminology gets more and more precise and doubles up as an explicit insistence on the risk to shape up into a fascist and cancerous body without organs, namely on the danger for a line of flight to turn into a death line, to be dragged to a black hole, to let yourself die or to wish to cause to die during the experiment[10] – as such often is the case with drug-users' experiences. So much caution is necessary to avoid the body without organs turning into this gland situated within ourselves and producing fascist and deadly secretions. To such extent, we can observe this phenomenon of capturing or immanent and absorbed mortification of the unconscious really being the core concern not only of schizoanalysis but also of any political philosophy.[11] In that sense, the withdrawal operated by the nucleic Oedipus complex no longer weighs much as opposed to that terror specific to the unconscious.

Despite that peril to the latter, fully spelt out, Deleuze and Guattari are definite indeed upon the fact that, by nature, 'the body without organs is not a dead body but a living one all the more swarming as it blew organism and its organisation'.[12] This is the meaning in which it can be perceived as an egg; its function is to convey, produce and distribute intensities in such a way that the return to repulsion always generates new attractions. This is where what is essential lies and such is the first meaning of the death drive: not at all the compulsion to disintegrate or return to the motionless state of matter but catatonia as a revival or relief, the ultimate and unliveable tip [*pointe*] of life. In such conditions, we can understand better that the authors could denounce death as being a drive without any contradiction whatsoever: '*Nous n'invoquons aucune pulsion de mort. Il n'y a pas de pulsion interne dans le désir, il n'y a que des agencements. Le désir est toujours agencé, et il est ce que l'agencement le détermine à être.*'[13] Here, Deleuze and Guattari create a new concept, that is, they philosophize indeed by impregnating the 'death drive' notion, so common in psychoanalysis, with a new meaning so that psychoanalysis ceases to be an avatar of renascent spiritualism or a new form of a 'fair' idea which would merely satisfy itself with performing in a subtler and slier way what the State, morals or the church have kept doing since the beginning anyway.

Moreover, we should notice that all those analyses are inseparable from the Deleuzian notion of subjectivity. 'Desiring machines do not die': only empiricists who have never quite understood what the 'ego' means can venture into such utterances. Indeed, it is obvious in some respects that I will die one day. So what is that thing which insists on and resists dying? Which subsists 'eternal', even if we have to specify the difference between eternity and immortality again a bit further down? The notion of impersonality must provide us with some key to its interpretation.

What distinguishes schizophrenization of death from genuine schizophrenia is that the dissolution of personality occurs *beforehand* and implies no break from the world – this is an 'English style' break, as Deleuze likes to say, in order to accurately distinguish it from French and German philosophers in some sort of geography of thinking, the former having focused on the cogito and the latter on the transcendental ego. What matters is that the experience of death as a widened experience be inseparable from taking the dissolution of ego into account, the inanity of any subject as a substrate, that is, as anything that would be pushed underneath as a support for all mental experiences. That being said, we can see that the subject of dying is nothing to be afraid of since it is an epiphenomenon itself, an ever-changing remnant that keeps forming and disassembling. Even more so, death is desiring and insuring this constant desubjectivation for the unconscious, thus avoiding reducing life to classical philosophical categories: conscience, mankind or the persona.

Experimenting death, experimenting the body without organs (BwO) as the ultimate limit, as what is beyond reach, as what remains once everything has been removed, precisely allows for such ongoing dissolution preventing intense movements of desire to be chained to already constituted subjects. Therefore, death experience is envisaged in the precise sense of circulation between a BwO and partial objects leading to a widened experience in which I stop living as a fixed form: 'perhaps … I am the thing that divides the world in two … thin as foil, I'm neither one side nor the other, I'm the middle, I'm the partition, I've two surfaces and no thickness … I am the tympanum …', Beckett says in *The Unnamable*. Such is the theory of the unconscious too, the sense of the assertive usage instead of the exclusive and limitative one, of the disjunctive synthesis. If the unconscious knows no 'no', this is primarily due to the fact that, contrary to Freud's intuition, it is not oppositional but differential, never dropping what it sometimes seems to be excluding: 'trans-lifedeath', 'trans-sexual', Deleuze and Guattari say, rather than exclusive disjunctions 'either, or' ('dead or alive', 'male or female', 'gay or straight').

In order to understand that paradoxical promotion of the death experience better, as a prerequisite to the feeling of a widened existence, let us twist the argument and remember an anecdote, which is not so really. In Deleuze's view, Resnais's best film is not *Hiroshima mon amour* or even *L'année dernière à Marienbad*, both of which are masterpieces, but a little-known minor film: *L'amour à mort*. Its plot is quite simple and its narrative straight: a man dies and a forensic pathologist records his death. The woman who loves that man and whom he loved remains in a state of shock when he suddenly comes back to life.

Yet, in one of his lectures, Deleuze says that a thinker, a philosopher too is one of those zombies, one of those ghosts rightly or wrongly believing two things: that he is dead and that he came back to life. But the way he lives is not common. Since he comes back from the dead, his way of living is quite particular. In other words, he stands between two deaths: apparent death and real death. A death he went through from within, a death awaiting him outside. The real one is the one from within; the apparent one, the one coming from the outside, merely by accident. Naturally, the latter is no trifle. Saying that my death is nothing is not sufficient, it actually is something and it even is the ultimate event. That empirical death enabled philosophy to produce its finest pages, for instance those written by Seneca in his Letters to Lucilius about death being on one's heels, on the shortness of life and the subsequent necessity not to waste it. What Seneca wants is a strong soul: 'Relax the straightened limits of the time which is allotted me. Show me that the good in life does not depend upon life's length, but upon the use we make of it; also, that it is possible, or rather usual, for a man who has lived long to have lived too little.'[14]

So the philosopher doubtlessly believes that he is heading for death awaiting him outside. But, more to the point, when the outside gets deeper, attracting the within, he stands in between two deaths. There lies what is essential. Between apparent death and death to come, the philosopher casts a flash of life. He is a zombie indeed but only a zombie can sing life. Only death experience can give us a widened experience, as all writers of terror managed to feel. Coming back from among the dead, I am singing life. This is philosophy, Deleuze says through another of his outstanding utterances. Because I am coming back from among the dead am I singing life… In any case, what ought to be noticed is that as early as in *Difference and Repetition*, then in *Anti-Oedipus*, Deleuze established the difficult double-death theory, death as a model and death as experiment, which he borrowed from Blanchot, and where one finds the elegy of the idea that 'one dies', of impersonal death having evacuated the subject supposed to die.

How does genuine death untie and disassemble any subject by leading it to the body without organs through which it is? What is that death all about, which has nothing to do with me and upon which I have no power whatsoever? What would it remind us of? Why even merely talk about it? Here, an attentive reader must detect an important philosophical insight. Such is the process, such is thinking from outside which Deleuze inherited from Blanchot. Somehow, it is coming back from among the dead. Should it come from such a widened experience, thinking necessarily provides us with a taste for dying not so much from happiness but happily, not to pass away as is the case in passive nihilism but rather to never stop crossing thresholds, as larvae would.

What Deleuze calls subjectless subjectivity precisely is the subjectivity in which the ego is passive and derived. In the first synthesis of time in *Difference and Repetition*, we always are Actaeon through what we behold, even if we are Narcissus through the pleasure we draw from it. What this means is that the ego appears as soon as a furtive contemplation occurs somewhere, as soon as a contracting machine functions somewhere, able to extract a difference from repetition at some point. The ego has no modifications, else we would return to a subject-substrate conception; in itself, it is a modification, a pulsation or a beat between the body without organs and desiring machines. What we need to understand by death experience is experimenting this perpetual passage, this crossing of the limits of a well-constituted subject, this experience of a larval ego extracting difference from repetition in the first synthesis, this experience of a memory which is not instantly mine in the second and, lastly, the cracked I, shattered by the shape of time in the synthesis of the eternal return taking Thanatos out of Eros and excluding my own coherence. This is no longer 'I am dying', somebody's personal demise, but rather 'one dies'.

This is the reason why as early as in the *Logic of Sense*, Deleuze was already rejecting the false alternative: you either have fixed subjects or you collapse into an undifferentiated abyss. In fact, a passage through to the limit does occur. This tendency to no longer hold spiritual death and material death as co-extensive is found in Deleuze's constant call for embryology, whose truth is that it understood that only a larval subject is capable of supporting anomalous foldings and outspreading movements, where a constituted subject would most probably perish.

It really is tossing double or quits. Lost or saved. God's judgement or ethics of powers. From the viewpoint of utterances, because it is inseparable from what in *Difference and Repetition* Deleuze named the constraint of representation [*le carcan de la représentation*], the reflection on the nature of the order-word (*mot d' ordre*) puts us on to a similar path. Indeed, the command (which is a fundamental function of language according to Deleuze and Guattari) brings direct death to whoever receives the command or eventual death should they not obey or death that they must inflict themselves. A father's command to his son ('you shall do this', 'you shan't do that') is not separated from the small death sentence the son feels in his inner self. But in fact, the 'God's judgement system' as a whole is inseparable from such worn out, vampirical statements since such a system fulfils the function of splitting differences which grow more and more different by de-doubling them with fixed subjects, logical objects, predicates and relationships. As the magnum opus *Difference and Repetition* detects with such rigour, thinking must no longer be subjected to the 'quadruple constraint of representation',[15] so it can finally turn into thought of difference, where everything immutable is nothing but symbols and where thinking loathes the spirit of heaviness [*l'esprit de sérieux*] and the arbitrary limits it created: identity, analogy, opposition and resemblance. Those mediations are in fact detestable compromises, for royal means to tame, domesticate and make the dark abyss of difference expiate. Death, death is the sole judgement, the one that only knows frozen forms and the passing from one form to another, and which sets itself as a system[16]: '*chaque fois qu'une relation physique sera traduite en rapports logiques, le symbole en images, le flux en segments, l'échange, découpé en sujets et en objets, les uns pour les autres, on devra dire que le monde est mort*'.[17]

Against this arresting power of representation, but also against the idealistic conception of desire, Deleuze and Guattari rather give voice to another, a second kind death, death as a boosting element of the unconscious, as opposed to the death that makes everything alive speed towards suicide. For if circulation between a body without organs and machines precedes subjects, then it inevitably is a-personological and non-representative, that is, eternal, since nothing can die anymore that way: 'For death, provided we let it speak out, has nothing to say but itself: abolishing gaps, disassembling the verticality of hierarchies for the benefit of the undifferentiated horizontality of nothingness, it is what "levels out all accounts".[18] Placing such death at the core of the discourse amounts from asking this discourse to restore the undifferentiation it had interrupted by emerging as human speech, hence turning it into the weapon through which all will amount to the same thing once the presumed silence has been restored'.[19]

When considering that aspect of the order-word, we can indeed see that no matter how much death essentially concerns bodies, its immediacy and instantaneousness come from the genuine character of an *incorporeal* transformation. What precedes and what follows it may be a long system of actions and passions, a slow work of bodies; in itself, it is neither action nor passion, only sheer act and transformation the enunciation bonds with the statement. It is a sentence, or a verdict. 'This man is dead…'. For Guattari and Deleuze, we are dead already when receiving the command… Indeed, death is like an insurmountable and conceptual border everywhere; separating bodies, theirs shapes and their states and functions is like the condition, be it initiatory or even symbolic, through which a subject must change shape or state. A body always separates and distinguishes itself from another through something immaterial, and this something is death as the Figure.[20]

Such is the first aspect, considering the processes of subjectivations produced by a fully operational power [*pouvoir*]: death is imposed upon subjects, therefore forced to pass from one form to another. But Deleuze and Guattari precisely reverse logic so as to forestall death, which is forced upon us from the outside through *spiritual* death (and, paradoxically, the *genuine* one). We have stressed in what respect the subject-substance alone is capable of dying. In that sense, it is indeed already dead as soon as a change of figure is imposed upon him. But when we find what the ego really is, that is to say assembled and derived from what is given, being a mere reflection of a relation (but a figureless reflection or rather one that keeps changing figures), then we find the eternity of desiring machines and their never-ending flow.[21] Once we have conquered this outstandingly vibrant part, once we have ceased to live and to think of ourselves as an 'ego', the 'magic formula' that has been troubling us from the very beginning starts revealing its secret.

Thus, when we consider the second aspect of the command, flight [*fuite*] instead of death, it appears that variables there enter a new state, that of continuous variation. We are tackling the core of the problem here, linking death experience to broadened experience. The passage to the limit now appears as an incorporal transformation, which yet keeps on assigning itself to bodies: the only way not to remove death but to lessen it or turn it into a variation.[22] '*Trouvez votre corps sans organes, sachez le faire, c'est question de vie ou de mort, de jeunesse et de vieillesse, de tristesse et de gaieté. Et c'est là que tout se joue*'.[23] Naturally, we should not hammer this down but act with all necessary subtlety and caution. We invent self-destructions that cannot be mistaken for death drive. Disassembling an organism has never meant a self-inflicted death but opening the body to connections supposing a complex arrangement, circuits, conjunctions, separations and thresholds, passages and distributions of intensity, territories and deterritorializations measured like a land-surveyor or a cartographer would.

Then, caution (and not wisdom, as Guattari and Deleuze specify) is the ultimate art in any ethical test [*épreuve éthique*]: should we dice with death by disassembling an organism, we also dice with falsehood, illusion, hallucinations, psychological death by avoiding meaning and subjection.[24] This is why doing so is perilous, with a constant risk of taking us into a black hole. As we can read in *Mille Plateaux*, such caution is necessary for the plane of consistency not to turn into a sheer abolition or death plan; for involution not to turn into regression to the undifferentiated. Paradoxically, will there be no need to keep at least some layers, shapes and functions, a minimal subject to draw materials, affects and arrangements out of it?[25]

Therefore, we understand why schizophrenizing death is a perilous exercise but whose only goal is to revive life and why the return to annihilation leads us – if it is successful and if it is not impeded – to getting back to new attractions. The annihilation generated by the unproductive station of the body without organs is indeed quite different from the desire for the self-destruction of passive nihilism, which consists of a wish to disappear and dissolve into an undifferentiated world. For Deleuze, to learn how to die rather amounts to lead a perilous struggle against the arresting death of the God's judgement system. As David Lapoujade said: '*Il y a quelque chose de "trop fort" dans la vie, de trop intense, que nous ne pouvons vivre qu' à la limite de nous-mêmes. C'est comme un risque qui fait qu'on ne tient plus à sa vie dans ce qu'elle a de personnel, mais à l'impersonnel qu'elle permet d'atteindre, de voir, de créer, de sentir à travers elle. La vie ne vaut plus qu'à la pointe d'elle-même*'.[26]

Indeed, a body without organs is a model for death. As some writers have understood it perfectly, death is not a model for catatonia but catatonic schizophrenia gives death its model. The model of death appears when a body without organs rejects and removes organs – no mouth, no tongue, no teeth … all the way up to self-mutilation and suicide. Yet, there is no real opposition for Guattari and Deleuze between the body without organs and organs as partial objects; the only real opposition is that with the molar organism, which is their common enemy. In desiring machines we can see the same catatonic inspired by the motionless motor forcing it to remove, immobilize and quieten its organs but also to reactivate them and revive them through local movements, boosted by hard-working elements then functioning in an autonomous or sterile manner. Therefore, talking about death-wish qualitatively opposing life-wish is an absurdity. Death is not sought, there is only desiring death as a body without organs or a motionless motor and there is desiring life too, as working organs. Here, it is not two desires that are at work but two elements, two sorts of dispersed elements of desiring machines.[27]

We must pay particular attention to the relationship our utterance – the statement that desiring machines do not die – establishes with the Spinozist idea of a sensation of eternity. During the ethical test, I can indeed produce a relevant notion of myself by distinguishing my eternal essence and my existence over time. Is this ordeal not precisely what Deleuze has to offer us? We can thus say that death indeed is necessary but in a way belonging to accidents coming from outside. In heartrending pages, with great comforting power, Spinoza invites us to stop thinking of death as internal since it only disassembles the 'ego' produced by the extensive parts defining our existence over time; it concerns neither our singular eternal essence nor our relations: 'Desiring machines do not die'.

What does 'I am dead' mean then? There are no more extensive elements, no extrinsic ensemble belonging to me; I am stripped of everything. This means that my characteristic relations no longer are achieved; 'I am dead'. It means all that but that only. So, what does death not prevent? According to Spinoza, what death does not prevent is that my relations stop being enacted, but these relations have an eternal truth. They no longer are accomplished but we previously saw that they amply were independent from their terms, an idea Spinoza shares with empiricists. No extensive elements correspond to the intensive part anymore. Nevertheless, the reality of the intensive element as such remains. The eternity of essence, of the singular essence that makes me what I am, cannot be affected by death. Hence Spinoza's invitation to feel and experiment (and not just think or conceive) that, even though mortal, all too mortal, we all are eternal.

If a free man thinks of nothing less but death, he yet must constantly turn death growing inside into a simple empiric death which will come from outside so that *Anti-Oedipus* and later *Mille Plateaux* join the old tradition according to which to philosophize is to learn how to die. In other words, make death less and less probable. The more we form relevant ideas, the more we experiment active joys, the greater the remaining element that stays active is and the lesser becomes the element that dies and is touched by what is bad.

Notes

1 As much as possible, this chapter will refer to the French original. The English translation used here is the following: G. Deleuze and F. Guattari, *The Anti-Oedipus*, translated by Robert Hurley, Mark Seem and Helen R. Lane (Minneapolis: University of Minnesota Press, 1983), p. 331: 'The experience of death must have given us exactly enough broadened experience, in order to live and know that the desiring machines do not die'.

2 On the topic of disaster and the risks all hasty presentation of authentic thinking implies, cf. J. Derrida, *Points de suspension* (Paris: Galilée, 1992), p. 204: '*Imagine-t-on une pensée sans ce risque? La plus violente méprise, et le mépris, n'est-ce pas de requérir d'une pensée sa présentation immédiate, de lui refuser l'endurance d'une autre durée? Et même celle de l'imprésentable?*' ('Can we imagine thinking without that risk? Are the most violent mistake and scorn not to request from a thought its immediate introduction, to refuse enduring another time span to it? Even the unpresentable one?').

3 On this method, see G. Deleuze, *Nietzsche et la philosophie* (Paris: PUF, 1962), p. 3–6.

4 On the denunciation of those forces of negativity, cf. G. Deleuze and F. Guattari, *L'Anti-Oedipe* (Paris: Minuit, 1972/1973) (nouvelle edition augmentée), p. 132. [from now on quoted *AO*]

5 G. Deleuze and F. Guattari, *Mille Plateaux* (Paris: Minuit, 1980), p. 192. [from now on quoted *MP*].

6 *AO*, p. 320.

7 *AO*, p. 14. G. Deleuze and F. Guattari, *The Anti-Oedipus,* translated by Robert Hurley, Mark Seem and Helen R. Lane (Minneapolis: University of Minnesota Press, 1983), p. 8: 'Antonin Artaud discovered this one day, finding himself with no shape or form whatsoever, right there where he was at that moment. The death instinct: that is its name, and death is not without a model. For desire desires death also, because the full body of death is its motor'. Unfortunately, the English

translation misses here the classical reference to Aristotelian metaphysics, since Guattari and Deleuze literally evoke an unmoved mover.

8 *AO*, p. 14.

9 G. Deleuze, *Deux régimes de fous. Textes et entretiens 1975-1995* (Paris: Minuit, 2006), p. 21.

10 *MP*, p. 251: '*Mais pourquoi la ligne de fuite, même indépendamment de ses dangers de retomber dans les deux autres, comporte-t-elle pour son compte un désespoir si spécial, malgré son message de joie, comme si quelque chose la menaçait jusqu'au cœur de sa propre entreprise, une mort, une démolition, au moment même où tout se dénoue?*' ('why does the convergence line … shelter such special despair for its own account despite its message of joy, as if something threatened it as deeply as to the core of its own enterprise, death, demolition at the very moment when everything gets solved?' (our translation)).

11 On this matter, *AO*, pp. 36–7.

12 *MP*, p. 43.

13 *MP*, p. 280. 'We invoke no death drive. There is no inner drive within desire, only layouts. Desire always is organised and it is what organisation determines for it to be'.

14 Seneca, *Letters to Lucilius*, p. 49.

15 Deleuze, *Difference and Repetition*, p. 337.

16 *MP*, p. 135.

17 G. Deleuze, *Critique et clinique* (Paris: Minuit, 1993), p. 69. ('each time a physical relationship is expressed into logical relationships, the imaged symbol, the segmented flow, the exchange cut into subjects and objects, for one another, we will have to say that the world is dead').

18 Shakespeare, *Measure for measure*, p. III, 1.

19 M. Zarader, *L'être et le neutre. À partir de Maurice Blanchot* (Lagrasse: Verdier, 2001), pp. 276–7: 'Car la mort, pour peu qu'on lui accorde la parole, n'a rien d'autre à dire qu'elle-même: abolissant les écarts, défaisant la verticalité des hiérarchies au profit de l'horizontalité indifférenciée du néant, elle est ce qui 'nivelle tous les comptes'. Installer cette mort-là au cœur du discours, c'est demander à ce dernier de rétablir l'indifférenciation qu'il avait rompue en émergeant comme discours humain, c'est en faire l'arme par laquelle, le silence supposé rétabli, tout reviendra au même'. For Zarader however, this is one of the inconsistent conclusions Blanchot leads us to.

20 On this matter: *MP*, p. 136.

21 See for instance G. Deleuze, *Critique et clinique* (Paris: Minuit, 1993), p. 68: '*Cesser de se penser comme un moi, pour se vivre comme un flux, un ensemble de flux, en relation avec d'autre flux, hors de soi et en soi. Et même la rareté est un flux, même le tarissement, même la mort peut le devenir*' ('Ceasing to think oneself as an ego, to live oneself as a flow, an ensemble of flows, linked to other flows outside oneself

and within oneself. Even scarcity is a flow, even the drying up and even death can become so'.)

22 *MP*, p. 137.

23 *MP*, p. 187 ('Find your body without organs, know how to do this as this is a question of life or death, of youth and old age, of sadness and joyfulness. This is where everything is decided').

24 *MP*, p. 198. On ethical test: G. Deleuze, *Spinoza. Practical philosophy*, translated by R. Hurley (San Francisco: City Lights Books, 1988), p. 41: 'The ethical test is therefore the contrary of the deferred judgment: instead of restoring a moral order, it confirms, here and now, the immanent order of essences and their states'.

25 *MP*, pp. 330–1.

26 D. Lapoujade, *Deleuze. Les mouvements aberrants* (Paris: Minuit, 2015), p. 22. ('Something in life is "too strong," too intense, which we can only live on the limit of ourselves. It is like a risk that makes us not care so much about life anymore in its personal dimension but in the impersonal dimension it enables us to reach, to see, to create and to feel through it. Life is only worth it at its own cutting edge'.)

27 *MP*, p. 393.

9

From the Freudian Oedipus to the Lacanian Phallus and Beyond: The Objet a as a Desiring Machine

Harris Raptis

1

The 1970s had a double *experimentum crucis* in store for Lacanianism. In 1972 Deleuze and Guattari published *Anti-Oedipus*, denouncing the complicity of psychoanalysis as an institution with capitalism. In 1975 Derrida published 'Le facteur de la vérité', denouncing the complicity of Lacanian psychoanalysis with metaphysics. There are some interesting parallels between the two critiques, most notably the way they use the conceptual status and the function of the phallus in Lacanian theory and clinical practice as a 'ram' for invading the Lacanian field.

As Derrida traces the concept of the phallus in Lacan, he diagnoses that Lacan recognizes a privileged position for the phallus or, in philosophical terms, a typically *transcendental* position: the phallus is the 'privileged signifier'[1] that belongs to the chain of signifiers while simultaneously making it possible, thus constituting its transcendental condition of possibility. This is, Derrida points out, 'the strict definition of the *transcendental position*':[2]

> the privilege of one term within a series of terms that it makes possible and which presupposes it. Thus a category is called transcendental (transcategorial) when it 'transcends every genus' (*transcendit omne genus*), i.e. the list of categories of which it is nevertheless a part while accounting for it. This is the role of the phallus in the logic of the signifier. (FV, 477)

This omnipresence of a condition of possibility, this permanent implication, in every signifier, of the 'signifier of signifiers', of the 'unparalleled signifier' ('The Direction of the Treatment and the Principles of Its Power', É, 526, 537), claims

Derrida (FV, 477–8), attests to the transcendental eminence and insertion of the phallus in the signifying chain. And any anti-transcendental protestations on Lacan's part (see, for instance, '*On a Purpose*', É, 306) are mere instances of 'denegation' (FV, 478), as they come up against the following – perfect – definition of the (transcendental) phallus:

> For the phallus is a signifier, a signifier whose function, in the intrasubjective economy of analysis, … is destined to designate meaning effects as a whole, insofar as the signifier conditions them by its presence as signifier. ('The Signification of the Phallus,' É, 579)

The privileged transcendental status of the phallus in Lacan is the major find – and deconstructible motif – to have been contributed by Derrida's 'Facteur'. What was needed to establish it was some unshakeable, incontrovertible proof. Derrida ingeniously sought this proof in the testimony of Lacanian clinical practice. Where exactly does the preferential treatment of the phallus lie from a clinical point of view? In two words, in the refusal to equate it with a part-object. The phallus must not be 'treated as part object, subject like any other to the chain of substitutes' (FV, 478). This is, according to Derrida, the 'axial demand, the most insistent plea … in Lacan's sexual theory' (FV, 478), as well as the most incontrovertible evidence of the privileged, transcendental state of exception that the phallus enjoys in this theory.

Thus we are incessantly led (back) to what guarantees the unity between signifier and signified, always the *same* signifier, which does not allow of partition, the signifier of all signifiers: the phallus. This, in Derridean terms, 'transcendental signifier' is promoted by Lacan to a general equivalent of the symbolic order and inhibitor of its 'dissemination'.[3] The Lacanian logic of the signifier, and the related status of the phallus, would merely be the product of the integration of Freudian phallocentrism with Saussurian semio-linguistics (FV, 478). The name of this product: 'phallogocentric transcendentalism' or 'phallogocentrism' – in other words, one more link in the long chain of Western logocentrism.

Similarly, Deleuze and Guattari's critique denounces the 'transcendent' status of the phallus as foundation of the idealistic conception of desire as a lack[4] and as agency for repressing the revolutionary forces of the unconscious, curbing the dissemination of partial objects and reducing them to a phallically overcoded totality that equally distributes lack:

> It is clear that such a totality-unity is posited only in terms of a certain mode of absence, as that which partial objects and subjects of desire 'lack.' Consequently, everything is played out from the start: everywhere we encounter the analytic

> process that consists in extrapolating a transcendent and common something, but that is a common-universal for the sole purpose of introducing lack into desire … . This common, transcendent, absent something will be called phallus or law, in order to designate 'the' signifier that distributes the effects of meaning throughout the chain … . It is as if the so-called signifying chain, made up of elements that are themselves nonsignifying … were the object of a special treatment, a crushing operation that extracted a detached object from the chain, a despotic signifier from whose law the entire chain seems consequently to be suspended …: *we pass from detachable partial objects to the detached complete object* … . (AO, 72–3)

> The signs (sc. of desire) themselves become signifying under the action of a despotic symbol that totalizes them in the name of its own absence or withdrawal. Yes, in fact, there the production of desire can be *represented* only in terms of an extrapolated sign that joins together all the elements of production in a constellation of which it is not itself a part. … There desire is necessarily referred to a missing term, whose very essence is to be lacking. The signs of desire, being nonsignifying, become signifying in representation only in terms of a signifier of absence or lack. The structure is formed and appears only in terms of the symbolic term defined as a lack. (AO, 310)

To the Lacanian symbolic 'lack-of-being' (*manque-à-être*) of desire Deleuze and Guattari forcefully counterpose the 'Real', 'objective being of desire' (AO, 26–7), which, they claim, 'does not lack anything' (AO, 26).

This brings us to the point where the two critiques, Derrida's and Deleuze and Guattari's, diverge. For in order to make Lacan fit into the category of (phal)logocentrism, Derrida invokes exclusively the – fundamental, for the 'classical' Lacan – oppositional distinction between the Imaginary and the Symbolic and the primacy that the Symbolic holds in its context, foreclosing the Real and its related axioms. What if, over time, this distinction is complemented and rewritten and the symbolic primacy is dethroned by the increasing emphasis that Lacan ascribes to the Real? This does not seem to daunt Derrida, to whom the 'mobility' of the Lacanian discourse, for all the 'major rearrangements' or 'decisive reworkings' it brought about, follows an interesting yet continuous path (FV, 462). Yet the blind spot of Derrida's critique, that is, the Real and its attendant categories, is, as we will see, the starting point for Deleuze and Guattari's aspired appropriation or, in Heideggerian terms, for the 'appropriation' *and* 'overcoming' (*Verwindung*) of Lacan.

Eight years later (1980), in the second part of *Capitalism and Schizophrenia* under the title *A Thousand Plateaus*, the critical motif towards psychoanalysis (specifically towards Lacan, since in Deleuze and Guattari the phallus equals a rigid designator or definite description of Lacanian psychoanalysis, just as

Oedipus is a rigid designator or definite description of Freudian psychoanalysis) remains the same, merely articulated through a new vocabulary. The phallus is now the tree that grows in *A Thousand Plateaus* within the microclimate of psychoanalysis, which 'subjects the unconscious to arborescent structures … central organs, the phallus, the phallus-tree'.[5] Combining Derrida with Deleuze and Guattari, I would speak of the alleged 'phallo-arborocentrism' of the Lacanian unconscious.

Leaving aside the question of Lacan's virtual absence in *A Thousand Plateaus*, I would like to stress from the outset that, in what follows, I will limit myself to a discussion of the prominent yet critically ambivalent place assigned to him in *Anti-Oedipus*. However, instead of compiling, in the name of some Lacanian orthodoxy or academic technocracy, a list of counter-arguments to the anti-Oedipal critique sourced from the entire corpus of Lacan's writings and seminars, I will attempt to present *Anti-Oedipus* not as anti-Lacanian but, as Eugene W. Holland proposes, as a post-Lacanian work,[6] presenting the terms and the limits of Lacan's 'appropriation' *and* 'overcoming' by Deleuze and Guattari.

2

Patented by Deleuze and Guattari, schizoanalysis is derived from the historical contextualization of psychoanalysis (PLHCP, 292). Deleuze and Guattari do with Oedipus and the eponymous complex what Foucault does with Man in *The Order of Things* (1966).[7] Oedipus is a specific historical construct, with a beginning and an end. As Deleuze says: 'Oedipus … make the best of [it], because it's not going to last.'[8] Indeed, it did not last, since Lacan himself withdrew it already in 1960, if not earlier: 'the Oedipal show cannot run indefinitely in forms of society that are losing the sense of tragedy to an ever greater extent' ('The Subversion of the Subject and the Dialectic of Desire in the Freudian Unconscious', É, 688). In fact, ten years later Lacan would go as far as declaring that 'the Oedipus complex is of no use' and proposing that it be analysed 'as being Freud's dream'.[9] Today's decidedly post-Oedipal constellation of psychoanalysis bears the signature of Lacan.

To Deleuze and Guattari, the phallus in Lacan, which hovers above the pages of *Anti-Oedipus* and is alternately referred to as 'transcendent signifier', 'despotic signifier' or the 'object from on high', marks first of all a sign of progress in the task that Lacan undertook, to lead Oedipus to the point of its self-critique (AO,

268, 310); therefore, I would add, it constitutes one step in the ladder towards the schizoanalytic, machinic, molecular, anti-Oedipal – indeed, anoedipal – unconscious. In order to understand the nature of this progress, we must present – in outline – Lacan's reformulation and transcription of the Freudian Oedipus.[10]

In the beginning, according to the Freudian functioning of the Oedipus myth, there was the triangle of Father–Mother–Child. The highly complex relations among the three terms result in the child renouncing the object of his desire, that is, the incestuous desire for the mother. According to Freud, the operator of this renunciation is the father, who comes as a third term in-between the narcissistic imaginary dual unity of mother–child and prohibits incest under threat of castration. Under the law of the father, the child is called upon to 'assume castration' as the necessity of substitution in the object of his desire, after which the child's desire becomes 'normalized'.

Already in Freud, the Oedipus complex is complemented by the castration complex, and this points from the outset to the affinity between the phallic function, which is at stake in the castration complex, and the function of the father. This means that the Oedipal triangle is complemented by a term and a function akin to the term and the function of the father, that is, it is complemented by the phallus and the phallic function. In other words, what we have ultimately is not a triangle but a quadrangle; not 3 terms but 3+1. As pointed out by Deleuze and Guattari, Oedipus would be nothing without this additional term which acts as the 'triangulation's cause' (AO, 268), the 'formal cause of the triangulation', which 'makes possible both the form of the triangle and its reproduction: Oedipus has as its formula 3+1, the One of the transcendent phallus without which the terms considered would not take the form of a triangle' (AO, 73).

Lacan's patent lies in the fact that he reorganizes and reformulates, translates and transcribes all these Freudian data in terms of signifiers (and signifiers are functions, not images or persons – in this instance, the persons of the family and familialist Oedipal triangle: Daddy-Mommy-Child/little Oedipus). But what does it mean to speak of father and mother as signifiers? It means, as Jacques-Alain Miller tells us, that for both sexes the father is prohibitor, and for both sexes the mother is the primary object of desire. In the relationship between the function of the father and the function of the mother, the father enters as prohibition and law, and the mother as primary object and desire. What we have here is the substitution of the law of the father for the desire of the mother.[11]

From the Oedipus complex to the 'paternal metaphor' as a way of articulating the function of the father and the phallic function, as a unified formula for the

Oedipus theory and the castration complex; from the father to the Law and the 'Name-of-the-Father';[12] from the mother to the signifier of the primary object of desire but also to the maternal Other as the locus of the signifier ('The Subversion of the Subject', É, 688); from the child to the subject as a break between signifiers; from the usual geneticism of the theory of the stages of psychosexual development and the phallus as the object proper to the phallic stage to linguistic structuralism and the phallus as the signifier of symbolic castration ('Guiding Remarks for a Convention on Female Sexuality', É, 616); from images to structure; in sum, from the Imaginary to the Symbolic:

> Lacan does not enclose the unconscious in an Oedipal structure. He shows on the contrary that Oedipus is imaginary, nothing but an image, a myth; that this or these images are produced by an oedipalizing structure; that this structure acts only insofar as it reproduces the element of castration, which itself is not imaginary but symbolic. (AO, 310)

We have to do with as many transitions and reductions that reflect the progress effected by Lacan, which is – to borrow a term from Guattari's *The Anti-Œdipus Papers* – the 'linguistization' of the psychoanalytical field.[13] As Holland notes, this linguistic or semiotic turn in psychoanalysis as a distinguishing element of Lacanian thought is positively evaluated and, indeed, radicalized by Deleuze and Guattari (PLHCP, 292). What is denounced and condemned is the symbolic predominance of the Law and the Name-of-the-Father in the age of their capitalist 'reproduction' and 'revival'. This is the point where 'progress' gets reversed into 'regression' and 'archaism'; in order to understand the reasons behind this, we must stop briefly at some elements of the tripartite typology of Deleuze and Guattari's libidinal/political economy.

It may be reminded that the primitive territorial machine, the barbarian despotic machine and the civilized capitalist machine are not presented by Deleuze and Guattari as concrete historical stages of social evolution but as three different great social machines; as three different types of social organization, which correspond to three different types of symbolic organization and codification of desire (territorial coding, despotic overcoding and capitalist decoding, respectively). However, as Holland points out, only in despotism 'does the name-of-the-despot govern the entire Symbolic order'; only in despotism 'are the name-of-the-father and patriarchal domination in the nuclear family homologous with the name-of-the-despot and political domination in society as a whole' (PLHCP, 296). Hence the observation by Deleuze and Guattari that Lacan 'accompanies the signifier back to its source, to its veritable origin, the despotic age, and erects an infernal machine that welds desire to the Law, because, everything considered – so Lacan thinks – this is indeed the form in which the signifier is in agreement with the unconscious, and the form in which it produces effects of the signified in the unconscious' (AO, 209).

The only thing is – and this is where Lacanian 'progress' turns into 'regression' and 'archaism' – that under capitalism, where Oedipus appears at last as the very representation of desire, the Name-of-the-Despot has long ceased to govern the symbolic order, and the despot has ceased to represent and occupy its fixed centre, as in traditional power societies. In capitalism there is no such centre, no 'transcendent signifier' (in Deleuze and Guattari's terms) or 'transcendental signified' (in Derrida's terms), no established authority figure (father, god, king or priest). Deleuze and Guattari thus condemn Oedipal psychoanalysis as an archaism, albeit, as such, with a very specific repressive function within capitalism. As Holland writes, 'from the point of view of schizoanalysis ... the Oedipus is an archaic and reactionary despotism installed at the heart of the nuclear family under capitalism to re-contain the free-flow of desire unleashed by capitalist de-coding in society at large. And the institution of psychoanalysis is the repressive agency of last resort whenever the deteriorating nuclear family fails to ensure complete oedipalization all by itself' (PLHCP, 298).

There we have, as Deleuze and Guattari say, the 'three major planes of structuration':

> Oedipus as the imaginary reterritorialization of private man, produced under the structural conditions of capitalism, inasmuch as capitalism reproduces and revives the archaism of the imperial symbol or the vanished despot. All three are necessary – precisely in order to lead Oedipus to the point of its self-critique. (AO, 310)

Hence, they point out,

> the extreme importance – but also the indeterminate nature, the nondecidability – of the argument advanced by psychoanalysis's most profound innovator, which makes the displaced limit pass between the Symbolic and the Imaginary, between symbolic castration and imaginary Oedipus. For castration in the order of the despotic signifier, as the law of the despot or the effect of the object from on high, is in reality the formal condition of the Oedipal images that will be deployed in the field of immanence left uncovered by the withdrawal of the signifier. I reach desire when I arrive at castration! What does the desire-castration equation signify, if not in fact a prodigious operation that consists in replacing desire under the law of the despot, in introducing lack there at the deepest levels, and in rescuing us

> from Oedipus by means of a fantastic regression. … From the Symbolic to the Imaginary, from castration to Oedipus, and from the despotic age to capitalism, inversely there is the progress leading to the withdrawal of the overseeing and overcoding object from on high, which gives way to a social field of immanence where the decoded flows produce images and level them down. (AO, 268)

3

What Deleuze and Guattari question is the 'frantic Oedipalization to which psychoanalysis devotes itself, practically and theoretically, with the combined resources of image and structure' (AO, 53). They do admit, however, that Lacan's thought, in its incessant, schizophrenic mobility, did not go in this direction. Quite the contrary: if the aim for Deleuze and Guattari is the schizophrenization of the domain of the unconscious (AO, 53), then, they acknowledge, Lacan 'was the first … to schizophrenize the analytic field' (AO, 363). In what way?

As we said earlier, the anti-Oedipal critique concerns both the imaginary and the symbolic Oedipus, which would only be two sides of the same coin, the constituent parts of one and the same structural whole. Even if we go back 'from the images to the structure, from imaginary figures to symbolic functions, from the father to the law, from the mother to the great Other' (AO, 83), in truth we merely move in situ on the same hermeneutic horizon, misrecognizing and sublating the 'real' or 'true' difference (a recurring phrase throughout *Anti-Oedipus*). Where do Deleuze and Guattari locate it?

> Wouldn't the real difference be between Oedipus, structural as well as imaginary, and something else that all the Oedipuses crush and repress: desiring-production – the machines of desire that no longer allow themselves to be reduced to the structure any more than to persons, and that constitute the Real in itself, beyond or beneath the Symbolic as well as the Imaginary? (AO, 52–3)
>
> The true difference in nature is not between the Symbolic and the Imaginary, but between the real machinic element, which constitutes desiring-production, and the structural whole of the Imaginary and the Symbolic, which merely forms a myth and its variants. (AO, 83)

In short, the 'true difference' lies not between 'two uses of Oedipus' but between the 'anoedipal' Real and the 'Oedipal' structural whole formed by the Imaginary and the Symbolic (AO, 83).

To 'trace back from images to the structure', Deleuze and Guattari emphasize, 'would have little significance and would not rescue us from representation, *if the structure did not have a reverse side*' (AO, 308–9). It is this 'reverse side of the structure' that Lacan discovers, as he is 'not content to turn, like the analytic squirrel, inside the wheel of the Imaginary and the Symbolic; he refuses to be caught up in the Oedipal Imaginary and the oedipalizing structure, the imaginary identity of persons and the structural unity of machines' (AO, 308). This 'reverse side' has a name, and it is neither the Name-of-the-Father nor the phallic signifier but the name of an object: the Lacanian *objet α*, the 'object-cause of desire', according to Lacan's definition, in which Deleuze and Guattari see explicitly the precursor of their desiring-machines (AO, 309).

So Lacan erects not only an 'infernal machine that welds desire to the Law', but also (according to a phrase of Guattari's from his 1969 paper 'Machine and Structure',[14] which would find its way to *Anti-Oedipus* almost unchanged) an 'infernal machine' that 'erupts at the heart of the structural equilibrium': the *objet α* as a desiring-machine (AO, 83). These two machines mark the poles of Lacan's 'admirable' theory of desire, as praised by Deleuze and Guattari in a footnote: one related to the signifier, which institutes desire as a lack; and the other related to the *objet α*, which defines desire in terms of a real production (AO, 27).

As Guattari states unequivocally in his last work, *Chaosmosis* (1992), with the *objet α* Lacan would have initiated the theory of desiring-machines[15] and hence the machinic, schizoanalytic, anti-Oedipal – indeed, anoedipal – unconscious, which is an 'orphan' with no Father and an 'anarchist', as it defies his Law: it is not 'representative, but solely machinic, and productive' (AO, 311); it is 'no more structural than personal, it does not symbolize any more than it imagines or represents; it engineers, it is machinic. Neither imaginary nor symbolic, it is the Real in itself' (AO, 53).

Indeed, we cannot see how the *objet α* could have failed to attract the attention of Deleuze and Guattari, since Lacan introduces it literally as the 'outside' of all objects of the schizoanalytic, anti-Oedipal critique. As Lacanian psychoanalyst Dimitris Vergetis has suggested,[16] it is the emblem of the so-called drive-turn (*Kehre*) of Lacanian theory, which opens up another path for the participation of sexuality in the unconscious; a path that is not phallically trodden but follows the course of the 'partial drive' and its 'circuit', with the *objet α* as Real at its kernel.[17]

The participation of the libido in the unconscious is thus entrusted to the functionality of an object whose properties are able to cause the entire anti-Oedipal charge-sheet to collapse. For, as such, the *objet α* is:

First, *outside-phallic signification*: it is the element that 'naturalizes' the libido in the unconscious, not thanks to the phallus and phallic *Bedeutung*, not as signification or, negativized, as absence, but through its real, positive presence.

Second, it is therefore *outside-castration*, that is, *outside-sex* (FCP, 196–205): the *objet α* does not fall within the field of sexual difference and its theology – 'there is neither male nor female' *objet α*. Thus it designates, to use an expression that Deleuze and Guattari borrow from Marx, the 'nonhuman sex' (AO, 294–6) of desiring-machines, the molecular machinic elements, their arrangements and syntheses; consequently, it deconstructs what Deleuze and Guattari call the 'anthropomorphic representation of sex' (AO, 294–6, 308–10), that is, just as much the idea that there are two sexes as the idea that there is only one (the Freudian phallocentrism as androcentrism, as Derrida would say [FV, 480–3]). For, to Deleuze and Guattari, where psychoanalysis makes do with one or at most two sexes, schizoanalysis is the variable analysis of the *n* sexes in a subject.

Third, the *objet α* is *outside-language*, that is, *outside-structure*:[18] it is intransitive to the structure of language, impervious to the services of the signifying chain. In the words of Guattari, the concept of the *objet α* in Lacan may be nothing more than 'a vanishing point, an escape, precisely, from the despotic character of signifying chains' (CY, 81), containing 'the seed that allows to liquidate the totalitarianism of the signifier' (CY, 79); or, as he observes again in 'Machine and Structure', the *objet α* constitutes an otherness irreducible to and unable to be absorbed into the references of the structure, identical to itself, which relates to the elements of the structure only by means of splitting and leads language to a dead end (MR, 115).

Fourth, it is *outside-representation*, that is, *outside-image*: a specific characteristic of the *objet α* in Lacan is that it has no specular image ('The Subversion of the Subject', É, 693) – it is, according to an inspired formulation by Dimitris Vergetis, a 'vampire object'.[19]

In short, I would say that for Deleuze and Guattari the *α* is the 'purloined letter' of all Oedipal, oedipalized or oedipalizing misreadings, uses and abuses of Lacan's teaching.

4

The *objet α* would thus be the alpha of Deleuze and Guattari's theory of desiring-machines. Is it also the omega? We shall leave the question open to discussion, but not before initiating it by pointing out an interesting vacillation.

In *Chaosmosis*, Guattari acknowledges once again that with his theory of the *objet α*, Lacan had the merit of deterritorializing the notion of the object of desire.

He defined it, as he says, as non-specularizable, thus escaping the coordinates of space and time, and took it out of the limited field of the traditional partial objects (the breast and the faeces), to which the post-Freudians had assigned it, in order to relate it to the voice and the gaze. But he did not realize the consequences of his rupture with Freudian determinism, and didn't appropriately situate, as Guattari believed he should, his pioneering version of desiring-machines within incorporeal fields of virtuality, which would confer on it a machinic creativity of boundless potential (CM, 94–5).

Yet isn't this boundlessly multivalent virtualization and machinization, under the unbridled operativity of techno-media-science, that Lacan prophesied already in 1964, when he spoke of the voice, 'partly planeterized, even stratospherized, by our machinery', and of the gaze, whose 'ever-encroaching character is no less suggestive, for, by so many spectacles, so many phantasies, it is not so much our vision that is solicited, as our gaze that is aroused' (FCP, 274)? Because, indeed, as Guattari observes in *The Anti-Œdipus Papers*, technical machines liberate the potential schizo use of desiring-machines: 'Group fantasy in the audio-visual realm is produced from Hertzian waves, not shit or milk flows'; even though, he hastens to note, the audio-visual superego is dangerous because it's perverse, so it, too, has to be oedipalized (AOP, 153).

Nevertheless, Guattari must have been acutely aware, thanks to Lacan, of this destiny of *objets α* in the age of their techno-scientific and media-technological reproducibility: answering a question by Serge Leclaire on the occasion of a round-table discussion organized for the publication of *Anti-Oedipus*, he said that by opening the series of partial objects, beyond the oral and the anal object, to the voice and the gaze, Lacan signified his refusal to close them off and reduce them to the limits and the pulsional infrastructure of the body. The voice and the gaze, observed Guattari, escape the body, by becoming more and more adjacent to audio-visual machines (CY, 78). 'By becoming an "a" object, the partial object detotalized, deterritorialized, and permanently distanced itself from an individuated corporeity', he notes (CY, 79). But what is it that enables the partial object to *become* an *objet α*? This question brings us back to the question of the phallus and its function.

Let us take the example of the breast and the following sequence, as presented elsewhere by Leclaire. The object of need, caught in the network of the repetitions of demand, becomes the object of desire: the breast, real object, by becoming the signifier of oral demand, causes the *objet α* to emerge, that is, the breast as an erotic object, and the function of the phallus is the operator of this transmutation of the object of need into the object of desire. If the dimension of demand causes the dimension of desire to emerge, the phallic function is the operator that allows to connect desire with the field of the *objet α*, with regard to which the subject is defined as a cut.[20]

In conclusion: is the phallus really, as Deleuze and Guattari would claim, insofar as it overcodes each of the partial objects, the operator of their unification and totalization that equally distributes lack in the symbolic order? Or is it, precisely and conversely, the operator of deterritorialization with regard to bodily territorialization, the operator of the *becoming-objet α* of partial objects? And, more generally, as Slavoj Žižek observes, isn't the phallus what, far from tying us down to our bodily reality, sustains our very ability to 'transcend' this reality and enter the space of immaterial Becoming? Doesn't it designate the bodily cut that enables us to enter the domain of the incorporeal? Isn't it what, far from signalling our rootedness in the corporeal territoriality, constitutes the deterritorializing rhizome par excellence?[21]

Notes

* [I would like to thank Tony Moser for his assistance in preparing the English version of this essay.]

1 Jacques Lacan (2006), 'The Signification of the Phallus', in *Écrits*, trans. Bruce Fink (Norton: New York), 581 [hereafter É].

2 Jacques Derrida (1987), 'Le facteur de la vérité', in *The Post Card: From Socrates to Freud and Beyond*, trans. Alan Bass (Chicago: University of Chicago Press), 477 [hereafter FV].

3 Jacques Derrida (1972), *Positions* (Paris: Minuit), 112–21, *120.*

4 Gilles Deleuze and Félix Guattari (1983), *Anti-Oedipus: Capitalism and Schizophrenia*, trans. Robert Hurley, Mark Seem and Helen R. Lane (Minneapolis: University of Minnesota Press), 25–6 [hereafter AO].

5 Gilles Deleuze and Félix Guattari (1987), *A Thousand Plateaus: Capitalism and Schizophrenia*, trans. Brian Massumi (Minneapolis: University of Minnesota Press), 17.

6 Eugene W. Holland, 'The Anti-Oedipus: Postmodernism in Theory: Or, the Post-Lacanian Historical Contextualization of Psychoanalysis', *boundary 2*, vol. 14, no. 1/2 (Autumn, 1985 – Winter, 1986), 292 [hereafter PLHCP].

7 I owe this insight to my friend and colleague Dionyssis Kavvathas.

8 Félix Guattari (2009), 'In Flux', in *Chaosophy: Texts and Interviews 1972-1977*, ed. Sylvère Lotringer, trans. David L. Sweet, Jarred Becker and Taylor Adkins (Los Angeles, CA: Semiotext(e)), 75 [hereafter CY].

9 Jacques Lacan (2007), *The Seminar of Jacques Lacan Book XVII: The Other Side of Psychoanalysis 1969-1970*, ed. Jacques-Alain Miller, trans. Russell Grigg (New York: Norton), 112, 117 [hereafter OSP]. Deleuze and Guattari are familiar with these declarations of Lacan's (AO, 83, 53).

10 See the lecture given by Jacques-Alain Miller at the colloquium held at Marseille, 12 and 13 March 1988 under the auspices of l'École de la Cause Freudienne, 'Lacan et psychose', in *L'experience clinique des psychoses* (Nice: Z'éditions), 15–29.

11 See Jacques-Alain Miller, 'To Interpret the Cause: From Freud to Lacan', intervention at the 3rd Meeting of the Paris-New York Psychoanalytic Workshop, 9–10 April 1988, transcribed by Ann Prendergast and edited by Ellie Ragland-Sullivan, available online at www.lacan.com/symptom15/?p=326; published in the *Newsletter of the Freudian Field* 3 (Spring/Fall 1989): 30–50.

12 Lacan insists on the distinction: 'I spoke … of the paternal metaphor. I have only spoken of the Oedipus complex in that form' (OSP, 112). However, a more extensive note is called for at this point. As Colette Soler observes (see 'La malédiction sur le sexe', seminar 1996–7, lesson of 8 January 1997, University of Paris VIII, Department of Psychoanalysis, unpublished), despite the early Lacan's elaborations, which were heavily based on the Freudian view of the father, despite also the paternal metaphor under the Name-of the Father, that is, the linguistic form that Lacan gave to the Freudian Oedipus, investing the Freudian father with renewed prestige, over time Lacan's own view becomes increasingly removed from its Freudian origin. Freud identifies the law of the father with the castration of jouissance; Lacan does not ascribe castration to the father and his law. The function of the father is not to prohibit but, conversely, to 'unite (and not to oppose) a desire to the Law' ('The Subversion of the Subject', É, 698). The father-castrator is a fantasy (OSP, 125), while castration is an effect of language; an 'essentially symbolic function, that is, is conceivable from nowhere else than the articulation of signifiers', a 'real operation that is introduced through the incidence of a signifier, no matter which, into the sexual relation' (OSP, 124, 128–9). So as Dimitris Vergetis notes in the foreword to the Greek edition of Seminar XVII, Lacan 'de-legitimizes' castration in the sense that he disengages the loss of jouissance that castration suggests from the law of the father and the Oedipal prohibitions and links it to the functioning and mechanisms of the signifier. In the same vein, I would add that Lacan de-mythologized castration. He did this when he gave Oedipus the status of a myth that at once exposes and veils castration, and stopped making a law of it; he did this when he reread *Totem and Taboo* as a kind of fiction that Freud created to explain the structure and the inevitable effect of castration (OSP, 109–32). So it is very aptly that Jacques-Alain Miller tells us more generally that there is something of an irony of history in the fact that what made history was Lacan's reformulation and transcription of the Freudian Oedipus, that is, the paternal metaphor governed by the Name-of-the-Father, when, roughly from 1960

onwards, the whole development of Lacan's teaching goes in the direction of the deconstruction of the paternal metaphor; see Jacques-Alain Miller, 'The Other without Other', closing presentation at the NLS Congress in Athens, May 2013, transcribed by Dosia Avdelidi, revised by Anne Lysy and Monique Kusnierek, translated by Philip Dravers, available online at www.lacan.com/actuality/jacques-alain-miller-the-other-without-other; published in *Hurly-Burly: The International Journal of Psychoanalysis* 10 (December 2013). A whole series of elaborations by the later Lacan are inscribed in this horizon 'beyond Oedipus': when he gives the father the status of a *semblant*; when he defines the Name-of-the-Father as a *sinthome*, in other words as one mode of jouissance among others; or, finally, when he derides the paternal metaphor by saying that it is also a perversion, a *père-version*, a perverse version or turn towards the father (*vers le père*), according to the Lacanian joke (*Witz*). As Jacques-Alain Miller points out: 'This *Witz* of Lacan is a derision of Oedipus. The classical Oedipus was that which was opposed to perversion, the pervert being someone who had not achieved the Oedipal norm. Lacan's *Witz* serves to show that Oedipus itself is no more than a perversion … . For Lacan, saying *père-version* … is to reclassify Oedipus as a form of perversion. This is the end of the privileging of the Name-of-the-Father'; see the closing intervention by Jacques-Alain Miller at the Colloquium of the ECF in Nice, 22 March 2003, 'Gays in Analysis?', trans. David Hafner, *Psychoanalytical Notebooks*, Issue 29, February 2015: Sexual Orientation. As a consequence, 'there is no normality of desire. Unconscious desire remains attached, in fantasy, to jouissances that, in relation to the norm, idealized by psychoanalysts, remain intrinsically perverse. Perversion is not an accident that happens to desire. All desire is perverse in so far as jouissance is never in the place that the so-called symbolic order would like it to be' (see Jacques-Alain Miller, 'The Other without Other').

13 Félix Guattari (2006), *The Anti-Œdipus Papers*, ed. Stéphane Nadaud, trans. Kélina Gotman (New York: Semiotext(e)), 125, 129 [hereafter AOP].

14 Félix Guattari (1984), 'Machine and Structure', in *Molecular Revolution: Psychiatry and Politics*, trans. Rosemary Sheed (Harmondsworth, Middlesex, England: Penguin), 115 [hereafter MR].

15 Félix Guattari (2006), *Chaosmosis: An Ethico-Aesthetic Paradigm*, trans. Paul Bains and Julian Pefanis (Sydney: Power Publications), 95 [hereafter CM].

16 See Dimitris Vergetis, 'Kittler – Derrida: the dispute over the reading of Lacan', *αληthεια*, no. 4/5 (Spring 2010): 189–92 [in Greek].

17 Jacques Lacan (2004), *The Four Fundamental Concepts of Psycho-Analysis*, ed. Jacques-Alain Miller, trans. Alan Sheridan (London: Karnac), 174 ff. [hereafter FCP].

18 See Jacques-Alain Miller, 'S'truc dure', *Pas tant*, no. 8/9 (October to December 1985): 4–11.

19 See 'Kittler – Derrida: the dispute over the reading of Lacan', 176.

20 Serge Leclaire (1983), *Démasquer le réel: Un essai sur l'objet en psychanalyse* (Paris: Seuil/Points Essais), 36.

21 Slavoj Žižek (2004), *Organs Without Bodies: On Deleuze and Consequences* (New York and London: Routledge), 83, 85–6.

Part Two

10

For an Ecosophical Theatre*

Flore Garcin-Marrou

Rather than making a lot of assertions about the political conception and the positions of a theatre with ecological preoccupations, this chapter will rather offer a few hypotheses. If the engaged theatre has for a long time echoed the politics of the far left, what would a political theatre in line with today's anti-globalist, eco-socialist and ecological preoccupations be like? Similarly, how would a theatre no longer *disconnected* from a nature that it tried to throw off stage accept a 'green turning point', as it begins to experiment on stage with the becoming of human organisms interacting among themselves and with everything non-human surrounding them? Moreover, what would an ecosophical theatre be if, along with Arne Naess[1] and Félix Guattari,[2] we were to propose a non-scientific approach, more intuitive and sensitive, of an experience of the world where man is conscious of his 'alliance' (Searles[3]) with a milieu that is for the most part non-human and with which man feels connected?

In our lives we can appreciate the spectacle of nature, take shortcuts and breathe 'a little fresh air' from the backyard;[4] allow the logic of a thought to act on us like 'a wind that pushes us in the back'[5] to make ourselves sensitive to the lapping of the ponds and to the songs of frogs; notice that ideas come as we walk, that nature helps us to think, that our ideas surge up from the environment we find ourselves in. Rousseau visits and revisits his thoughts as he gathers plants in *The Reveries of a Solitary Walker*. Derrida, in *The Animal that therefore I am*, tells us about his experience with a cat that looks at him naked and that through his shameless look, strips him off his clothes – him, the philosopher – rendering him as helpless as a beast, provoking in him a feeling of annoyance, of shame, unbecoming, '*animalséance*'.[6] In *Le Versant animal*,[7] Jean-Christophe Bailly tells us of his emotion when, on a country road, a squirrel jumps up from the back of a clearing. This furtive irruption sets Bailly to worry about the possible disappearance of the wild world. The idea that runs through these examples is that the environment cannot be reduced to a mere frame or to a milieu, inside which or upon which humans would be active. There is a 'co-naturalness between human and non-human beings'[8] and this awareness of the non-human world is under a double menace: The fusion with this world (Thoreau's symbiotic experience with the wild nature in *Walden*) and the loss of the human world (the fears and the pathologies of urban life totally cut off from the living).

A thought born in plant gathering

This chapter is going to develop on two stages at the same time: the stage of thought and the theatre stage. I move jointly on these two planes because I take, in this reflection, the theatre to be the scenic projection of thought. What then would an ecological theatre be from the point of view of thought? Let us begin with Rousseau, the philosopher-botanist, who experiences thought as the art of promenade and dreaming. This is what we read in his first promenade:

> The leisurely moments of my daily walks have often been filled with charming periods of contemplation which I regret having forgotten. I will set down in writing those which still come to me and each time I reread them I will enjoy them anew. (Rousseau 1979: 6)[9]

If nature causes the spirit to wander, the fixing of memories in writing seems necessary, even if only for the pleasure of being reminded of the terms of the wandering of his mind. During his second promenade, Rousseau explains more carefully the effects that plants – their contemplation but also their being gathered – have on his mind and on the way he situates himself with respect to the world – in a state of alliance:

After lunch on Thursday, the 24 October 1776, I followed the Boulevards as far as the rue du Chemin-Vert which I took up to the heights of Ménimontant … taking paths across the vineyards and meadows … and stopped from time to time to look at plants in the vegetation… . One is the *Picris hieracloides*, belonging to the family of composite plants; and the other is the *Buplevrum falcatum*, belonging to the family of umbelliferous plants. This discovery delighted … me. Finally, after having looked thoroughly at several other plants I saw still in bloom… I gradually turned away from these minute observations so as to give myself up to the no less charming, but more moving, impression which the whole scene made on me. (Rousseau 1979: 13)[10]

Meditations and ideas come to Rousseau because he walks, observes nature, recognizes the plants that he has already collected in his herbarium during his earlier promenades. The plant world, although non-human, is familiar to Rousseau: he likes to feel their companionship, which is not the sole effect of the observation of nature – according to a typically romantic theme – but rather the result of a gesture that intervenes in nature, passing through the selection of species and their collection in view of their being shown in the herbarium. This alliance with nature is for Rousseau the expression of a 'plant friendship' (Starobinski 1971: 278).[11] As a result, the philosopher, besides being literally the friend of wisdom, would also be the friend of nature: a friend that would not only resolve to be a wise contemplator but also testify to the intrinsic necessity of introducing actively his mind to the things of nature, by means of plant-collecting. Being a surveyor of nature, he comes to recognize a plant, picks it up, finds its name and its species, dries it up and sticks it in his folder. He observes nature, arranges it and turns the dry plant into a 'commemorative sign' (Starobinski 1971: 281)[12] that makes a past state of mind surge up – a souvenir. The dried plant signals: it has its use, it is capable of 'waking up' an experience, both sensible and intellectual. Rousseau ends up writing in the seventh promenade: 'I no longer have anything but sensations' (Rousseau 1979: 98) revealed by the herbarium that represents an 'immediate memory' of those walks. And Starobinski writes:

> The collected leaf turns into a sign thanks to which a feeling is tornaway from forgetfulness and repeats itself, without ever losing anything of its original vivacity. (Starobinski 1971: 282; my translation)[13]

The page of the herbarium is therefore conceived as a projection surface, a mental stage from where an idea may surge and surge up again. The herbarium allows a reiteration of the eminently dramatized idea – having the same function as the theatre stage upon which every evening a play is being played and replayed. This is, at first sight, what a theatre of ecological thought could really be.

A thought born as waters lap

We find a second example of an ecological theatre in the thought of Gilles Deleuze, with different modalities and finality. In a text of 1967, Deleuze discusses the 'method of "dramatization"'.[14] He explains that our thought is a mental stage, where ideas begin as larval entities that come to hatch on a plane of immanence, where, later on, they live as conceptual personae with their own identity. The idea consequently lives in two states: a state of (larval) formation and a state of formulation. The idea is first intensive, and only later extensive. Later on, Deleuze resumes this discussion of the dramatization of the idea in a seminar on cinema that took place on 24 November 1981, where he investigates the quality of movement in space.[15] This is what he says: Movement is always motivated by an intensive factor which is then deployed in the extension of movement. Movement as a result follows the same process as the idea. We can easily see what movement is when it becomes visible to all, but how can we think of the 'intensive factor' at its origin? Deleuze explains that what is intensive emerges from a zero point of matter, from an obscure matter, a swampy and gloomy ground, from which fumes and emanations are exuded – a nameless space, where an essentially non-organic life exists, as well as ideas having not yet found their forms. Deleuze speaks of 'smoky parts', of 'pestilent marches': a *no-place* where matter, on its zero degree level, is agitated and constantly lapping.

To think with the lap, or by means of lap – this is what an ecological theatre could be from the point of view of the Deleuzian thought: a theatre that would not be held at the surface of things, but would rather be *under*neath them, *before* their formulation. Obviously, this theatre of the marsh or of the swamp would not be a classical theatre, it would refuse all frames and every composition. This theatre of the marsh would rather act as a force of decomposition sending the sign over to a swampy, non-organic and brute state. No more straight lines, but rather broken ones, diagonals and ideas in crazy speeds. Things that look intoxicated…What a world! What anxiety! Deleuze exclaims in his seminar… . But at the same time, what an invitation to life!

A larval theatre

We find a third example of the ecological theatre in Gregory Bateson's thought, in his discussion of the 'ecology of the mind'.[16] Focusing on epistemology, Bateson investigates the way we conceive ideas and form aggregates of them. The American anthropologist asks: 'How do ideas act on each other? Is there a kind of natural selection that determines the survival of certain ideas and the extinction or death of others?' Ideas can be formed only according to the milieu from which they emerge. For Bateson, as well as for Deleuze and Rousseau, ideas come always from *an organic underneath, from an infra-stage* of thought. If ideas begin by swarming in swamps, what causes the loose mud to turn into a dry surface? Must we always wish that our ideas get fixed in this dry surface? The theatre of thought that Bateson promises is a theatre of the loose mud, of that which has not yet reached the classical stage surface, and rests disorganized and inorganic. The paradox then of the ecological theatre is in its will to bring to the stage what, according to the orthodox norms of theatrical representation, is supposed to come *before representation*. The ecological theatre would be representing therefore that which, for a long time, has not been considered as part of the representation.

That which should not be seen in representation is exactly what Pirandello produces in *Six Characters in Search for an Author*, what Pitoëff stages in 1923, what the spectator Artaud sees and writes about in the journal *La Criée*. In Artaud's story, we are told that Pitoëff's actors, in search of an author, surge up on the stage wearing white make-up. Being real larval entities, like those of Deleuze in the *Method of Dramatization*, they come to acquire an identity. These swampy entities wish that the theatrical stage could 'dry them up', help them accede to a form. These characters in search of an author are 'larvae in search of a mussel to slip into'.[17] Artaud sees them as typical actors of his theatre of cruelty: larval actors wearing 'different human bodies', living 'in the depths of tombs in places historically, if not geographically, out of suspicion'.[18]

These are the first suggestions that we can make for a hypothesis of an ecological theatre, the interest of which would be to border on what is not human.

Hypotheses for an ecological theatre: Schechner/Quesne

Let's situate ourselves on the theatrical plane. What would the dramaturgical characteristics of an ecological theatre be like? We are not without historical references. Richard Schechner, following Kaprow and the avant-gardes of the beginning of the twentieth century, wrote that the 'environmental theater' rests on six fundamental principles:[19]

1. The environmental theatre is an ensemble of transactions connecting diverse materials (the public, interpreters, text, sense, stage, technicians) that form *a continuum*. It is therefore derived from an aesthetics 'built on systems of interactions and transformations and on the capacity of coherent wholes to contain contradictory parts',[20] either inside the theatrical frame or outside of it. We must in such a case reach a state of *relational* theatre that often solicits the theatrical senses of sight and hearing but also the more intimate ones of taste, touch and smell. It is a question of a relational aesthetics, aiming at the

deconstruction of the frames and the conventions of the orthodox theatre that separate the stage from the auditorium and then, in order to increase the interactions, at the strengthening of the empathic link between stage and auditorium.

2. The environmental theatre rests on the idea that the entire space is used for the performance. Ever since Greece, a *special place, inside the theatre* (the stage itself) has been reserved for the performance. But the space of the environmental theatre must favour a continuum between actors and spectators. This is the case, as many ethnologists have shown, inside a ritualized context, even if the modalities of participation or exclusion are many and different. Schechner uses as an example the film *Danse et transe à Bali* (1938) of Margaret Mead and Gregory Bateson that shows how the performance moves through space and comes to meet the people. The front of the stage is then adjustable. The space is defined by the action that is being deployed. Schechner notes that, among the spectators, some pay attention, others do not. The space breathes and the public changes places according to their sensory reception. In a Western context, such an elasticity of the stage constituted by the action can be found in street marches.
3. The environmental theatre takes place inside *a 'found space'* that does not tolerate the outside, the function of which is to delimit the space of play. Schechner refers to Bauhaus: a few of its members were thinking about 'new organic spaces'[21] that could encircle the spectators. He also refers to the original ideas of Frederick Kiesler (1896–1966), designer between 1916 and 1924 of the *Théatre Infini*, capable of accommodating 100,000 persons, and aiming at the composition of a 'natural milieu',[22] proper to the theatre. Kiesler deplored the fact that until now we have been content with assembling the public and the actors inside artificial spaces. Here is the idea of a nature, not natured but rather dramatized, the counterpart of which would be the fictional stage.[23] Finding an environmental space is constructing an organic and dynamic space, where materials do not get dissimulated but rather explored and exploited. Their organization may then be left to chance.
4. The fourth axiom of the environmental theatre specifies that the attention of the spectator is flexible and variable. Against the uniqueness of the point of view of the orthodox theatre, the environmental theatre adds two more points of view: The 'multiple point of view' occurs when many events take place at the same time, in different places; the observation must in these cases be readjusted, it must choose. The 'localized point of view', where the fact that only a few spectators have access to what is happening goes against

the idea that the theatre must project the action to everybody. Schechner concludes with this idea: 'The environmental theatrical space becomes like a city whose lights switch on and off, where there is circulation and where one can grasp scraps of conversation.'[24]

5. The fifth axiom recommends that 'each of the components of the spectacle speaks its own language'. Schechner then asks: why must the human interpreter be more important than the other constituents of the spectacle? Is it because he is human? We find here the will to make human and non-human signs coexist on the basis of a sensory equality.
6. Finally, the text participates in the *continuum* of the spectacle without ever being more central. The theatrical experimentations of Schechner's Performance Group have attempted to take theatre out of its hermetic places, and by working on relations and interconnections, to reconnect it with society. The environmental theatrical act rests on a continuous mode of exchange, away from the stage, in accordance with parameters of visibility and reception that do not stop fluctuating. The environmental theatre becomes in this case, 'a refuge place, a place of disruption and instability, the origin, potentially, of radical changes in the social topography'.[25]

Let us now move to another, more contemporary proposal of a theatre that could be qualified as ecological: the theatre of Philippe Quesne. In a conference at the University of Avignon in 2010, this director confirmed that the question of nature is one of the main themes of his work.[26] His group is called *Vivarium Studio* and has had the same actors for ten years, with Quesne trying to constitute an affective ecosystem. His thematics determine the course of his productions. In the *Festival entre cour et jardin* in Bourgognes, Quesne installs a camp of antiglobalists at the edge of a lake filled with black water. In 2005, he stages *D' après Nature* in the Theater of Bastille. The same year, he leads an artistic tour called *"Action in a natural milieu"* in the Parc de la Villette, which is repeated in 2006 in the form of '*Brief Reflections on Nature's Presence in an Urban Milieu*'. In 2008, *La Mélancolie des dragons* and in 2013, *Swamp Club* participate as well in the elaboration of an ecological aesthetic.

From an environmental point of view, Philippe Quesne, being concerned about the ecological and carbon impact of his tours, chooses his décor from ordinary materials. Indeed, his group does not travel by bus, the way that certain theatrical productions cart along monumental decors throughout Europe. For the *La Mélancolie des dragons* tour, the Vivarium Studio frequented the green spaces of the cities they visited in order to have access to the branches that constituted their décor. The desire to consume less and to use the local natural resources allow the establishment of new models of production. And this leads to the creation of a network of living exchanges where a reflection in contradistinction to the globalized world can be constructed, soliciting the local powers more often than the state political artistic institutions.

From a social point of view, Philippe Quesne puts, in each of his spectacles, communities of small humans asking themselves where their destiny leads them. The elaboration of the action is collective, not hierarchical. In 2008, *La Mélancolie des dragons* staged men standing still on the snow. The story was being invented by the actors. There was nothing concrete to do and nothing really happened. The whole group agreed to believe in ridiculous things. They decided to repair the ozone layer. Quesne thought that as soon as seven individuals believed in something, there was hope. The action presented was of a different nature than the dialectical drama that moved ahead as long as contrary forces confronted each other. What we may call 'eco-drama' is a decreasing drama (of a politico-aesthetic decrease) that operates a de-dramatization of theatre. It invites us to abandon our habitual understanding of theatre, forged by centuries of Aristotelianism that forces us to expect that something is going to happen (and Beckett was the first to present us with the fact that perhaps nothing would happen in the theatre in the *Waiting for Godot* that took place in front of a dead tree!) The gathering of these actors, but also the gathering of the public that solicits the theatrical representation, function like a core or a nodule, a nebula, a flea market in a public space, a public rounding up of the Assotiation pour le Maintien de l' Agricululture Paysanne, a feast of neighbours: These are gatherings that generate opportunities for material or sensible exchanges, as they carry always the idea that humanity is not totally lost.[27]

An ecological factory

The environmental or ecological theatres intervene in the fabric of the theatre. I would like to advance a few hypotheses about the effects that ecology has on the actors and the way they play. The quality of the ecological gesture calls forth different acting techniques. The actors should no longer be inclined to organically mimic nature – on the contrary, to repeat Deleuze's words, the expressions of the face should turn swampy, the gestures discontinuous, the changes of place intoxicated. A return to animality has always been a part of the actors' formation, allowing, with the solicitation of the instincts, a venue different from the psychological approach to the character: the animal form can maintain the actor in a dualist conception of corporeality (in all theatre courses, for example in the workshops of Jacques Lecoq, actors and actresses work on their becoming-dog and becoming-bird). The animal, like us, is structured according to a binarization, left–right, but also according to the structure, ventral–dorsal. Having actors experiment with becoming-plant would allow them to reveal new problems. The proximity of the actor to the vegetable is more singular. The difference between vegetable existence and the animal world would reside in the meteorological and seasonal constraints, on reproduction, in their capacity to convert directly the solar energy, in the fact that plants emit neither sounds nor words, that they change rather than escape, that they are of one piece (having neither outside nor inside), that they live like non-places in a state of undivided, unlimited and uncentred existence, and in that they have a diversity of sexual systems with the presence of male and female parts in the same organism.[28]

The experiments of Esa Kirkkopelto, professor of theatre in Helsinki, dragging her group to explore becoming-mushroom, becoming-germinations, becoming-mountain, are destined to develop new forms of theatre and new training for the actors.[29] Kirkkopelto calls these séances 'Secret Retraining Camps' where the participants have the opportunity to try new exercises in an environment both protected and directed. These sessions are not performances but rather sessions of free exercise, not seeking any spectacular effect, not playing with any dialectic of the seer and the seen, but rather aiming at the production of simple movements and the formation of human and non-human constellations. They start with the principle that the world wanting to be nothing but humanist would today be a symptom of exhaustion.

Here is one more example of a body-actor run through by the vegetative: the butô dancer Min Tanaka, theoretician of what he calls 'meteorological body' (Bodyweather). In the film that Josephine Guattari and François Pain made of him in the La Borde clinic, Min Tanaka draws his force from the earth, the territory, the stables and the swamps that surround the clinic.[30] A few hours away, southwest of Tokyo, Min Tanaka has created a farm (the Body Weather Farm) where the dancers are also farm workers: everyone there pursues a rigorous physical training in search of his own dance that is coordinated with the actual labours of the running of the farm.

An ecological narration?

Ecology may also, through contamination, experiment with narration, for example, with that which theatrical studies have designated as 'landscape-piece', inaugurated by Gertrude Stein and theorized by Michel Vinaver. Vinaver opposes the landscape-piece to the machine-piece that proceeds through the chaining of causes and effects. The landscape-piece moves through crawling and juxtaposition. The spectator is invited to stroll in an intertwining of spaces and times. In his piece *La Demande d' emploi* (1971), we find four opening situations that do not connect on the narrative plane. The spectator seems to be inside a forest; it is up to him to change his perceptual habits, to find his way in the midst of trunks that do not cross each other, but are, at any rate, planted *in the same soil*.

The text acquires its own ecology: there are *oikoi* – places where people live, places where organisms have relationships with their environment. They are palimpsest milieus that absorb the writing of others, gather together images and sounds and create literary ecosystems. Gertrude Stein's landscape-pieces are long *continua,* deriving from a *natura naturans* the form of which is always indissociable from the growth of the action. The form is never achieved: it proliferates and then perishes. It is always on the way, in a state of becoming, a work in progress. These landscape-pieces do not talk specifically about nature, they are *in themselves natures*: the organic world dictates forms of writing, so that we can imagine writing that is according to lops, foliage or root systems. Writing according to the modality of a tree leaf, for example, is writing in search of the greatest extension of its exposed surface. In order to write according to the modality of the root, Deleuze and Guattari experimented with the rhizome, but there are many other kinds of roots with different structures that would be interesting to propose as exercises in writing workshops.

What is interesting here is that we move from the writing *of* nature (when the leaf serves as a pictorial motif) to an ecological writing, the way that Lawrence Buell defined it.[31] Four criteria set it apart: 1.The environment plays in it a role of the first order and not only the role of decorum. 2. Man's interest is not the only one presented as legitimate. 3. Writing takes into account man's ethical responsibility towards the environment. 4. The environment is thought of as a process and not as a constant. Ecological writing goes beyond the mere description of a landscape the way it was customary to find in the exploration stories of eighteenth-century voyages. The description of a landscape, after all, is subservient to the human regard that colonizes the territory. To consider an ecosystem according to the territory, along with its social, cultural and political environment and its interactions with the non-human elements is perhaps to achieve *a post-colonial ecological writing*, where the predominance of the human over the living is criticized, even abandoned, in the will *to move from the ego-centred* to the *eco-centred.*

However, it is not only the theatrical text that experiences the challenges of a critical ecology; plateau writing, the writing at work in the performance is also impacted by the 'green turning point'. Allan Kaprow defines these *events* as environments. Richard Schechner discusses and experiments with an environmental theatre. John Cage creates ambulatory concerts. Bonnie Baranca offers many examples in her work *Ecologies of Theater*[32] where John Cage begins to resemble Rousseau when the author describes him as a naturalist-composer harvesting the sounds of the world, whether human or vegetable, mineral or industrial, wanting to make the musical composition into an ecology.

These creations turn into a kind of theatrical production (*mises en scène*), or better still, cultural production (*mise en culture*) able to build 'greenhouses' in order to cultivate the time of the spectacle, an ecosystem on its way to being constituted. The 'as if' which is at stake in theatre is no longer anthropo-centred but rather concentrated on the multiplicity and the complexity of nature: animals, plants, minerals turn into a sensible universe that gives way to dramaturgy.

An ecosophical theatre?

We have now reached our last proposal. The artists that we mentioned talk about an ecological theatre deriving not only from a thematic or protective ecology – normative, guaranteeing the right equilibrium among the species living on the earth (the kind of ecology that Arne Naess qualifies as superficial ecology). They are also for a progressive ecology, productive of new subjectivities, generative of an existential, social, political and aesthetic *praxis*. This is why the term 'ecosophy', proposed by Naess and later on forged by Guattari, seems to us capable of playing a role in the future elaboration of what an *ecosophical theatre* could be.

The ecosophical posture has the particularity of treating the environmental, social and subjective dimensions in an *absolutely global* manner, in view of a progressive reformulation of our relations to the world. The dimensions cannot be treated separately from one another. The ecology of the mind aiming at the reconstruction of individual subjectivities 'lead[s] us to reinvent the relation of the subject to the body' (Guattari 2000: 35).[33] Social ecology reconstructs subjectivity in its relation with society. Environmental ecology tries to protect nature and to elaborate rules of coexistence with the non-human. The necessity of ecosophy starts from this premise: the ecological deterioration due to techno-scientific transformations implies a deterioration of the modes of human life. Thus, the ecological crisis must find answers in the reorientation of subjectivities. What Guattari proposes is that this reorientation must be achieved, not by scientific means, but through the means of 'new ethico-aesthetic paradigms[34] … just as Greek theatre and courtly love or chivalric romance were once adopted as models or rather as modules of subjectification'[35] (ibid.: 38). It is really a new 'ecological drama' that can ground an ecosophy with an ethico-political character. Together with Guattari, we could postulate that the hypothesis of an ecosophical theatre would be a necessary 'narrative detour' that 'through the annals of myth and ritual or through supposedly scientific accounts, all of which have as their ultimate goal a dispositional mis en scène, a bringing into existence' (ibid.: 37) permitting the establishment of new 'supports for existence' and creation. The ecosophical theatre, consequently, offers itself as a laboratory of innovative modes of existence and aesthetic paradigms, social reconfigurations and original communitarian harmonies.

Let us then propose a few venues for experimentation. The ecosophical theatre could be a theatre of micro-experience that plunges the body of the spectator inside a corporeal ecology, transforms stages into ecosystems and makes theatre into an agent of sensibilization and modification of our subjectivities. This could generate dramaturgies of immersion: outdoor theatres that count on a non-antagonistic or non-competitive relation (Bateson) with the surrounding world, greenery theatres, places temporarily managed for the theatre, with the end of restoring an interaction, body–mind, nature, in opposition to the Cartesian vision. Julien Previeux's 'Clandestine Theater'[36] could be the site of such an ecosophical experimentation. This two-part sculpture is inspired by the tools for the detection of enemy planes built by the British army during the 1920s. They are cement walls, the acoustics of which allowed one to hear the approaching planes. Previeux, for the Anglet Biennale, created two replicas of these instruments that delimit a game space on a grand green expanse, where the acoustics permit us to communicate from one point of the exposition to another, without raising our voice. We rediscover the possibilities that Schechner suggested for the environmental theatre: interconnections, sense solicitations, multiplications of points of view, etc.

However, these theatres would be lacking a purely political dimension. What other forms could then be proposed? It seems to me, first of all, that the ecosophical theatre, since ecosophy is born from the failure of the dualisms between man and nature, has the particularity of not making use of dialectics. Political ecosophy as a result is the one that has the possibility to maintain a productive and desiring tension between man and nature. But, in doing without dialectics, are not the proposals of the vegetative theatres risking to create ecosystems staged inside cloches, sheltered from cold contradictions, forms of pacified and harmonized heterotopias, where the actors, like laboratory rats, move about on a test tube stage, subjects of an aesthetic experimentation in places cut off from the dialectics of History? What kind of politics does the ecosophical theatre induce?

Richard Schechner proposes, in the pages he sets aside for the environmental theatre, that this kind of theatre finds a possible crystallization in guerrilla theatre, the proper of which is to find a place of the urban tissue, in the outdoors, in order to stage a politicized situation and to denounce it. But, according to Schechner, guerrilla theatre restores a stage where the marches for freedom succeed in eliminating all temptations to fix a stage inside the urban space. The marches in this case constitute a theatre of changing places, where the spectator chooses his own point of view, does not ever stay in a fixed place, and where the action is not restrained by the limits of a defined territory, because it is organized according to the mass of agents that walk in the street. To describe these marches only from the political point of view is being reductive. Schechner insists on their aesthetic and theatrical dimension. The marches are performed for the sake of those who are on the street, those who will be seeing them on television or reading of them in the newspapers. The manifestation that integrates nods, nodules, loose theatrical conglomerations (we could designate them as 'ecosophic street stages') create an elastic space that is able to be modulated, a space that introduces completely original relations – to the extent that they are modelled from life – between those who march, those who pass by the march, those who watch and those who choose not to.[37]

Translated by Constantin Boundas and Susan Dyrkton.

Notes

* A French version of this essay has been published in the revue Degrés no 163–164, Bruxelles, autumn-hiver 2015.

1 Arne Naess, *Ecology, Community and Lifestyle: Outline of an Ecosophy*, trans. David Rothenberg (Cambridge: Cambridge University Press, 2003).
2 Félix Guattari, *The Three Ecologies* (London: Bloomsbury Academic, 2005). See also Félix Guattari, *Qu'est-ce que l' écosophie?* (Paris: Lignes/Imec, coll. Archives de la pensée critique, 2013); also *Chimères*, no. 76 (2012) "Ecosophie", edited by Manola Antonioli.
3 Harold. F. Searles, *The Nonhman Environment: In Normal Development and Schizophrenia* (International Universities Press, 1960).
4 Gilles Deleuze and Claire Parnet, *Dialogues*, trans. Hugh Tomlinson and Barbara Habberjam (New York: Columbia University Press, 1987).
5 Gilles Deleuze, *Negotiations: 1972-1990*, trans. Martin Joughin (New York: Columbia University Press, 1997)
6 Jacques Derrida, '*The Animal that Therefore I am (More to follow)*', in *Animal Philosophy: Essential Readings in Continental Philosophy*, ed. Mathew Calarco and Peter Atterton (London: Continuum, 2004), 113.
7 Jean-Christophe Bailly, *Le Versant Animal* (Paris: Bayard, 2007).
8 Guy Trastour, 'Communauté et Ecosophie', *Chimères* 70 (2009): 17.
9 Jean-Jacques Rousseau, *The Reveries of the Solitary Walker*, trans. Charles E. Butterworth (New York: New York University Press, 1979)
10 Ibid.
11 See Jean Starobinski, 'Les amitiés végétales', in *Jean-Jacqes Rousseau: La Transparence et l' obstacle* (Paris: Tel, Gallimard, 1971), 278.
12 Ibid., 281.
13 Ibid., 282.
14 Gilles Deleuze, ' The Method of Dramatization', in *Desert Islands and Other Texts. 1953-1974*, ed. David Lapouzade, trans. Michael Taormina (New York: Semiotext(e), 2004), 94–116.
15 La voix de Gilles Deleuze en ligne, http://www2.univ-paris8.fr/deleuze/article.php3?id_article=82 (accessed 10 October 2015).
16 Gregory Bateson, *Steps to an Ecology of Mind. Collected Essays in Anthropology, Psychology, Evolution and Epistemology* (Chicago: University of Chicago Press, 1972).
17 Antonin Artaud, 'Six personnages en quête d' auteur à la Comédie des Champs Élysées', *La Criée* 24, Mai 1023.
18 Antonin Artaud, 'Le théâtre de la cruauté', in *Oeuvres Completes II* (Paris: Gallimard, 2004), 1661.
19 Richard Schechner, 'Six axiomes pour le théâtre environnemental', [1967, rev. 1987] in *Performance, Expérimentation et theorie du théâtre aux USA*, trad. Marie Pecorari (Montreuil-sous-Bois:Editions Théâtrales, 2008), 121–47.
20 Ibid., 121.

21 Ibid., 133.

22 Ibid., 133.

23 Schechner quotes Kiesler: 'The entire structure is shut in a double fuselage made of steel and opaque welded glass. The scene forms an infinite spiral. The different levels are connected with elevators and platforms … The structure is a system of elastic construction resting on cables and platforms that are inspired by the construction of bridges.' Schechner writes that this grand environmental theatre resembles the environment of the American shopping mall.

24 Ibid., 143.

25 Ibid., 119. Anne Cuisset's introduction.

26 The University Lessons proposed by Laure Adler, 'Midi-Minuit. Cultivons notre jardin'. 15 July 2919. https://www.youtube.com/watch?v=Kwe12kgj40k (accessed 7 July 2015).

27 Guy Trastour, 'Communauté et Ecosophie', 10.

28 See Karen Houle, 'Les différentes symétries des plantes', *Chimères* 82, L' Herbe (2014): 155–67.

29 See the presentation of Esa Kirkkopelto's works on the Labo site LAPS: http://labo-laps.com/presentation-des-travaux-desa-kirkkopelto/ (accessed 3 September 2015).

30 The film is available from YouTube. First Part: https://www.youtube.com/watch?v=VgErye7jXbl Second Part: https://www.youtube.com/watch?v=lrHgwSRTjKO (accessed 02 October 2015).

31 Lawrence Buell, *The Environmental Imagination: Thoreau, Nature Writing and the Formation of American Culture* (Cambridge, MA: Harvard University Press, 1995).

32 Bonnie Maranca, *Ecologies of Theatre* (Baltimore: Johns Hopkins University Press, 1996). Maranca classifies under the name 'Ecologies of Theater' the following actors: Gertrude Stein, Robert Wilson, John Cage, Meredith Monk, Isak Dinesen, Herbert Blau. Under the name 'Natural Histories of Drama': Rachel Rosenthal, Heiner Muller, Maria Irene Fornes. Besides Bonnie Maranca, Anglo-Saxon research has spent more effort than the French on the question of the conditions of the possibility of an ecological theatre. Here is a non-exhaustive bibliography: CLESS, Downing, 'Eco-Theatre, USA: The Grassroots is Greener', TDR: *The Drama Review* 40, no. 2 (1996): 79–102/ *Ecology and Environment in European Drama* (New York: Routledge, 2010). Kershaw, Baz, *Theatre Ecology: Environments and Performance Events* (Cambridge: Cambridge University Press, 2007). May Theresa, *Greening the Theater: Taking Ecocriticism from Page to Stage*. PDF: http://pages.uoregon.edu/ecodrama.files/file/Greening%20the%20Theatre.pdf Bronislaw Szerszynsji, Wallace Heim and Claire Waterton, *Nature Performed: Environmental Culture and Performance* (New York: Blackwell, 2004).

33 Félix Guattari, *The Three Ecologies* (London: The Athlone Press, 2000), 35.

34 Guattari's conception of the 'new aesthetic paradigm' may be summarized as follows: In order to revolutionize the familial, social, urban and ecological practices, in order to reinvent new ways to be and to act, the individual must observe the artists and be inspired by their capacity to invent a new subjectivity with every new work that they create.

35 Félix Guattari, *The Three Ecologies* (London: the Athlone Press, 2000), 38.

36 Parpen, cement. Dimensions: 6.5m by 16m by 2.8m/ Technical Conception: Kerwin Rolland. Photographs in the Gallery Philippe Jousse http://jouisee-entreprise.com/fr/art-contemporain.oeuvres/le-theatre-clandestin/ (accessed 02 September 2015).

37 This essay will be developed in a book. *Ecosophie théâtrale*, written by Flore Garcin-Marrou and Philippe Quesne, and in the issue 90 of Chmères, jointly edited by Charlotte Hess, Flore Garcin-Marrou, Valerie Marange and Valentin Schaepelynck.

References

Antonioli Manola ed. (2012), 'Ecosophy', *Chimères* 70.

Antonin Artaud, 'Six personnages en quête d' auteur à la Comédie des Champs Élysées' *La Criée* 24, Mai 1023.

Bailly Jean-Christophe (2007), *Le Versant Animal*. Paris: Bayard.

Bateson Gregory (1972), *Steps to an Ecology of Mind. Collected Essays in Anthropology, Psychology, Evolution and Epistemology*. Chicago: University of Chicago Press.

Buell Lawrence (1995), *The Environmental Imagination: Thoreau, Nature Writing and the Formation of American Culture*. Cambridge, MA: Harvard University Press.

Cless Downing (2010), *Ecology and Environment in European Drama*. New York: Routledge.

Cless Downing (1996), 'Eco-Theatre, USA: The Grassroots is Greener. TDR', *The Drama Review* 40: 2.

Deleuze Gilles (2004), 'The Method of Dramatization', in David Lapouzade (ed.), Michael Taormina (trans.), *Desert Islands and Other Texts. 1953-1974*, 94–116. New York: Semiotext(e).

Deleuze Gilles and Claire Parnet (1987), *Dialogues*. Translated by Hugh Tomlinson and Barbara Habberjam. New York: Columbia University Press.

Derrida Jacques (2004), 'The Animal that Therefore I am (More to follow)', in Mathew Calarco and Peter Atterton (ed.), *Animal Philosophy: Essential Readings in Continental Philosophy*, 113. London: Continuum.

Guattari, Félix (2000), *The Three Ecologies*. Translated by Ian Pindar and Paul Sutton. London: The Athlone Press.

Guattari, Félix (2013), *Qu' est-ce que l' écosophie?* Paris: Lignes/Imec, coll. Archives de la pensée critique.

Houle, Karen (2014), 'Les différentes symmétries des plantes', *Chimères* 82, L'Herbe, 155–67.

Kershaw, Baz (2007), *Theatre Ecology: Environments and Performance Events.* Cambridge: Cambridge University Press.

Kirkkopelto, Esa, works on the Labo site LAPS: http://labo-laps.com/presentation-des-travaux-desa-kirkkopelto/ (accessed 03 September 2015).

Maranca, Bonnie (1996), *Ecologies of Theatre.* Baltimore: Johns Hopkins University Press.

May Theresa, *Greening the Theater: Taking Ecocriticism from Page to Stage.* PDF: http://pages.uoregon.edu/ecodrama.files/file/ Greening%20the%20Theatre.pdf

Naess, Arne (2003), *Ecology, Community and Lifestyle: Outline of an Ecosophy.* Translated by David Rothenberg Cambridge: Cambridge University Press.

Rousseau, Jean-Jacques (1979), *The Reveries of the Solitary Walker.* Translated by Charles E. Butterworth. New York: New York University Press.

Schechner, Richard (2008), *Performance, Expérimentation et théorie du théâtre aux USA.* Translated by Marie Pecorari, 121–47. Montreuil-sous-Bois: Editions Théâtrales.

Searles, Harold (1960), *The Nonhman Environment: In Normal Development* and *Schizophrenia* International Universities Press.

Starobinski, Jean (1971), *Jean-Jacques Rousseau: La Transparence et l' obstacle.* Paris: Tel, Gallimard.

Szerszynsji, Bronislaw, Heim, Wallace and Waterton, Claire (2004), *Nature Performed: Environmental Culture and Performance.* London: Blackwell.

Trastour Guy (2009), 'Communauté et Ecosophie', *Chimères* 70: 17.

11

The Transversality of the Oasis Skateboard Factory Alternative School

Gary Genosko

Throughout his career Félix Guattari referred to the accomplishments of radical French teacher Célestin Freinet, whose work he discovered through his youthful outings in the hostelling movement with pedagogue Fernand Oury, the brother of his long-time collaborator at La Borde, Jean Oury. The institutional pedagogy movement in France dovetailed with the institutional psychotherapy practised at La Borde – paying critical attention to how institutions generate subjectivities – although the followers of Freinet and Oury were not often able to cooperate. Nevertheless, formations of subjectivation were engendered in an original way through Freinet's use of a classroom printing press, in a way complementary to how the institution itself and its organizational diagram were foregrounded in the grid, the table of rotating duties and personnel assignments at La Borde. Inspired by Freinet, Guattari adapted practices designed for schoolchildren in rural France in the 1920s and 1930s to the psychiatric clinic, developing the process over his career there from the mid-1950s to the early 1990s.

Looking across institutions and bringing diverse historical practices into a contemporary context, I want to report on my participation in a downtown Toronto alternative school that is built around the mediating technology of skateboards. I don't mean simply riding skateboards, although that is not a simple matter at all; I mean delivery of state-mandated curriculum from the ground up by means of the construction, design and marketing of different kinds of boards and an immersion in youth street culture through the production of buttons, zines, graffiti, T-shirts and of course, skateboards. I want to provide in a preliminary way a contemporary schizoanalysis of the mediations, institutional constraints, transversal extra-academic challenges and successes, as well as the prospects for its students and teachers, of this small, one-room, alt-high school.

I will begin with a few reflections on Freinet's techniques and methods and then turn to the skateboard factory, where I participated during 2011–12 in the life of the school as a member of the community council and a specialist in publishing.[1]

Skateboarding is not among the sports that Deleuze and Guattari discuss, but this has not prevented their readers from linking their thought with a rhizomatics of street skateboarding and smoothing of urban space through temporary repurposings of rails, benches, walkways and stairs, not to mention lines of flight along a vast concrete phylum (Fine 2013); rhizomatic resistance is a potent theme in describing youth skateboarding against the controlled space of the skate-park (Leafgren 2009: 180–1). A study of skate punks in California is inspired by Guattari's remarks on the many kinds of deterritorialization of dominant realities that machinic intensities can provide, such as boarding in empty suburban swimming pools (Butz 2012: 212). Yet from the time that Iain Borden (2003) published his study on architecture and skateboarding to the present, boarding has been in some cities partially integrated into urban renewal schemes, education and health curricula, adopted as a strategy for building youth social capital around the globe, and its business successes celebrated. This is the broad context of my study: skateboarding's entry not so much into the mainstream, but as a controlled substance of socialization within the well-established alternative streams of high school education in Toronto. The very link between skateboarding and curriculum is an inspired Guattarian gesture of experimentation taken by founding teacher Craig Morrison, in the context of the Arts and Social Change programme he designed in the Oasis alternative school in 2006, before the programme jumped into its own 'one room schoolhouse' rented in the Scadding Court Community Centre in downtown Toronto in 2009. Despite its high public profile and positive media coverage, and the numerous awards the school has garnered, Oasis Skateboard Factory has not been successful in acquiring a designated space of its own that doesn't require cleaning, repacking and locking up at the end of each day, and the school must raise through sponsorships and partnerships money in order to supplement its modest official budget of around $5,000/year from the local school board.

Transiting, then, from the printing press to the skateboard, I pass through Freinet's so-called natural method of pedagogy that was largely a trial and error process without lessons favouring active rather than passive learning that he thought of as a 'way of life' (1968: 120). Clearly in line with the active school tradition, but diverging from the more production-oriented and industrial education models, Freinet claimed that a pupil's desire for greater perfection in visual expression and power over representation could be augmented by the use of a printing press, among a whole battery of technological devices and their associated techniques; however, for schools without the requisite budget, any number of pre-digital duplicating machines would suffice, which during the period in question beginning in the 1930s, would have used a stencil, as in a mimeograph, or a limograph. Whatever the choice, getting one's hands inky was a rite of passage for Freinet's young grade-school students. Stencil tech was relatively cheap and non-electrical, not to mention non-colour, delivering lines with some shadows; the copies could then be hand-coloured. The creation of copies permitted each student in the class to compile a book of his or her own work, a Book of Life, and include works by fellow classmates as well; in addition, each pupil could create a free text of their own akin to a diary, as well as contribute to the school newspaper. Individual work plans balanced with collective responsibilities. The original student publications played the role of school syllabus and attracted the wrath of both Ministry of Education officials and socialist politicians because Freinet ignored board textbooks and didn't teach the classics, either (Acker 2007: 60). Eventually he would build one hour of mandated exercises into his daily school timetable, with the option for another hour developed to 'old pedagogy' at the end of the day (Beattie 2002: 22ff). Freinet also developed a system of cards (*fichier documentaire*) that held information such as newspaper clippings about a variety of topics and were catalogued by subject as a classroom resource, and used in a variety of lessons.

The desire of pupils to create and to communicate their own original vision, full of their own personality and character, was at the heart of Freinet pedagogy. Freinet also promoted the use of linocut techniques of engraving and running off copies as they produced better results especially for illustrating newspaper articles (1968: 123). Freinet used these student publications for the purpose of interscholastic communication, beginning modestly with fellow travellers, and growing as he refined his methods. Packages of Books of Life were exchanged between schools in France and the lives of children from diverse parts of the country were shared and used as lessons and sources of material for classroom activities. The exchanges were regular and they were used to deepen interest and were supplemented with maps, postcards, regional foods, etc. At the outset, Freinet exchanged Books of Life between participating schools, formalizing the exchange with questionnaires and delivery dates, but he then wanted each school to print a high-quality illustrated newspaper for interscholastic communications. School newspapers are a staple of high school and university campuses, but Freinet believed both primary and middle years could also participate. The mature centrepiece of Freinet education is a school print shop with a movable metallic type press; the Gutenbergian legacy is obvious without becoming a techno-fetish. He does not consider the printing press to be a panacea, but leans heavily on 'modern techniques' as a source of enchantment and magic for pupils and a means to integrate them into contemporary social processes (1968: 309), neither reducing the lessons to 'education by work' nor 'technical apprenticeship' (1968: 251–3). The production process is not manual, Freinet claimed, but 'intellectual and spiritual' because it deconstructed the work–play distinction in an atmosphere that was egalitarian and democratic. The school print shop is a place of collective production (1968: 174). It is also a place of working to a deadline as newspapers would be produced weekly. The newspaper was posted on a wall as a mural and was subject to collective review giving rise to congratulations, criticisms and requests.

In order to facilitate group communication and collective decision-making, and build the life of the school, Freinet constituted a cooperative council consisting of students and teacher – the multi-age and -ability Freinet school had only one teacher. He built this event around the posting and 'common discussion' of the newspaper, but it was a democratic body with power to make decisions about certain expenditures. Although the teacher played an important role and held a veto, the formation of the assembly as a self-directed group was first and foremost at stake so that its projects may be articulated and pursued and responsibility for them taken together. The council instituted the communal life of the school. Freinet's spouse Elise introduced a vegetarian diet for the boarders and day students, including – in the late 1930s – refugees from the Spanish Civil War.

Freinet identified himself as a proletarian educator, joining the French Communist Party in the 1920s and participating in rural cooperatives and teacher unions; his autonomous school in Vence, a small medieval village, founded in 1936, catered to small numbers of students of different ages many of whose parents were immigrants. Freinet believed he was operating in the Soviet Artek tradition of summer camps (with a full film studio on site) (Beattie 2002: 140) and enthusiastically participated in the youth hostelling movement. His rural location held its own dangers when reactionary forces marshalling local anti-Soviet sentiments were able to remove him from his public post in 1932–3. Freinet was also ill-adapted to pedagogical theories emanating from Paris, namely the institutional pedagogy movement that grew out of different conditions and adopted a highly theoretical language inherited from psychoanalysis. The fraught relationship between Freinet and institutional pedagogy – the latter recognized as a strand of the former, but without the focus on teaching materials, and more concerned with professional qualifications, academic research and problems of urban high schools that lacked a community – yet establishes an explicit crossover between Freinet techniques and Jean Oury's experiments with adult patients at Saumery (1949–1953) and then La Borde.[2] Experimentation necessitated by material privation is part of the standard version of this history, but so is the communist utopia of revolving intellectual and manual tasks, declassification of specialities, communitarian organization, non-hierarchical clubs, which culminates in something like the grid, the double-entry bookkeeping system that Guattari adapted to managing work assignments and durations through the categories of time and task in relation to existing role definitions (doctors, nurses, non-medical staff, patients, families, etc).

The implementation of the grid at first placed Guattari in the role of 'grid maker' (Dosse 2011: 57) and expressed his democratic centralism as an organizational principle, but one that would change over time as the system mutated and became more sophisticated, that is, less logical and rational, and more subject to distributed monitoring and decision-making. For Guattari, 'The grid is a double-entry table that allows for the collective management of individual assignments in relation to tasks. It is a kind of regulatory device for the necessary deregulation of the institution' (1998: 4). This abstract machine that is expressed on paper bears little overt relation to the printing press as a concrete object, but both are machines that articulate affects and assignments, by exposing resistances, enabling recognition of limitations, requiring negotiation, heightening shifting valorizations, and emergent singularities, towards the production of new kinds of subjectivities and the collective auto-engendering of institutional life with various degrees of formation.

Complementary forms of transversal experimentation (Guattari 2003) exist between the Freinet classes articulated around concrete machines and the collectively produced journals and newspapers and the grid at La Borde (rewriting the doctor–patient relationship), in as much as they enabled the formation of subject-groups, in addition to the multi-level communication opened up by the cooperative council that rewrote the student–teacher relationship by centring the classroom around the press itself rather than orienting itself to the teacher and his lecture podium. Individual and collective auto-engenderings of the institution do not necessarily result in archivable artefacts, but these are durable records of desiring-productions. The situation at the Oasis Skateboard Factory (OSF) is not so far removed from these concerns. The position and authority of the teacher is not decentred, but remains intact, although traditional performances at the head of the class are minimized. The presence of the founding figure also poses a quandary about succession should either he or his co-teacher Lauren Hortie depart. A similar quandary about whether anyone practises schizoanalysis may be posed after Guattari and Jean Oury's deaths.

A standard curriculum must be delivered, a daily schedule made available for parents and for purposes of transparency and accountability; occasional disciplinary problems do arise with a class consisting of around 20–25 students in the age group of 16–20 years. But the challenges faced by at-risk, marginal youth are multiple – homelessness directly and regularly affects OSF students in some measure, although the class composition of a given cohort is variegated. Grades must be assigned and submitted according to the requisite achievement level scales and learning outcomes, not even Freinet could swerve around such requirements. Yet the OSF is, as co-teacher Lauren Hortie observes (2015), 'not in a school building … There's no bell. We do not sing the national anthem'. The setting in a community centre with its diverse all-ages clientele in an impoverished neighbourhood next to a large and notorious public housing estate, social services, a pool and skating rink, as well as the lively small-food businesses outside on the sidewalk, is a far cry from a school layout in which the distance between any point on the property to the principal's office may be the measure of an alienated student's life. OSF caters to re-engagement students who are short on high school credits and cannot graduate, which does not mean that they can graduate from OSF, since they may lack credits that are not available there. As a result, only a portion of the class graduates directly from OSF each year, an event that is treated as a special honour and held at skateboard design shop Roarockit. OSF students are said to be with tenderness 'misfits' who have either dropped out of mainstream schools or are currently faltering in some manner. OSF has an enviable success rate when it comes to students earning class credits in English, art and business, but it does not offer a full range of high school subjects. The recent trend is that greater numbers of OSF students are receiving their high school diplomas from OSF.

And an entirely different 'object' mediates school life – the skateboard. The cultural status of the board remains linked with a subcultural ensemble signifying rebellion, despite its accommodations and services performed in the name of socializing youth. This is how Morrison and Hortie get 'buy-in' from the students by putting them into contact with the subculture they live, or at least emulate, and translating the conflict with law enforcers and property owners most urban boarders have experienced into a model of how to succeed in the spirit of cooperative associations; for instance, in the Student Design Team which does work with community partner–clients (like Kensington Market retailer Longboard Living) and, ultimately, by establishing sole proprietorships of some size and shape, although this is not a guarantee but a tactic of passage in adulthood. However, the 'object' is not given, preformed and readymade. It must be created from kits provided by partner Roarockit design. This is the DIY ethos at play in delicate balance with the entrepreneurial mission of the school. Yet DIY is filtered through a careful lesson plan in skateboard design and art history and technique development. There is open recognition that OSF teaches entrepreneurial skills. This is a bulwark against high youth unemployment rates. While Morrison admits 'we are really about products', he qualifies this with the observation that 'for at-risk youth, that product allows for opportunity for engagement. If you're without a product you don't have a feedback loop'. Student success is OSF success and vice versa, but this success for a large measure takes place by means of contingent arrangements with outside sponsors. Part of the public face of this success is that it is embedded in business, which is ironic, as Morrison comments: 'why this is a moment when we're popular and supported, it's because we teach business … I frickin hate business'. Hortie explains that by business what is meant is the development and marketing of a 'personal brand'. Design has the flavour less of an order word that freezes and more of a password that unthaws. For Morrison, students design their lives and worlds; they sell their boards and their services, not to mention their zines, buttons and t-shirts; they make contracts and fulfil them. They learn to pass by transforming intensity into extensivity. They are mentored by volunteers in the advertising sector, by artists and designers. For instance, a much publicized mentoring arrangement with global ad agency Anomaly in 2013 provided direct feedback about pitching proposals and business strategies (Krashinsky 2013). Yes, OSF students make products and sell them, just as Freinet did when he developed a printing press and sold it to his followers, publishing instructions in his journal on how to assemble it, and neither are anti-capitalist projects. But OSF teachers and students engage in critiques of consumerism and dominant norms, including local political issues, and gender biases in skateboarding culture.

OSF has refocused itself on deploying the skateboard as an 'engagement tool for girls', as Morrison puts it, and the gender imbalances in classes have dramatically improved from the early years that were dominated by teenage boys. A leadership project undertaken by three OSF students in 2011 ('Heels on Wheels') was funded by an external grant from Change Our World (Ministry of Education, Ontario) and was primarily educational, addressing girls' empowerment through skateboarding within the alternative school system (http://changeourworld.ca/submissions/category/9) in Toronto. The self-determined presence of young women in skateboarding magazines is still marginal, but reports about women's organizations and events are more regular, and women's histories in skate communities have been documented dating from the 1960s (Porter 2014), providing missing reference materials that can be existentially impactful.

The self-entrepreneurial subject is produced by finance capital in the wake of the evacuation of social supports, precarization and immaterialization of labour. Is the skateboard school caught up in this process? It would seem so, yet entrepreneurialism does not generate a monolithic subject, because the process that is initiated contains components that also characterize subject-groups, namely, openness and assumption of risk, and the successful confrontation with alterity; we see this in the confrontations with the enemies of the subculture in the guise of powerful civic politicians who scapegoat urban youth (skateboarders, graffiti artists, bicycle messengers, squeegee kids). The construction of the mayor as a castrating master whose blind demands and punishments one cannot evade teaches only passivity and capitulation, and does not as Guattari insists allow one to get past such 'pseudo-phallic' phantasies and gain a critical insight into the gender dynamics and economic interests structuring political life. To have the students acknowledge the socio-economic forces impinging upon their decision-making, and thus to see that they are also subjugated groups waiting to be heard, but by whom exactly remains unknown. OSF is not, of course, an analytic milieu, so these lessons are not on the table alongside the spray paint cans and tubs of wood glue, yet they are glimpsed through the many ways that social life explicitly finds its way into their classroom, and how the leading groups of 'seniors' manage it, responding by imprinting onto successes or by retreating into silence and avoidance. Early in the reign of 'crackhead' mayor Rob Ford, OSF students contributed a lively flow of street art mocking him and at least one student even built their personal brand around their pointed political critiques.

In the pages of Concrete Wave, a local Toronto magazine and OSF partner in which students have published their written and graphic work describing links between boarding and creativity ('Lost in Translation' 2012), we see an example of how consumption of style within the subculture is modified by a collective contribution that contains ideas first tried out in classroom zines and visual design exercises. Publishing in a magazine is productive work that reflects shared interests in the culture, even though writing is a challenge for many students. Connecting with the skateboarding print universe, and taking responsibility beyond an assignment, a move towards a new becoming writer was initiated by modifying their position as audience/readership – in which many of the students counted themselves and their friends – to contributor. Although this material is not re-integrated into the classroom as the foundation for lessons in the Freinet tradition, it is evidence of the strong connections that the students build with subcultural vehicles and various community organizations, for instance, the local downtown independent businesses where their non-riding boards are hung by clients as signage and wall art. A recent OSF exhibition ('Youth are Revolting') and auction of boards at the gallery space in the Gladstone Hotel combined fundraising for a school trip and school promotion of its mentorship programmes with local artists.

On any given day when class is in session at the centre of the makeshift classroom may be found a portable sawhorse, with a vise holding onto a recently glued seven-ply maple skateboard. Rough edges are hand-sanded. Running commentary is provided by fellow students. Sawdust is in the air and on the floor. Turpentine bristles nose hairs; spray paint cans, tubs of wood glue, styrofoam board moulds litter the tables. Not single desks and seating plans, but shared, movable tables. Painter's tape is being pulled off of boards at some tables, stencils refined and applied, and spray paint applied out of doors. Over in the 'kitchen' area, the toaster trips a breaker and the ancient computers crash. For certain groups, power tools are devalued and hand sanding is a preference for small-scale production. There is a story here and it has to do with prevalence of broken equipment in middle school and high school woodworking shops. Lunch suddenly appears in the hands of a student's grandmother. Some kids go out for a cigarette. A visiting graffiti artist shows up and commences work with a student on a new design. It is always quiet when exacto knives are in use. Full-scale diagrams are spread out on the tables. Portraits on bits of broken skateboards are stored in a milk carton, awaiting upcycling. The soundtrack of the classroom is scraping and sanding, with occasional bursts of music from portable personal music systems. In full swing the classroom is not centred on a teacher at the front of the room. Interactions with Morrison and Hortie are sporadic, individual and problem-based, but consultations are scheduled and progress towards set goals is emphasized and monitored. There is an unpredictable nature to the class, subject to tangents, diversions, debates, peccadilloes. Yet one-on-one consultations are taking place between teachers and artists and other guests. Projects tend to be layered and overlap. Students are taking time out to write their contributions to the school's Slo Skate Zine. Often this is a painful, academic process, but some of the students are highly skilled writers and advance rapidly. Most figure out that the desire to interview a skate or art star is risky. Requests are emailed. Anxiousness and disappointment are inevitable, but these too are usable. The best approach is to request an interview with someone they believe will respond. Non-responses are sometimes integrated into the report as badges of honour: 'As you can image, Shepard Fairey [OBEY] is currently over-booked .... Regrettably he must decline your invitation to participate.' Some connections in the skate and street art worlds are forged, questions sent, and answers read, and rewritten in a report format about a person, an organization, an event. The zine eventually comes together. The process is low-tech, classic alt-press production techniques, maybe without the waxing and porcelain rollers! Not everything is like this. OSF has a manual screen-printing station. It can screen on grip tape and offers this service through a local board shop.

A skateboard is not a printing press! There are many skateboards in various states of composition and decomposition in OSF on any given day. A skateboard is a diagram and not a code. It is exploratory, whether in production or on the street. In passing from the virtual to the actual, the diagrammatic function of the skateboard is filtered by a gamut of factors from the curriculum to its layers of veneer, but taken together they are productive of new realities. OSF itself changes in relation to the skateboards made in and for it, and for others outside, both lost and found, to force new sensations together all across the city. Every skateboard begins with a package of raw materials and is conjoined to a sketch for a brand that travels along a pedagogical passage all the way from warm-up work to the finished board and beyond into the streets or onto the walls of small shops, art galleries and private homes. Students at OSF are transmitters of a skateboard's potentialities. Their rhizomes extend well beyond the classroom's walls and are thrown outward by curricular prerogatives such as seeking sponsors for boards, negotiating designs, gaining an honorarium on sales participating in pop-up shops; or instead of cash, donations are brokered, and philanthropic giving by students or sponsor is encouraged. The entrepreneurial skills acquired at OSF do not reduce a skateboard's diagram to education as work. As Morrison observes: 'We're reframing hands-on skills so that they're not just a working class characteristic'. Freinet's critique of 'education by work' struggled against its utilitarian framing and denigration of manual labour with its 'potential for an ulterior social production' (252). Instead, he considered his goal to be 'schooling by life, for life, by work' (282), an achievement in which each child would make the school his or her own. Here, OSF wants to distinguish itself from tech-training or vocational training that overcodes social subjects as non-academic tradespeople, despite the intense machinism that crosses both work and play. The 'victory lap' phenomenon, during which local high school students take a fifth year to refocus themselves into a non-professional career, often involves a proto-apprenticeship in the trades, often with strong artisanal dimensions.

OSF focuses on materials, their manipulation and transformation into products. It plays on the myth of the one-room schoolhouse with a rented room, but its marginality is never in doubt as it still has to hope that the yearly budget process will actually guarantee that enough wood will be available to build skateboards. Let's not forget these boards are canvases for young designers. OSF is not a segregated school as it is open to the outside and has complex relations with many social scenes and actors, including major institutions. In 2012 a group of OSF students were artists-in-residence in the afterschool programme at the Art Gallery of Ontario where they staged skateboard construction workshops. This kind of relationship modifies their role as students and opens them to a variety of encounters. However, the school term, and the various deadlines that have to be met, are constraints of the skateboard diagram that set up the conditions for exploration. A new diagrammatic extension is the annual NYC school field trip, which exploits industry contacts, opportunities for pop-up shops, and fundraising.

OSF students are academically successful with high class pass rates (between 90 and 100 per cent). The courses offered across grades 9–12 in a typical slate (2015–16) include Youth and Culture Studies; Skateboard Design; Creativity and Social Entrepreneurship; DIY Media and Publishing; Street Art. These may be taken for credit in specific areas (history, geography, English, business, art) or on a credit recovery basis, in whole or in part, on an individualized basis or in a remedial cluster. These designations are part of the school board's prerogative to assist struggling students without forcing them to repeat the same courses they have already failed.

OSF helps students to take advantage of interactions with the outside and in doing so attempts to maximize its transversality and organizational complexity. Transversality is known to exist in every institution; although it is not quantified, it is a 'coefficient' that modifies local variables. As a coefficient, transversality is linked to degrees of blindness within an organization, and what it takes to calibrate it may be considered a 'tool' in its service, although Guattari was not fond of such a term. Transversality always runs up against institutional inertia – primarily with reference to school board politics around curriculum, a given cohort can choose social regression. The fact of the non-school-property location of OSF, which is seen by both teachers and students as high in transversality, also necessitates that nothing is left in place at the end of the day, limiting project continuity and therefore introducing another pressure of conformity from the outside of the community centre and its rental arrangements.

The figures of the entrepreneur and leader are deployed against inclinations to retreat from encounters with openness, with all of their contingencies, as threat management and preservation of scarce resources. Over the course of a year, and from year to year, relational configurations change and new challenges arise, while some conditions linger. The negotiation of otherness is a core requirement of success at the school, and in this it needs to be recognized that traumas do arise such as deaths within the skateboarding community in Toronto (Gillis and Powell 2012; Anderssen 2012). How such an event mobilizes the class and its sub-groups to reaffirm their existence or face decaying into subjugation in a hostile environment that lessens feelings of security will shape outcomes during that period of crisis and for some time after.

The spatial independence of the school, the flexible cultural affinities between teachers and students, the unfurling diagram of the skateboard as a means of enhancing encounters, establish new points of reference, and reduce inhibitions, while not reducing all such encounters to exchange values – although this is an ever-present monodimensionalizing threat even when it is a necessity of survival – together constitutes the transversality of the OSF. Skateboards that are not for riding but for visual and sculptural expression are not so easily captured by a skills discourse because, after all, the manual skills required to assemble a skateboard kit are not especially advanced but, instead, de-reify subcultural commodities for the students with the lesson that they can themselves make the signs of the subculture they desire; yet, skateboards retain some elements of uncontainability when and if they are put back on the streets, but always in the shifting contexts of political representations for the public control of youth subcultures. As an abstract diagram, the skateboard is not exhausted by its riding, and it is embedded in a formal and informal assemblage of teachables like street art and self-publishing, but also sharable musical, food and fashion choices, and all of the practices within the alt-arts universe including tattooing, piercing and other body modifications, and small-scale craft production (even broken boards are recycled as canvases for new expressions). As a transversal tool, skateboard subculture in the broadest sense in its academic context within OSF and beyond its walls provides students with much more than entrepreneurial self-management skills, but serves as a meta-model not only for a participatory critique of skateboard subculture, in other words, as acumen that is carried through a self-invented, creative but institutionally structured entry point into the very subculture already inhabited in a variety of ways by OSF students and teachers. Yet as Guattari (2011: 68–9) recognized, in taking into account the analyses of early education by Anne Querrien and Liane Mozere, the issue is how capitalist labour power is manufactured through compliance, acceptance and pleasure, appropriately 'tooled' (he did not mention entrepreneurism, but it is worthwhile underlining). While Guattari was ever watchful for phallocratic and other forms of repressive sexuality, at the very least it may be said that OSF not only takes a critical position on gender politics, but is less in the business of forbidding anything; however, it is probably just as guilty, and just as susceptible, on the question of how funding is used as a disciplinary device cultivating dependency on contingent windfalls. Finally, it is appropriate to think of a double re-entry at play: returning to school but also re-entering the subculture with new critical goals and conditions of contact. OSF doesn't flirt with a failure-based entrepreneurial wisdom, because most of the class has already known rejection and its deleterious consequences. Skateboards provide existential supports for subjectivity's enrichment and reinvention, yet must grapple with the calculated deployment of entrepreneurism that simultaneously threatens and promotes transversal relations with an outside that is paradoxically both active and passive in its influences; the phantasies attached to the teachers and school board must be flushed out, and the mixing of teenage molecules in the many temporary reassurances of sex, drugs, and rock and roll are full of lessons whose value is only accessible for those prepared not to evade them.

Acknowledgements

I am grateful for the invitation of Hélene Frichot to the Deleuze Camp 2015 Daughters of Chaos on the island of Utö in the Stockholm archipelago where I taught a course on 'How to Build an Institution' and presented a section of an earlier version of this chapter. The graduate students who were attending the camp lectures and credit class in transversal writing not only accepted my challenge to assemble a skateboard kit in a very compressed time frame and without really knowing one another, but also to reflect upon the exercise as an organizational event in private conversations and public demonstrations.

Notes

1 In addition to my own experiences during 2011–12, and my attendance at the 2015 fundraiser at the Gladstone Hotel 'The Youth Are Revolting', I make extensive use of an interview conducted by Ariel Fieldin and Michael Barker with OSF teachers Craig Morrison and Lauren Hortie, 'The Innovators', Notes from the Field (2015). http://notesfromthefield.ca/talking-with-teachers-in-alternative-schools/oasis-skateboard-factory/.

2 Through the diverse fields of anti-psychiatry, David Cooper's experiments in the ward known as Villa 21 in Shenley Hospital during the mid-1960s are representative of how the prospects of diffusing psychiatric roles come up against the entrenched authority of physicians, as well as demands by patients that those who provide care are qualified. Breaking what Franco Basaglia (1987) called the 'circle of power' in the psychiatric institution, in which power and aggression are internalized by doctors, passed along to nurses, and then turned against patients, requires recognition of how the cycle reproduces itself and how it may be broken through a common struggle in which there is solidarity between the 'healthy and the sick'. Basaglia's development of a staff and patient's daily assembly at the psychiatric hospital at Gorizia reduced formal distinctions by giving patients a voice, with a rotating chair selected from elected patients, and collectivized responsibility for finding solutions to a number of issues in the institution that were no longer perceived as individual. Marked by spontaneity and disorganization, the assembly helped to realize Basaglia's negation of the institution as an overturning that called it into question and forced it into crisis. The central strand that crosses anti-psychiatry, Freinet pedagogy as well as institutional pedagogy and analysis such as it was practised at La Borde, is the displacement of the authority of the doctor and teacher.

References

Acker, Victor. (2007), *The French Educator Célestin Freinet (1896-1966): An Inquiry into How his Ideas Shaped Education.* Lanham: Lexington Books.

Anderssen, Erin. (2012), 'Skateboarders becoming a force to reckon with on streets', *The Globe and Mail* (16 May).

http://www.theglobeandmail.com/news/national/skateboarders-becoming-a-force-to-reckon-with-on-streets/article4184416/

Basaglia, Franco. (1987), *Psychiatry Inside Out: Selected Writings of Franco Basaglia*, translated by N. Scheper-Hughes and Anne M. Lovel. New York: Columbia University Press.

Butz, Konstantin. (2012), *Grinding California: Culture and Corporeality in American Skate Punk*. Bielefeld: Verlag.

Beattie, Nicholas. (2002), *The Freinet Movements of France, Italy, and Germany 1920-2000*. New York: Edwin Mellen Press.

Borden, Iain. (2003), *Skateboarding, Space and the City: Architecture and the Body*. London: Bloomsbury.

Dosse, François. (2011), *Deleuze and Guattari: Intersecting Lives*, translated by D. Glassman. New York: Columbia University Press.

Fieldin, Ariel and Barker, Michael. (2015), The Innovators: Interview with Craig Morrison and Lauren Hortie, Oasis Skateboard Factory, Notes from the Field. http://notesfromthefield.ca/talking-with-teachers-in-alternative-schools/oasis-skateboard-factory/

Fine, Hunter H. (2013), 'The Skateboard Dérive: A Poststructuralist Performance of Everyday Urban Motility', *Liminalities: A Journal of Performance Studies* 9/3 (June): 1–20.

Freinet, Célestin. (1968), *La méthode naturelle 1. L'apprentissage de la langue*. Neuchatel: Delachaux and Niestlé.

Gillis, Wendy and Powell, Betsy. (2012), 'Cabbie charged in skateboarder's death', *The Toronto Star* (15 May).

http://www.thestar.com/news/gta/2012/05/15/cabbie_charged_with_murder_in_skateboarders_death.html.

Guattari, Félix. (2011), *Lignes de fuite: Pour une autre monde possible*. La Tour d'Aigues: Editions de l'Aube.

Guattari, Félix. (2003), 'La transversalité', in *Psychanalyse et transversalité: Essais d'analyse institutionnelle*. Paris: La Découverte.

Guattari, Félix. (1998), 'La grille', *Chimères* 34: 1–14.

Krashinsky, Susan. (2013), 'A different kind of school board', *The Globe and Mail* (7 December): M4.

Leafgren, Sherri. (2009), *Reuben's Fall: A Rhizomatic Analysis of Disobedience in Kindergarten*. Walnut Creek, CA: Left Coast Books.

12

The Production of an Anxiety Dream Space Machine

Eric Harper and Charity N. Mwaniki

In my history lessons I look at a map of the world, run my fingers along the surface, and stop at: Sudan, Palestine, Uganda, Zimbabwe and wonder how there aren't any open bleeding holes in the paper, wonder how the gaping wounds in the soil of these lands, lands that have been fed misery and pain, do not show up, and do not transfer onto my fingers.

Hana Aylid (2015)

Many years have passed since the politicization of madness, yet now more than ever we need Schizoanalysis so as to be alive to the signs of life lost. The apprenticeship of the signs is to be found within the howls of wretched of the earth 'I can't breathe![1]' This is the cry of life and the cry our time, the untimely call of the future within the present seen on the streets of Syria, witnessed by the 'Black Lives Matter' movement and protests around Grenfell Tower London. This is the *sign* of the madness of our times, one in which the wretched of the earth and wretched earth cannot breathe. The sacrifice of life in which the earth as a breathing machine suffocates alongside those lifeless bodies washed onto the shores of Europe while trying to seek asylum. Now the ships of modernity, which carved capitalist maps onto the earth, are transformed into the spaceships of future. Spaceships for the select few who are granted air conditioned space to breathe as the earth is turned into an alien space.

We accept that there are those who find it helpful to think of their experiences, called schizophrenia or psychosis as an illness but there are others who do not and who would like to create other kinds of spaces to breathe that sidestep the Western 'language game' of diagnosis, medication and symptom management. Once trapped within these language games of truth the person's likelihood of recover without long-term medication and continuous hospitalization is seen as improbable and implausible. These truth games are framed by the intersection of those authorities who assume the right to define what mental distress is and right to negate the ways other cultures frame madness.[2]

The problem we wish to address is the ever increasing construction of docile bodies and the chemical imprisonment of those categorized as psychotic. It is the problem of 'the increasing medicalisation of depression and suicide not only as the state's response to a perceived new public-health crisis but potentially also as the spread of a form of diffused governance that substitutes everyday commonsense categories and practices for rational and technical ones so as to vitiate the moral and political meaning of subjective complaints and protests' (Biehl, Good and Kleinman 2007: 3). The label 'psychotic or personality disorder' is to attempt to fix the place within which this body can move, think, feel and even dream. Only when the person internalizes this oppression is the work of confession and confinement complete.

None of us and all of us know what madness is, for it is just too easy to call someone mad in a casual remark or accusation, as in a burst of anger. Yet it is only a few in society who are granted the right and the power to act on your madness. Sanctioned, medicated, locked-up and turned into a numbed, docile body with a lifelong label – psychotic, borderline.

We cannot know what madness is nor do we aspire to do so, is the call of *Anti-Oedipus,* but what they do know is that when madness is transformed into mental illness or psychosis it is a form of colonization that occurs under the semblance of therapy, analysis and support. Yet we are conditioned to be on the lookout for those who deviate from the 'normal', those to be stigmatized, marginalized or contained. Isn't this also maddening? Our very own prison and fight to remain subjected to self-servitude and obey the superego and the internalized panoptical ever watchful eye/I.

Alongside this there is the everyday invitation to foreclose other cultural world views that consider what is labelled as psychotic and mental illness as something of value. For example shaman practitioners in African and Native American societies invite madness. Rituals and plants are used in ceremonies that alter states of consciousness and induce madness. Moreover 'suicide as social protest and resistance is a historical reality among Chinese. Only under the impress of the current phase of globalization is it beginning to be reinterpreted as the result of a mental disorder' (Biehl, Good and Kleinman 2007: 3).

'Producing-machines, desiring-machines everywhere, schizophrenic machines, all of species life: the self and the non-self, outside and inside, no longer have any meaning whatsoever' (Deleuze and Guattari 2003: 12), so that the shaman, I, we, present and past, ancestors are all simultaneously present and absent, the pure form and time of Aion, becoming-imperceptible. 'A pure becoming without measure, a veritable becoming mad, which never rests, it moves in both directions at once. It always eludes the present' (Deleuze 2013: 3).

The work of madness in Western and modern society is framed by paradoxical demands that destroy good sense and common sense thereby resulting in maddening spaces that drive people crazy. We ponder how a term, such as psychotic, is used as a way to control society and remove those who don't follow or understand social norms. Paradoxically it appears that, all too often, it is acts that are outside the normal that get viewed as crazy, yet at the same time everyday taken-for-granted normal acts with maddening effects do *not* get labelled as crazy. Again we ask, what is madness, who is mad and who has the right to call another psychotic and refuse asylum?

The current treatment vogue within the mental health profession is building recovery capital yet this occurs at the very moment capital is in crisis and so-called recovery resources found in the community are getting cut back, due to the austerity agenda. Many clients in crisis want safe spaces to retreat into (asylum) but the weekly agenda of psychiatric meetings is about freeing up costly bed space. There are the occasional references to staff getting attacked, in some situations stabbed, or a client who killed himself, but this increase in the number of suicides, since the cutbacks in services, is not part of the agenda. The real agenda of these meetings is to populate a flow chart so as to cover the cracks in the surface presentation. The flow chart is administered by timelines which can evidence throughout and tightly managed border control. The spreadsheet aims to decode and replace the incorporeal body and metaphysical surface, capital in the place of an ontology of suffering, thereby ensuring money is spent paying back the debt of speculative capital.

The work of madness covers the cracks through a sacrifice, making people crack and taking 'responsibility' for this breakdown. Stated another way, the fashionable covering of bare life with shamefulness is marketable when dying of shame is diagnosed as self-inflicted. The logic forcing this shameful death is a double bind that constructs a cruel nonsense that somebody is called up to embody, the sacrifice needed to uphold the sense inscribed in the ordering of things on the surface. As regards double binds, consider the example of good practice guidelines call for partnership work, especially with so-called dual diagnoses, but services are overstretched and erect barriers that stop referrals. One effect of this is an engagement in more extreme behaviour to make the gatekeepers aware of their distress. In this regard we need to ponder how the mental health process of seeking asylum, safe spaces, parallels the asylum-seeking process of trying to land on European soil!

The official policy/ideology is client consultation but in practice the person's needs are not listened to. The focus is on what risk they pose to society. What is witnessed over and over, when meeting somebody having a mental health crisis, are two questions that dominate the discussion: 'Are you taking your medication' and risk – 'Are the voices telling you to hurt anybody, are you able to say no to the voices, do you have the means to kill yourself' The focus is on treatment compliance (shorthand for taking medication and chemical imprisonment).

Addiction to prescribed medication and how this produces mental health distress while perpetually hovering as an obvious but unspoken question is erased with talk of the need for a meds review or a conclusion that 'they are treatment resistant' or 'perhaps they are personality disordered and not psychotic'. The addiction to prescribe is especially the case when people seek help from burned-out medical practitioners who need to evidence cost-cutting expenditure – referral to therapy is expensive! – or when people return from the acute wards, pumped up with drugs, usually over a week or two. When returning to the community and showing signs of agitation, one wonders if this is drug withdrawal, mental health distress or a combination of the two and/or failed respite/asylum.

Nothing changes yet everything changes as the doors close or 'they' are put onto a new regime of medication with often unforeseen side effects. What one is seeing are people adrift at sea, including the captain of the ship of fools, guided by the illusion that each new drug trial, often conducted in Africa, will offer a map. Medication without building a safety net, that is, without having access to recovery resources/community support, goes nowhere; it circulates and as Matt Lee (2016) states 'imprints itself deep into the flesh – pity the genes, cells and microbiology that are unable to escape this circulator process'.

The policy talk is one of equality and diversity yet black males in the UK have over the past thirty years received *very* different treatment compared to white men. For example, the police will get called out as the first line of treatment, followed by imprisonment. The second line of intervention – drug treatment or getting sectioned. No talk of therapy or community services and therapeutic communities as these men are bad, mad and dangerous and clearly terrorists if they are also Muslim.

None of this is unknown, the research has been known since the early 1990s yet the stigma of mad, bad and dangerous still prevails and isolates these individuals.

Services place barriers for people from non-Western cultural backgrounds and fail to understand the cultural, community and family context and use of rituals that many non-Western people use to negotiate mental distress. Traditionally mental health services have focused on benefiting those individuals who come knocking at the door asking for help and failed to engage in community outreach work. The underlying assumption is that the person is both familiar with and able to benefit from 'our way of doing things'. This alienates many marginalized people who feel held to ransom by a system of compliance that they either cannot or do not want to comply with.

There is both an ever increasing production of new symptoms – compare the number of symptoms in the first DSM to the current DSM – and an engagement of suffering through drug trials. Drugs are a cheaper form of imprisonment. Treatment by drugs is not confined to people with mental health symptoms but also includes putting those with illegal drug addictions onto a legal addiction-script. It is at this disjunctive synthesis between drugs and mental illness that the work of madness manufactures new hybrids – *contemporary construction sites of madness* – found on the streets, in the day centres, homeless hostels and prisons.

The issue of drug use consuming and rearranging the person's entire life, the life of the addict, most evident in psychological and/or physical addiction, is the *same* model of support offered to people with mental health challenges. Instead of only thinking about how drugs or alcohol use may escort or intensify mental health symptoms, should we not also be asking how can people get through the day without drugs or alcohol[3] and the loss of rituals, in other words, capital as a pure presence without break? What is it like to live in a society without moments of break, as seen in rituals and dream machines? Moreover, it is a society that prescribes drugs and alcohol as the only consumer choice in the capitalist rituals that do exist. This reconfiguration of the moments of break through the capitalist appropriation and decoding of the spaces of ritual with consumerist demands subordinates the senses of belonging. The social bond is not only linked to identification to an 'imagined community' – Benedict Anderson's nationalism – but also to the new god of capture, the virtual planes of market forces which function as site of habituation – a thoughtless process in the name of thinking – in which an organism appears to no longer respond to the repetition of stimuli within that environment. Habituation, in Deleuze and Guattari's terms, territorialization, results in a decreased response to stimuli because it has become familiar or is expected.

The front line staff will spend 60–70 per cent of their time in front of a computer screen populating a spreadsheet. The hated paperwork becomes a safe haven to hide from actually spending time with people. The paperwork enables the spreadsheets to flatten out the cracks in a similar way that the analyst hides behind the 50 minute hour and demands payment. This system can only work if practitioners consent to the codes, bar codes barring life and thoughtfulness. The ordering signifiers from the heights above as part of the organization's induction policy and the corporate model imposed on the work habits manufactory surveillance. These lifeless and depersonalized bodies replicate the habit of thinking the Others thought[4] from the heights.

Spreadsheets and collusions set ceilings about what can and cannot be thought and thought by whom. The cover story that gets constructed from this endless paperwork and therapeutic regulation is an alibi to cover up a murderous hatred projected onto those called mad, bad and sad, what Richard Klein (1995) calls a hatred of those forms of enjoyment that are not the same as mine. We are, as Foucault states in the preface to *Anti-Oedipus*, 'civil servants of Truth' and with our titles psychoanalyst, psychiatrist, social worker, mental health worker, researcher and our language mystification we impose the discourse of the master. It is this process of speaking for and speaking in the place of the other, as Chris Oakley (2006, personal communication) has noted, that drives people crazy.

> The psychotic does not think but it is the product of thought, indeed, can only have thoughts that have been implanted in him, or her, by the 'other.' Rather than being the actor on the stage he or she has become the stage on which the other's play unfolds. (Oakley 2012: 174)

The transformation of madness into psychosis is a deceptive copy that presents a surface without cracks and in so doing brackets out madness to the depths. This administrative coding creates a series – mad, bad and sad – part of a broader series, dangerous, criminal, dirty and infectious, irrational, alien, animal. Madness within this categorization is no longer an event, singularity, as it has no *life* outside of a series of binary oppositions through the construction of equivalence.[5] This social surface, sense of order, relies heavily and paradoxically upon nonsense.

The history of madness, or for that matter, homelessness forms part of the evolution of racism within the West into bio-politics. State sovereignty thus becomes 'the imperative to protect the race' (Foucault 1997: 81) from the impure, unhygienic and irrational – biological racism. The archaeology of this colonial capture is to be found in the intersectional diagram of the slave ships, ships of fools and camps of modernity, including the labelling and burning of witches.

Madness and acute anxiety go hand in hand. We concur with Haya Oakley (2003) who argues that anxiety and fear is central in the treatment of madness, the fear of the analyst and the client. The anxiety/fear of the client, practitioner, family, community and state construct madness, in much the same way that the unconscious is a group production. The intersections of these conflicting discourses shut down mental and/or physical spaces into which the person can retreat and think; instead, they impose thoughts and enforced coding.

We accept that anxiety can make my world an enclosed space without room to move, a narrowing of the breath as one swallows the codes. It is an alienated body, which in words of Fanon, can no longer question or move, become a joyful passion as Spinoza calls for. Instead of a body that invites new assemblages through its movement it becomes an organized body, one that is alienated and apart, not part of the social scene. What is foreclosed or alienated is the logic of sensation, the thought from the outside, what Freud would call primary process thinking or Bion the alpha elements in dreams This sense of alienation and self-disconnection produces a breakdown of a sense of control[6] as one enters an enigmatic and alien world of the heights and depths, in Wilfred Bion's vocabulary, a cruel and murderous superego driven by a hatred of reality producing a world filled with bizarre objects, intangible emotions and a cruel no-breast – a place where a thought could have been.

Acute anxiety is to be intensely present, a series of intensities that produce a cracking surface – for Bergson the virtual dream time that breaks with habit and invites new habits[7] – that demands immediate attention. As Deleuze's *Logic of Sense* shows us, nothing is more fragile than the surface but at the same time there is a corresponding metaphysical surface that anxiety opens onto. This is a 'pure presence without absence' (Richard Klein 1999), it is no longer the time of Chronos, but time is experienced as standing still, transfixed to the moment yet fragmenting. Paradoxically, it is catatonic yet with thoughts racing faster and faster and faster. With each failed attempt to bring about a sense of calm the speed of thought increases and produces unforeseen associations which jump and break with the conventional linguistic pathways that allow ideas not held before. This involves a temporary break, a kind of pure memory/dream space that is not fixed but which expands,[8] a florid state of engagement with another time and reality that alienates the person from others and which often makes it impossible for him or her to get through the day and manage practical tasks.

We 'enter the storm' 'carved into the depths of the bodies' which create with 'breath-words' and 'howl-words' that are tonic, an 'organism without parts'

(Deleuze 2012: 101), a body without organization. From speech to voice, sounds, phonemic letters, the esoteric and portmanteau ear and I/eye that transports one into what Laing calls inner space. The body is consumed, no longer eating or sleeping or cared for and isolated, while the mind is engaged and active. The result is a meltdown of the individual's capacity to function as society requires and demands. That is, suspended/frozen in action with thoughts moving a thousand miles a minute. In the body, with the limbs that never moved an inch, for the whole hour that went by in a flash, a moment missed, that was never registered by the mind but recorded by the universe.

The person is as fascinated and transported by what he or she can *see* or *smell* as by what he or she can *hear* or *taste* or *touch*; to be is defined by *voice* and *eyes*, *skin* and *noise*, the blurring of discursive and non-discursive process, the primacy of the statement and visibility which at the same time is irreducible to representation as Deleuze outlines in his embrace of Foucault's intimacy and compassion for madness. It is to enter a foreign and strange world of the depths that are marked by invasiveness and a sense of depersonalization, pre-individual singularities, yet at the same time, as noted by Richard Klein (2000) there is a personal sense of involvement in the surrounding events which signify something, some kind of sign, but with no precise sense.

This state of acute anxiety is often accompanied by a metamorphosis of one's surroundings, the becoming animal-spirit, pig-spirit, god's whore, and sun-ray, to 'dismantle the face' (Deleuze 2005: 13) with the screaming mouth which is 'the hole through which the entire body escapes' (Deleuze 2005: 19) – from the logic of sense to the logic of sensation. One response to the metamorphoses is agitation, a restless pacing up and down the depths in which the body tries to find a sign of guarantee, perhaps the father or a yellow pot or seagull with a message, on the lookout, like a tic, parasitic, for something, anything, like alcohol, food, sex, the organized delusion, anything, to take these feelings away and distract one. In this scenario alcohol, self-medication, slowly dismantles the present, as do other drugs like heroin – an 'extraordinary hardening of the present … one lives in two times, two moments' (Deleuze 2012: 179). There is a slowing down of thinking, thought, taking us to another place, space, in which one can intensely be somewhere else. Illicit drugs and alcohol often partner madness, for intoxication does the work of grammar, the copula, enabling some kind of social bond.

To find the connection that is lost, where thoughts overflow, where the mind is a landscape of wonderings and the body seems abandoned, foreign, jacked.

There is now anxiety to desperately bring into operation, production these now separate, disconnected things, fragmented selves, mind-machine and body-machine. Simultaneously in the past and the future, the time of Aion, without the burden of the present, a time where all possible worlds exist simultaneously. Alcohol use in the end was the only way R.D. Laing could endure the cracks of life for he could address step three in the AA resentments.

Another response to anxiety is the transformation of cracks and wounds, Bousquet's and Nietzsche's refusal of resentment, docility, the call of life, vitality. Nietzsche scorns the self-deception of those who assert a sense of superiority over that which conquers them and in so doing denies vitality, life. Opposing this and following Spinoza and Nietzsche anxiety is no longer flight or fight response, but 'lines, planes or bodies' (Spinoza 1987: 98) of escape that involves a transversal of the codes of governance, a site of intensity that explodes apart, taken-for-granted, represented with maps of intensity that strive to increase the body's power of acting by forming new assemblages. Anxiety as a form healing metamorphosis, the metamorphosis[9] and movement from and between molar into molecular and molecular into molar, simultaneous, joined and forever apart, as seen in the Mobius strip, in which the surface/depth and inside/outside are the same. This transversal and eternal is the same for the surface/depth, inside/outside. This transversal and eternal repetition, metamorphosis of molar into molecular and vice versa, is what creates the cracks of breath.

Within the phenomenological tradition, for example Medard Boss and Rollo May who follow Kierkegaard, anxiety involves a beyond, the unsettling or even destroying of the present security, which gives rise to the tendency to deny the new potentiality, a dizziness when confronted by the revelatory possibilities that take one outside the comfort zone. The uncanny re-birthing for Otto Rank and Eastern philosophy that invites a tuning, into another order of complexity. Anxiety is no longer a closed space but the reality of freedom as a potentiality before this freedom has materialized. A new possible assemblage, but this very possibility involves a rearrangement of container and content and the relations of the part to the whole, one in which 'the subject of the Search is finally no self' (Deleuze 2008: 84). The cells and vessels of the search of anxiety, its incommensurability and non-communication, are 'distances, but distances that fit together and intersect' (Deleuze 2008: 84).

Dream space like anxiety provides a potential deterritorializing, a refusal of representation and vertical hierarchies. In Foucault's reading of Binswanger he points out that the dream is space in which we are most alone, but this private space, retreat, is protected, in that it is always, and can only ever be, a solitary experience not corrupted 'If you're trapped in the dream of the Other, you're fucked' (Deleuze). Hijacking a dream and turning it into a nightmare like the space on Cable Street, 12 Cable Street: what was initially proposed as a museum of women's history became an attraction about Britain's most notorious murderer of women. The entrance has blue plaques that are fake English Heritage signs 'commemorating' suspected culprit George Chapman and the fourth victim, Elizabeth Stride. This is the building that was once owned by Ali until 2012 and photographed by Christian Petersen. 12 Cable Street has been in the news since its open dates with protests and demonstrations.

For Foucault (1992: 35) the problem with psychoanalysis is that the dream image is exhausted by interpretation and the 'morphological structure, the space in which it deploys itself, its temporal rhythm of development, the world which it bears with it, all count for nothing if they are not allusions to meaning. In other words, the language of the dream is analyzed only in its semantic function.' The dream beauty illustrates the process of the fold, the folding and unfolding of those lines imprinted on the flesh thereby allowing a molecular movement between the world of affect, sensations and un-thought concepts – maps crafted with diagonal lines. There is a metamorphosis in which any dominant monad – majority thought or molar element – soon finds itself confronted by the minor elements, the obscure details of the dream that disentangle attempts to organize the dream space with vertical hierarchical points of view.

Dream spaces offer us a movement from a passive place, diminished power of action, a 'sad passion' to an active state of becoming, the possibility of a beyond, a crossing. They are always at the border, spaces that open and close simultaneously, a way of going into an event, to take one's place in it as a way of becoming something other, present and absent, young and old, at the same time.

The anxiety dream wakes you up as does any big dream! Bion correctly states it is within the analytic session that analyst and client must dream. This is to echo the importance of dreamtime and dream spaces, something long known in non-Western societies. When somebody presented hearing voices it was understood in Xhosa culture as a calling of the ancestors. As such they needed to undergo a rite of passage and become a healer (*sangoma*). Their sense of self during this journey was an assemblage of the person, the family, community and ancestors and there was a positive value and status attached to this rite of passage (as opposed to a knee-jerk anxiety/fear-based reaction resulting in the chemical imprisonment of the person), one in which the person felt supported by the community and non-anthropomorphic and thereafter held a usual function in the society. Sadly in the colonization of Africa the medical model and human-centred world view has for the most part replaced this rite of passage, except in some rural areas.

Psychoanalysis as a revolutionary machine has failed as it cannot count beyond 4 – mother, father, child, phallus/signifier – yet now more than ever we need to befriend dream machines without interpretation. A dream space is a liminal state and transversal that invites an altered state of conscious which is in-between dream and waking consciousness. The location of dream space is similar and different to Foucault's heterotopia, a space that is often connected with temporal discontinuities that can either involve a break with the time of Chronus or involve the time of Aion, linked to the time of festival.

Dream space can function as a laboratory, experimentation,[10] a radical way of experiencing your own world, being alive to yourself and life through a 'joyful passion' of thoughts, sounds, images, sensations, smells that invite an increase in the movement, the speed and slowness, longitude and latitude of the multiple plateaus. One potential outcome is the unfolding of creative space in which the dreaming body can move, question, play and dream, as opposed to 'existing' as a representation. The dream space can only produce when there is a refusal of representation, history, myth or language, as the productive molecular elements are always in excess of any history, myth, archetype and narration and drive beyond the reality principle or language. This does not mean that dream spaces ignore history, myth or language, they obviously do not, they use these, but as sensations, lines, sounds, smells, tastes, colours, that shade in and dance across with other moving bodies; force fields that shape maps that open onto other maps, spaces. Mental and/or physical spaces into which people can retreat and play. If a dream space has any kind of language it is what Guattari calls the asignifying one that refuses and resists a grammar that structures and codifies experience according to social convention. The dream space is a site of experimentation with a life force which unfolds within a plane of immanence as opposed to submitting to a transcendent ordering principle.

Dreams and dream spaces, like art, create percepts[11] and affects that produce sensations, affects, and intensities in attunement with concepts that are provocations and respond to the wall, the problem of docility. This creative deterritorialization is akin to Winnicott's transitional space, where things come to pass, on the border between images, words, sounds, smells, colours and thoughts, a border that is imperceptible, as Deleuze and Guattari (2004) put it, but always multiple, never simply this or that. Winnicott speaks of transitional space as the simultaneous experience of me and not-me but he does not go far enough as the disjunctive always includes an AND – mother *and* child, child *and* teddy, dream *and* awake, sleep *and* image *and* smell *and* sounds *and* the herd of animals – a kind of flow where things come to pass, evolve, transform, take shape and slip into one image among others.

Dreams and dream spaces are the last escape from violence. The loss of the capacity to dream is to be caught up in the Other's dream, an invasive representation of the present that fixes the body and imprints itself on the flesh. We should not only focus on what the dream spaces communicate but instead enjoy its creation, resistance. This is a spatial act and a site of movement that frees life from what imprisons it – these habitual modes of operation and perception, a body without organs, without organization or dominance of one organ. What is radical is the movement, the flows, the unfolding of the dream space-time, hence the need to observe the way the dream and dream space hopefully changes over time, with new images, stories, sensations. Being (difference) and time (repetition) play in the dream. This flow is sister to anxiety which is why we have anxiety dreams and why there is anxiety about collective dreams of political groups, as with one of the groupings to have formed around the police killings in the United States who uses the name Dream, a collective call to '*have a dream*' or '*imagine a world*' earth that can breathe air not contaminated by the codes of capital.

Dreams resonate through our sensory being and reverberate right through our waking moments. Images go beyond language and representation through a regimen of signs. A captivating flow of images calls to us, our-primal-animal-selves which for Elisabeth Grosz 'produce and generate intensity, that which directly impacts the nervous system and intensifies sensation' (Grosz 2008: 3) and territorialize and continually frame and reframe through our imaginings.

Attempts to only understand the dream world through representation kills the dream space. Pallasmaa (2005) traces vision historically within Western culture and privileging the eye over the other senses linking it to power, knowledge and ethics. This, Pallasmaa argues, places the eye as narcissistic and nihilistic, in which the dominance of vision tends to fixate and totalize. This follows Bachelard (1964) who notes that poetry engages all the senses bringing us back to the present, the happening, so as to furnish us with a body of dispersed images at the same time.

Gaston Bachelard's *Poetics of Space* calls for a living of the poem when we read it (Bachelard 1964: xxvii) and an opening to the image without any psychological reductionism. By living the poem we read, we have salutary experience of emerging. To live the poem is a creative challenge, a process that involves developing new habits which include the forgetting of our rationalistic learning. The poetics of space for Bachelard is encountered through daydreaming so that 'images touch the depths before it stirs the surface' (Bachelard 1964: xxiii). It is the primitiveness through poetry and not the detailed description of space that stirs in our daydreams.

There are many examples of spontaneous and organized dream spaces. A dream space or anxiety dream machine can be found in many shapes and sizes when the becoming-imperceptible comes with the 'pure relations of speed and slowness' (Deleuze and Guattari 2004: 297) between bodies, particles and molecular movements and brings about deterritorialization as seen with the dreamachine.[12]

Dream spaces of escape that bring us back to ourselves by allowing us to dream, like Ali's Place that was located on Cable Street till 2012. For about thirty years Ali's Place served tea and *khat*[13]/*qat* to regulars in East London (such spaces are also called *Mafrish* or *khat* shop), an area that has a historical connection to Somali and Yemeni sailors working the docks of East London. Ali's Place was named so by photographer Christian Petersen as the space/shop didn't have a name earlier. Petersen documented the space and got to know the men who frequented this space and their strong friendships and affection for one another. Until 2013, before the ban on *khat/qat*, spaces such as Ali's Place were all over the UK; mostly, men from Yemen, Somalia, Ethiopia, Iran, Libya – to name a few – socialized here.

The *Mafrish* cafe has a twin function: it provides people with access to *khat* – a form of self-medication – and at the same time enables people to coexist, to be in pain but also be in relationship with others. This ritual space enables them to live with their pain, something that is especially difficult when people feel homeless, especially those who've endured war and torture. It is a refuge in the face of been driven mad and having come from a brutal and traumatic war and epistemic violence attached to the asylum-seeking process. These dream spaces enable the person to establish a paradoxical social bond without going mad, a rite of passage constructed by the community.

Such spaces are now hard to find as they have become illegal after *khat* was banned in September 2014 and classified as a Class C drug. But isn't it 'crazy' that alcohol and nicotine, which are more addictive than *khat*, cause more harm and cost the National Health Service (NHS) more, are not considered bad for society? Isn't it 'mad' and frightening that this space, like Ali's Place, that produced recovery capital is now foreclosed? It is a cost-effective treatment option and provides a space that helps those seeking asylum. We call for communal dream spaces for 'the true container is not the cup but the sensuous quality, the flavour' (Deleuze Proust and Signs 200: 78). Bion approximates this with the concept of alpha function in dreams. This kind of machine is a 'production of partial objects, fragments without totality, vessels without communication ... if dreams appear in this group it is by their capacity to telescope fragments, to set different universes in motion and to cross, without annulling enormous distances' (Deleuze Proust and Signs 2000: 97).

In conclusion, madness is never one thing, but a moment among other moments. Many of these moments are ordinary in the everyday normative sense, but one of these extraordinary moments is a waking dream state. Dream space aims to open[14] up new connections, assemblages, for example, the peer support approach by the Hearing Voices Network. The alternative to a social embrace of this is having no space to breathe, a terrifying acute alienation, isolation, disconnection and trauma. Madness becomes a sad passion and psychotic hell when it remains trapped within an enclosed 'black hole' of disconnection. The failure to provide a witness, read the signs, leaves the person at sea within the fragments of the waking dream as her communication is rejected or ignored by the community as simply psychotic talk and not seen as a dream process trying to undergo some kind of transformation.[15]

The work of madness invites movement in the face of confinement and alienation. It is a movement from alienation to the love the alien hence it is closely connected to the way that a dream space is often experienced as something uncanny. As Matt Lee (2016 personal communication) points out, the alien always affirms a double life – virtual and actual, conscious and unconscious, reactive and active, individual and collective – which is to say, is always multiple. However, when this enforced encounter is contained by the Western history of negation, master and slave, it is appropriated, or worse colonized by external impingements.

The thread between what is alien and alienating lies along the lines of a body and it is here that the life of the organism can turn on itself. The body is 'that which questions' and whose entire existence is continually put into question and when that is constricted by containment it 'forecloses the question of existence and in doing so prevents "life" from flourishing by choking the breath out of the body' (Lee 2016).

Following the work of Sunny Tsai we embrace Nietzsche and Zhuangzi invitation to think alongside snakes, fishes, birds, snakes, the wind, butterflies and other pipes of the earth, the pre-individual. Once upon a time, Chuang Chou (Zhuangzi) dreamt he was a butterfly, fluttering hither and thither and he was conscious only of his happiness as a butterfly, unaware that he was Chou. Upon waking he did not know whether he was then a man dreaming he was a butterfly, or whether he is now a butterfly, dreaming he is a man. Between the human and a butterfly there is necessary difference and its repetition, which is an instance of the thought from the outside, the transformation. Richard Klein (2010) following Lacan responds to Chuang-tzu butterfly with the surrealism proposes that it is not so much the making of poems as the transformation of men into living poems. The fluttering wings and splashes of colour are in the words of Sunny Tsai the stillness within the running water, knowing the stillness is also flow, a place free of the baggage of capitalist that suffocates us and instead open to the intoxication of the waters of life.

The problem of Zhuangzi and the butterfly can be either/both how to dream twice, or/and how to wake up twice, to be sober twice: waking up from a dream by dreaming or/and starting dreaming by waking up again. The twice dreaming/waking makes a repetition with difference, a habit between two habits. Is it a habit to be able to be mindful of the crossing, of the flow between flows? There is surely a stillness of the running water, an awareness that is aware of both states, and the betweenness. There is not only this or that habit, this or that addiction, but also the betweenness, what is between two addictions, when the waking up, the dreaming is felt in its flowing instead of immersed in flows that are actually static, intoxication that is an habit but no longer intoxicating or transforming. To be between lines, between structures, the emergencies and endings of structures. It takes so many waking-ups and so many dreamings, but what makes the difference is what is in between. To become living poems. Poetry does not exist in one line or the other but in between lines. One should not try too hard to become one line. But the point is to become the resonance of lines, the leap before habit, the quietness inside a flow (Sunny Tsai, personal communication).

Notes

1 The last words of Eric Garner 14 July 2014, Staten Island, New York.

2 The experience of hearing voices among different cultures, as Tanya Luhrmann discovered, involves significant cross-cultural differences https://newrepublic.com/article/119017/schizophrenia-experience-and-symptoms-differ-between-cultures

3 What they do not tell you at rehab is that addiction will not stop until capitalism is transformed. Addiction is central to the workings of market forces.

4 In the place of thoughtfulness we have the contracting and expansion of market forces into physical and psychological habits resulting in a pandemic of thoughtlessness – a 'process without a subject' which for Althusser is an ideological condition. (Louis Althusser – translated by Ben Brewster – *Montesquieu, Rousseau, Marx. Politics and History*. Verso Books 1972 page 185). This thinking habit normalizes the repetition of the frames of capital which in turn affects what we think.

5 Nietzsche's struggle in many ways anticipate the dual diagnostic categorization that many young men and women in London find themselves subjected to. Were he alive today he would have been strongly encouraged to substitute any illegal drug use for script comprising antipsychotics and/or mood stabilizer and any hint of opiates, using on top, would have resulted in him been placed him on a methadone script. Bombed out and only able to surface at about midday, for these drugs are merciless, he would have then been encouraged to go to a day centre. At best he might have been asked by some well-meaning alienist (old term before psychiatrist came into existence) what is it about him that is causing him to isolate himself and feel alienated.

6 What frightens many people who hear voices is not what the voices tell them but the lack of control over the voices. Moreover, not everybody who hears voices finds this a negative experience.

7 This idea came about through a conversation with Charlotte Williams Foster who is working on Bergson, Deleuze and Whitehead's conception of habit.

8 Ibid.

9 Frankie Macey (personal communication) points out that Kafka understood the metamorphosis of the dream in ways that Freud was unable to.

10 Freud consulting room ends up as a dream space, one comprised of man, dog and ancestral signs of the depth, his archaeological objects. This is Freud who now turns to the Wolf and no longer has the wolf turn to man.

11 See Deleuze On Philosophy in *Negotiations*.

12 Artists Brion Gysin and William S. Burrough along with Ian Sommerville created the dreamachine. 'The purpose of the Dreamachine is to stimulate imagination, image formation and visionary experience … with the intention of disseminating the design widely to "bring about a change of consciousness in as much as it throws back the limits of the visible world and may indeed, prove that there are no limits"', Dream Machines, National Touring Exhibitions (2000). Dreamachine prototypes were made in 1960 and instructions for making the machine were published in 1962 in the *Olympia* magazine. Made out of cylinder cardboard with cut-out slots placed on a record player with a light bulb in the centre tuning at 78 rpm, Dreamachine is 'viewed with the eyes closed: the pulsating light stimulates the Optical nerve and alters the brain's electrical oscillations…. It is claimed that

using a dreamachine allows one to enter a Hypnagogic. This experience may sometimes be quite intense, but to escape from it, one needs only to open one's eyes' (Wikipedia).

13 *Khat* is a plant, an amphetamine-like stimulant; when the leaves and stem are chewed it is said to cause excitement, loss of appetite and euphoria.

14 As another example of opening up space see the 'Open Dialogue' approach which is an innovative approach getting used in Finland.

15 For example in a project for people diagnosed as both psychotic and having a drug addiction, it was only when staff began to understand that there were moments when speaking to them that Mr M was dreaming while awake that they opened up the possibility of a productive transformation. They began to understand that he was using the dream in a similar way to art image, to communicate something very real, causing him terrible distress but also inviting life and transformation.

References

Aylid, H. (2010), *Scarf Magazine – Freedom to Wonder*. London.

Bachelard, G. (1964), *Poetics of Space*. London: Orion Press.

Biehl, João Guilherme, Good, Byron and Kleinman, Arthur. (2007), *Subjectivity: Ethnographic Investigations*. Berkeley: University of California Press.

Deleuze, G. (1995), *Negotiations*. New York: Columbia.

Deleuze, G. (2005), *Francis Bacon: The Logic of Sensation*. London: Continuum.

Deleuze, G. (2008), *Proust and Signs*. London: Continuum.

Deleuze, G. (2012), *Logic of Sense*. London: Bloomsbury.

Deleuze, G. and Guattari, F. (2003), *Anti-Oedipus*. London: Bloomsbury.

Deleuze, G. and Guattari, F. (2004), *A Thousand Plateaus: Capitalism and Schizophrenia*. London: Continuum.

Foucault, M. (1994), 'Dream, Imagination and Existence', in Michael Foucault and Ludwig Binswanger (eds), *Dream and Existence: Studies in Existential Psychology and Psychiatry*. Edited by Keith Hoeller. New York: Humanities Press.

Foucault, M. (1997), *The Politics of Truth. Hermeneutics of the Self*. Edited by Sylvere Lotringer and Lysa Hochrorth. Los Angeles: Semiotext(e).

Foucault, M. (1997), *Technologies of the Self*. In *Ethics, Subjectivity and Truth. Essential Works of Michael Foucault*. Edited by Paul Rabinow. The New Press.

Foucault, M. (2003) *Society Must be Defended. Lectures at the College De France, 1975-76*. Penguin Books.

Grosz, E. (2008), *Chaos, Territory, Art, Deleuze and the Framing of the Earth*. New York: Columbia University Press, p. 3.

Klein, R. (1999), *Personal Communication*. London.

Klein, R. (2000), *Personal Communication*. London.

Kelly, R. (2015), *Black Rainbow: How Word Healed Me – My Journey Through Depression*. Publisher: Hodder & Stoughton.

Oakley, H. (2003), *Personal Communication*. London.

Oakley, C. (2006), *Personal Communication*. London.

Oakley, C. (2012), 'Where did it all go Wrong,' in *R. D. Laing 50 years since the Divided Self Herefordshire*, PCS BOOKS, Limited.

Pallasmaa, J. (2005), *The Eyes of the Skin: Architecture and the Senses*. London: Wiley-Academy.

Spinoza, B. (1987), *Ethics*. Hertfordshire: Wordsworth.

wikipedia https://en.wikipedia.org/wiki/Dreamachine#cite_note-4

13

The Relationship inside the Psychiatric Institution between the Clinic and the Politics of Emancipation, according to Félix Guattari: The Experience of 18Up

Katerina Matsa

Daphni. The vast asylum with 2,500 mental patients under treatment, the 'cuckoo's nest' of post-Junta Athens. Big walls separate it from its surroundings. Locked doors, patients tied with bands or even chains onto their beds, 30–40 people crammed in each room, deplorable conditions of health and nutrition. Some pavilions look like concentration camps. 'Pavilion 11, an absolute horror: 95 people, some completely naked, others dressed up, screaming': this is what Félix Guattari wrote in his *Journal of Leros*, when he visited Daphni on his way back from Leros, in the context of a vast European programme of deinstitutionalization. The ambience is marked with an excessive, despicable violence, directed against helpless patients.

At the Athens State Mental Hospital in Daphni, later relabelled as Psychiatric Hospital of Attica, an 'institution of violence', a radical venture was undertaken in the 1980s: the creation of '18 Ano',[1] a project where the clinical and the political were to be intrinsically interrelated and the therapeutic praxis was to be, among other things, also political in nature. The goal was to create a groundbreaking centre for alcohol and drug treatment, in the aftermath of the ideas of May 1968, on the basis of Claude Olievenstein's psychoanalytic view of drug addiction, and taking as a model Félix Guattari and Jean Oury's La Borde clinic. Initially, '18 Ano' was a pavilion just like any other within the psychiatric hospital, its only difference being that its population consisted of alcoholics and drug addicts.

In this pavilion, during the 1980s, a novel – for Greek standards – therapeutic proposal was formulated in order to confront addictions on the basis of psychotherapy and art; this was a proposal to articulate therapy and the political, treating therapy as an act of emancipation. This was also the time when the 'community of therapy' model, such as 'Ithaki', which functioned on behaviourist principles, was promoted by the then PASOK government and the media as a panacea.

For the founding group of 18 Ano in which I participated, as a young psychiatrist back then, having just returned from France, Félix Guattari was a constant source of inspiration. Guattari was a revolutionary, an anti-Stalinist, an admirer of Leon Trotsky's *My Life*, a militant, for some time, in a small Trotskyist group, an active participant in the revolutionary event of May 1968, and at the same time a collaborator of the great psychiatrist Jean Oury at the La Borde clinic; he was a fervent supporter of institutional psychotherapy, a political activist and a psychoanalyst; and, to use Gilles Deleuze's expression, he was a constant reference for a politicized minority of psychiatrists.

As Jean-Claude Pollack (2007) puts it, Guattari was always a supporter of minorities and of becoming-minority, against all norms, political or others. His everyday life was a constant back and forth between activism and therapy. Guattari was against the authority of the expert who is supposed to hold the privilege of knowledge, against limiting oneself in the strict competences and roles of the nurse, the psychologist or the psychotherapist, against medical authority, against corporatism among the workers, against all hierarchical structures. He was always open to the unexpected, the Event.

All these features played a major part in the arduous process of transforming the old Pavilion 18 of '18 Ano' into a model clinic, as Guattari himself characterized it in his *Journal of Leros*:

> And like a *deus ex machina* or a happy end, here we are in a model clinic for thirty drug addicts and alcoholics. Director Mrs. Katerina Matsas set it up out of nothing fifteen years ago. The interior walls were built and painted by the personnel and the patients. Here, all methods of individual and collective therapy are used: music, psychodrama, relaxation techniques. (Guattari 2015: 57)

A small revolution was required in order to change things in the field of the clinical treatment of drug addiction. Everyday life was organized around the Collective Group (Le Collectif), in which all patients and therapists participated (we called it the 'Clinic Group'). The role of therapist was acknowledged to anyone who worked, in any way whatsoever, in the clinic, from the chief psychiatrist to the janitor. Many intense discussions were required in order for the nursing personnel to accept to abandon the white outfit, the trademark of the asylum, and operate on a basis of equity, out of the common hierarchical structure. Much hard work was also required in order to change the outlook of the place: paint it, put curtains, tablecloths, vases for flowers, organize a common lunch for everyone involved, use of forks and knives – and not just spoons for every kind of food, as was the common practice around the psychiatric hospital – let the patients' beloved little dogs and kittens walk freely around the premises, create a general therapeutic ambience, and make this transitional space 'good enough', as Winnicott put it. That is, a space with clear limits that the drug addicts and alcoholics under treatment could accept precisely because they know that these limits are there to protect them.

In this public and free facility, services of actual *care* were provided to addicted persons, both drug addicts and alcoholics, who were now able to integrate themselves into the therapeutic process. For the first time, as a result of many struggles, addicted persons were acknowledged as subjects capable of taking decisions for themselves – and not destined to have parents, prosecutors or psychiatrists decide for them – about their treatment and their lives. The emphasis was put on the notion of the therapeutic relation and the therapeutic continuum. The chain of command, medicalization and standard descriptions of duties were abolished in practice. Everyone and everything within this context were to serve the multifarious needs of the person that suffers and asks the facility for help. Role complementarity became a way to bring therapists closer to one another, and to permit them to develop bonds with the patients too. Many thematic groups were also integrated into the process of therapy: pottery, dance therapy, primitive expression, individual and collective psychotherapy, poetry and theatre. Therapy was not reduced to a simple administration of the psychic material, nor was it in itself a work of art. However, according to Guattari, it did have to evolve in developing the same kind of creativity that characterizes Art.

Treatment had been 'drug-free' from day one, using no medicines or placebos. Psychiatric medication was used very rarely, under a psychiatrist's close supervision, only in cases where there was a coexistent severe psychopathology.

All groups operated within a 'constellation of group', as Guattari put it, producing important therapeutic work. This is because the process of therapy, the treatment process, is also *political* in nature, and may be interpreted as an act of emancipation, since addiction is the pathology of freedom par excellence.

Art has been from the very beginning a catalyst in this process of emancipation. In its dialectical relation with treatment within the therapeutic context, Art gives access to the imaginary and the symbolic, thus contributing to the production of a new subjectivity, emancipated from the chains of addiction or from any other form of bondage.

'Playful and creative experience through visual arts, music, theatre or dance is the main form of communication between therapists and patients. Art-Therapy is a verbal and symbolic experience of the self, in the protected and safe context of the relation' (Duchastel 2005: 30). Art-therapy creates new universes of reference, contributing thus to the production of a plural and multivocal *subjectivity*, according to Bakhtin. The cornerstone of life in the therapeutic context is the Collective that organizes everyday life and gives meaning to the clinical praxis. Says Guattari (2000: 69):

> By means of these transversal tools [*clefs*], subjectivity is able to install itself simultaneously in the realms of the environment, in the major social and institutional assemblages, and symmetrically in the landscapes and fantasies of the most intimate spheres of the individual. The reconquest of a degree of creative autonomy in one particular domain encourages conquests in other domains – the catalyst for a gradual re-forging and renewal of humanity's confidence in itself starting at the most miniscule level.

Of course, Guattari is talking here about the subjectivity of the group, not about an Ego or a Superego. Subjectivity is always transindividual, not individual. Its production is interlinked with the conquest of collectivity, and it forms the main goal of the therapy. In the clinical praxis, the content of the term 'therapy' is posited as a Foucauldian 'care of the self'. The addicted persons are asked to assume for themselves the care of their selves, to become able, through their treatment, to function not just as subjects of the therapeutic process, but as social subjects too.

The Collective Group organizes all relations and interactions between therapists and patients, the encounters between active and interactive subjects. Life in the therapeutic context bears the mark of psychoanalysis, dialectics and Marxism. This is not psychoanalysis understood as a rigid edifice, but, in Guattari's words, as an elucidation of the social and cultural dead ends in which, and against which, we fight. The discourse uttered is therapeutic, but also political, ideological, thoroughly anti-institutional.

Everything happening in this context has a meaning that needs to be found collectively, and becomes a question for the whole team, which is aware of course that there is also something beyond meaning, something that will be forever elusive.

The group is constantly faced with the danger of activism for activism's sake, which tends to reproduce itself as a reaction against the absolute inertia of the 'total' psychiatric institution, as Goffman labelled it, and the typical passivity of addiction.

The subject-group, as defined by Guattari, within the institution of 18 Ano has a perspective, a world view, a task to perform, as well as important imaginary dimensions. In practice, it becomes able to make its actions meaningful in its own way, to resist in its functioning all the inclinations to institutionalization that exist in every institution, to be active and participate in the forming of new ideas and practices, fulfilling thus its desires. The subject-group utters its own speech about everything that happens in its context, in a constant interaction with the social and cultural environment. The subject-group must also be able to act as a subject of history, through its own emancipatory action. Thus, in May 1999, during the NATO bombing of Yugoslavia, 18 Ano therapists and patients of the social rehabilitation phase of treatment travelled to Belgrade in order to carry humanitarian aid (medicines and first-aid materials) and make their cultural intervention at the Belgrade Institute of Mental Health, where therapists and patients from both institutions painted together on the same canvases, expressing thus their creative imagination amid the bombardments.

The subject-group is in constant dialogue with all the different groups within the therapeutic context, articulating all the particular activities in a total subversive act, open-ended and aimed at transcending social alienation, of which an extreme form is drug addiction. Since its foundation, 18 Ano has been populated by groups that brought together therapists and patients, groups of therapists (personnel) and groups of patients (psychotherapy, drama therapy, occupational therapy, photography, sports training, art, etc.)

Collective functioning and a spirit of emancipation in a department of the Daphni asylum was back then a bright spot amid the surrounding darkness: internment, locked doors, isolation, suppression through psychiatric drugs (usually, in enormous quantities) or through mechanical enchainment, an absolute neglect of patients, psychiatrists self-content in their authoritative monologues, and lonely, unhappy and usually violent nurses acting as guards of the patients. According to Guattari (2015: 108), every group has a *manifest* content that has to do with the coordinators, the subjects and the attitudes of the members of the group, and a *latent* content that must be constantly decoded.

Transcending the dichotomy of verticality and horizontality, Guattari (2015: 112–13) refers to a *transversality* that has to do with the communication between different levels and directions. The 'coefficient of transversality' is low when communication is only formal, and high when communication is real, authentic.

A high coefficient of transversality has a decisive impact on the institution, influencing in a positive way the climate, the exchanges, its real mode of operation. Transversality exists only in the subject-group, which assumes the meaningfulness of its own acts, and resists any inclination to fixate itself on the social map, any predisposition towards stereotyping, repeating itself. The space in which it moves and from which it draws the meaning of its acts is the space of risk, the space of the *socius* and the imaginary, where new ideas and practices are gestated and born, or rejected and left to die; the space of the rhizome, where all certainty about the present, the past and the future emerges and explodes as well.

It follows that the subject-group has a revolutionary potential, though it may lose it at any time, becoming thus a subjugated group *(groupe-asujettie)*; yet the opposite is also possible.

This is why the subject-group has to be broadly open 'onto the socius and the Cosmos' (Guattari 2000: 60). Its members must be tied to each other, so as to secure maximum cohesion for the group, to develop maximum solidarity, and at the same time to become increasingly different from themselves. The very functioning of the group must be an ongoing process of bringing forth the singularity of each member (Guattari 2000: 61), the singularity of the person, which the therapist must respect, listen to and try to communicate with as he or she accompanies them during their therapeutic process.

The subject-group is always faced with the danger of its 'bureaucratic sclerosis', in Guattari's words. This can happen when it unknowingly turns to dispositions that are opposed to transversality. For transversality is the support of the group's desire, the place of the unconscious of the Subject of the Group. The danger is escaped when the meaning that emerges within the group is faced with the non-meaning, the absence of meaning, death, becoming thus the group's driving force for an activity that has nothing to do with death and everything to do with life.

A central aspect of the therapeutic process is psychotherapy within the therapeutic context, the so-called institutional psychotherapy. Institutional psychotherapy, which was founded by the Catalan anti-fascist psychiatrist Francesco Tosquelles at the Saint Alban psychiatric clinic, and developed by Jean Oury and Guattari at the La Borde clinic, is one of three types of psychotherapy, along with individual and collective psychotherapy, in the process of producing a new subjectivity.

Tosquelles distinguished between the institution and the asylum. The asylum is alienating because it is destined to inertia, and has to transform itself by transcending its resistances. This is what the process of deinstitutionalization is all about.

Institutional objects are transitional objects, according to Winnicott. The function of transitional objects may be performed by all kinds of encounters, the workshops, the operations, even the spaces of the therapeutic context, which then becomes 'good enough' (Winnicott), and the patients become the subjects of their own emancipation. According to Oury, institutional psychotherapy is the use of every kind of means for the everyday struggle against anything that may divert a collectivity towards a concentration-camp-type structure.

On this basis, institutional psychotherapy challenges the structure of asylums and constantly fights against the biases that promote discrimination. The false antinomy of internal and external only perpetuates walls made either from bricks or from ideas.

This means that within a context, a therapeutic institution, there is a need for a constant analysis and re-examination of what happens at any moment; critical thinking must be developed, and the strategy and plan of therapy for each patient must be constantly reworked, since every person is a special and singular case. This process is in its essence a permanent revolution.

For Guattari, desire becomes a driving force when it involves, in a social aggregation, the Social Other. This is because desire in Deleuze and Guattari is not situated in the field of lack, as in Freudian and Lacanian psychoanalysis, but is *machinic*, a positive force that shapes a new relation of the natural and the political.

Our personal and collective course in 18 Ano, comparable in many aspects with the pathlines/itinerancies (Kouki 2015) of the great artist Fernand Deligny, a friend of Guattari and Oury, followed paths that intersected, came together or diverged, and eventually converged at the ultimate goal of the emancipation of these extremely alienated persons that join in the therapeutic process.

It was along these lines that life within the context was organized, as an open-ended one, and the institution was kept alive, so as not to let its activities degenerate into a deadly repetition such as the one of the drug use, a stereotyping that cancels their subversive content (Guattari 2000: 39).

18 Ano was developed as a space of culture and creativity, a transitional space, as defined by Winnicott. This space is constantly discovered and created by the patients. It is discovered as a possibility, subversion, rupture, an openness to the new and the unforeseen. It is created as a transition to the new way of life, as liberation of flows of desire, by introducing desire itself in its social dimension, away from codes and territories (*deterritorialized* desire).

As a transitional space where the same and the other coexisted and conversed, 18 Ano became the space where sentiments of transference and countertransference circulated freely and were studied by the whole therapeutic group. The therapeutic group was called to reflect, to converse, to dream. 'Freedom is therapeutic' was the principle that inspired 18 Ano, as well as the whole movement of deinstitutionalization.

The venture was undertaken inside Daphni, the largest psychiatric clinic in the Balkans, the authoritarian institution par excellence, which institutionalizes not just thousands of mental patients, but all societal fears of madness, of the incomprehensible, of the dark side of human existence. Daphni as an 'institution of violence' and repression has always been hostile to anything new, novel, or radical. From the very beginning, it was highly suspicious and biased against 18 Ano, trying to suppress many novelties in its bureaucratic cogs. The unavoidable clash with the institutional mechanisms and the institutional practices in the nearby pavilions, the theoretical confrontation with the academic establishment and biological psychiatry, the fight for the deinstitutionalization of the clinic, assumed back then by a small minority of mental health practitioners, including members of the 18 Ano therapeutic team, the constant clash with rigid government policies, all this gave the venture a huge boost, at a historical juncture when Daphni was sinking to barbarism – a situation that Guattari himself found shocking when he visited the place – and the Greek society was experiencing the beginning of the end of the post-Junta dream and of all expectations for a social revolution.

This was the 1980s and 1990s, when heroin invaded for good the Greek society, and the best of the youth, boys and girls who sang for revolution and believed in it, faded away, their expectations frustrated, from an overdose.

This was also the time when the 'modernists' of PASOK came to power, and 18 Ano put up a huge fight in order to entrench its own existence and functioning.

The therapeutic group of 18 Ano had to confront the whole of the psychiatric establishment, as well as the state and the mouthpieces of the dominant ideology, which constantly reproduced social stereotypes about the drug addict as an incurable, chronic patient for whom the only 'possible cure' was the administration of substitutes, as a dangerous and permanently delinquent person. The struggle against this system, which was also conducted through the pages of the review *Tetradia Psychatrikis* (Papers of Psychiatry), published from 1984 to date, presupposed the cohesion of the members of the therapeutic group of 'Over 19' as well as the forming of alliances with various social actors, artists, scientists, intellectuals, trade unions, families, the local government, always against the mechanisms of social control and the preservation of addiction as a way of life.

For 18 Ano, treatment is a process of constant change of the addicts' existence, of their psychological functions, of their way of approaching the world and themselves in it, their way of relating to other people, of thinking, of expressing themselves, of organizing their lives on new grounds. Treatment cannot be anything else but an act of emancipation, requiring a fight against everything that opposes change and liberation from all kinds of chains.

From these big and small clashes that became ordinary through the years, 18 Ano drew force, consolidated itself and was able to effectively defend its values, the life, the dignity, the collectivity, the 'legacy' of institutional psychotherapy, the dream of social and individual liberation. 18 Ano was able to communicate the message that substance dependence is a social phenomenon that combines multiple factors and has social, psychological, cultural and various other dimensions; that drug addicts are not incurable, dangerous patients, and their proper place is not in prison. The communication of this message was decisively promoted by patients who had a successful treatment, who were able to actively participate in society and, having been 'cleansed' for good, to fight for their lives on a basis of equity with everybody else, organizing collective acts of social solidarity.

The values of 18 Ano, its structuring and foundational references, its revolutionary vision, are its 'legacy', as Guattari would have it.

The great danger for any such context of constant reinvention of the new, for every context open to change, whether big or small, is to fall under the domination, at a certain historical juncture, of the fear of change, to come to view change as disaster, and let the institution be petrified in an eternal repetition of the same, of treatment as a rigid routine, hiding under the guise of the old, radical form an actual adaptation to institutional order and 'voluntary servitude' – a process through which the subject-group fades into a subjugated group. In this case, what is endangered is the visionary, subversive, revolutionary character of the therapeutic praxis itself.

Yet such a loss creates the 'shadows of legacy', in Guattari's words, that may darken such a luminous venture.

Note

1 '18 Ano': The upper (in Greek: 'Ano') floor of the Pavilion 18, where psychotic women were hospitalized in the ground floor and addicted men in the upper floor.

References

Duchastel, A. (2005), *La voie de l' imaginaire*. Montreal: Les editions Québecor.

Guattari, F. (2015), *From Leros to La Borde*. Translated into Greek by E. Kouki. Athens: Koukkida.

Guattari, F. (2015), *Psychoanalysis and Transversality. Texts and Interviews 1955-1971*. Translated by A. Hodges. Cambridge, MA and Los Angeles: The MIT Press/ Semiotext(e).

Guattari, F. (2000), *The Three Ecologies*. Translated by I. Pindar and P. Sutton. London and New Brunswick, NJ: The Athlone Press.

Kouki, E. (2015), 'Grammes Porias/Periplanisis' ['Pathlines/Itinerancies'], *Tetradia Psychiatrikis* [Papers of Psychiatry], 127, January to April.

Pollack, J.-C. (2007), 'Félix ante Félix', in Manola Antonioli, Pierre Antoine Chardel and Hervé Regnauld (eds), *Gilles Deleuze, Félix Guattari et le Politique*. Paris: Du Sandre.

14

Double Bind: On Material Ethics

Andrej Radman

We are made of contracted water, earth, light and air – not only prior to the recognition or representation of these, but prior to their being sensed. Every organism, in its receptive and perceptual elements, but also in its viscera, is a sum of contractions, of retentions and expectations.[1]

Deleuze, *Difference and Repetition*

The task of abstraction … is to liberate the virtual subject – the designated force of thought – from the trap of the material. But this liberation is conducted precisely by utilizing the resources of the material, with the aid of its tendencies, properties and parameters, that determine and govern the behavior of the material system and, correspondingly, constrain the dynamic of thought, forcing it to revise its formation and to triangulate new affordances for conception and action.[2]

Negarestani, *Torture Concrete*

Introduction

Ethics is derived from the Greek word *ethos* meaning dwelling or habitat. But rather than the question of *where*, the emphasis must be placed on the question of *how*, on habit. Habit is not to be regarded as a mere passive knee-jerk response to a stimulus, but as a creative power. It is more than obvious that we cannot be said to *have* habits. Rather it is habits that have us. Moreover, it is habits that we *are*. The Urdoxa of 'transcendental unity of perception' prevents an account of the genesis of sense. As the feminist philosopher Rosi Braidotti has argued, the enabling 'power to' as *potentia* needs to be distinguished from the hindering 'power over' as *potestas*. We see this as a plea to set environmentality apart from governmentality:

> I do not think it acceptable … to raise any issues related to ethics or to morality independently of considerations of power and power relations. … At times contemporary moral philosophy comes across as comfortably installed in a consensus about the *context free* nature of its deliberations. As a materialist nomadic feminist philosopher, I want to stress the urgency of rewriting issues of power. …[3]

Aesthetics has to be rescued from the province of reactive undisciplined sensuality. In order to do so, as the political theorist Jane Bennett argues, we ought to stop overlooking and 'underfeeling' a realm between a striking reality and a stricken body. This third realm she calls *sensibility*, '*this* aesthetics – aesthetics as sensibility-formation – has implications for ethics that are irreducible to fascism, hedonism or indiscriminateness. For as a form of *askesis*, a sensibility establishes the range of possibility in perception, enactment, and responsiveness to others' (original italics).[4] The approach draws on the Foucauldian practice of the self, 'in its Greek sense of self-discipline rather than a Christian sense of self-denial'.[5] The founder of 'ecosophy', French psychotherapist and lifelong accomplice of Deleuze's, Félix Guattari, coined the term *Ethico-Aesthetic* precisely in order to underline the inseparability of action and perception.[6] The neologism was his subtle way of arguing that it is practice and experimentation that actively shape the subject. Until recently the *sentient* had been considered as a mere supplement to the *sapient*. The ranking order in major philosophical systems clearly reveals a historical bias towards the cognitive over the affective. But as the literary theorist Terry Eagleton remarked, it is in the manner of such lowly supplements to end up supplanting what they are meant to subserve.[7]

Ecological thinking

We start from the hypothesis that the digital turn in architecture effectively reproduces the duality of mind and body, removing the former from contexts of engagement with the environment while treating the latter as no more than a kind of recording mechanism, converting the stimuli that impinge upon it into data to be processed. The Cartesian view of action as the bodily execution of innate (or acquired) programmes is replaced with the kindred albeit more contemporary cognitivist view of perception as the operation of the mind upon the deliverance of the senses. The architecture theorist Ingeborg Rocker protests the reductionist tendency in the parametricist disregard of sociopolitical issues:[8]

> Only if architecture and urbanism are viewed from more than one – currently the formal – vantage point, only if sociopolitical as well as technological-material and organizational aspects are taken into the equation, will parametricism be able to achieve … changes to our modes of thinking, designing, and producing the architecture and urbanity. …[9]

Parametricism in its current state, in other words, is too formal and hence not abstract enough. Let us recall that the opposite of the concrete is not the abstract but the discrete. Even though the champion of parametricism Patrick Schumacher has in the meantime conceded the problem, the question of formalization of the non-discursive remains open at best.[10] We cannot but reiterate Guattari's puzzlement from thirty years ago: 'But where does the idea that the socius is reducible to the facts of language, and that these facts are in turn reducible to linearizable and "digitalizable" signifying chains, come from?'[11] It is for this reason that we want to revamp the legacy of radical empiricism in general and that of James Jerome Gibson's ecological perception in particular.[12] Gibson similarly cautions: 'We cannot hope to understand natural stimuli by analogy with socially coded stimuli, for that would be like putting the cart before the horse.'[13] The American psychologist vehemently rejected the reductionist information-processing view, with its implied separation of the activity of the mind in the body from the reactivity of the body in the world, arguing instead that perception is part and parcel of the total *system* of relations constituted by ecology. Let us follow Guattari and call it ecologies in the plural: environmental, social and psychical.[14] As the author of *Nihil Unbound* Ray Brassier underscores, the structure of reality includes but is not exhausted by the ego-logical structure of discretely individuated objects:

> The question is why those who are so keen to attribute absolute or unconditional reality to the activities of self-consciousness (or of minded creatures) seem so loath to confer equal existential rights upon the unconscious, mindless processes through which consciousness and mindedness first emerged and will eventually be destroyed.[15]

Perceivers get to know the world *directly* by moving about and discovering what the environment affords rather than by representing it in the mind.[16] Hence, meaning is not the form that the mind contributes to the flux of raw sensory data by way of its acquired schemata. Rather it is continually becoming within the relational contexts of engagement. 'The materiality of each organism, its historical thickness, and the density of its internal and external relations, rule out any dualism between "software" and "hardware" that is specific to the notion of computer programs.'[17] Because everything starts from the sensible, the cognition is extended and not interiorized or centralized, embedded and not generalized or decontextualized, enacted and not passive or merely receptive, embodied and not logocentric, and affective and not unprovoked. Architects should pay close attention to the pan-experientialist implications of the 4EA approach (extended, embedded, enacted, embodied and affective) that dispenses not only with the biological/social dichotomy but also with that between evolution and history.[18] The key is to expand the explanatory framework 'out of our heads'. According to the social anthropologist Tim Ingold this approach explains human capacities as the properties not of genetic or cultural programming but of the self-organizing dynamics of developmental systems:

> It follows from this approach that if people raised in different environments perceive different things, this is not because they are processing the same sensory data in terms of alternative representational schemata, but because they have been trained, through previous experience of carrying out various kinds of practical tasks, involving particular bodily movements and sensibilities, to orient themselves to the environment and to attend to its features in different ways. Modes of perception, in short, are a function of specific ways of moving around … these forms of motility are not added to, or inscribed in, a preformed human body, but are rather intrinsic properties of the human organism itself, developmentally incorporated into its modus operandi through practice and training in a particular environment. Hence capacities of perception, as of action, are neither innate nor acquired but undergo continuous formation within processes of ontogenetic development.[19]

The actual content of architecture is thus movement and not message. It is movement that is space-making and thus literally ontogenetic. This is why, according to Gibson, learning is but the education of attention, based on continuous variation and selection rather than enrichment through schematization.

Nomadic ethics

The current affective turn renders some traditional issues obsolete but introduces new problems, most notably those concerning the 'source of normativity'. After all, as Deleuze and Guattari diagnose in the first volume of *Capitalism and Schizophrenia*, 'unlike previous social machines, the capitalist machine is incapable of providing a code that will apply to the whole of the social field'.[20] When pondering the issue of whether there can be a material ethics, Deleuze advanced an infamous tongue-in-cheek proposal that morality needed to be replaced with physics. What he meant, of course, is that the source of any critique must not come from the outside as in a transcendental intrusion: 'the conditions of a true critique and a true creation are the same: the destruction of an image of thought [cliché] which presupposes itself and the genesis of the act of thinking in thought itself'.[21] It needs to operate at the level of production of the very concept (or affect), at its own terms. 'Thus the question is not how architectural criticism can serve architecture, but of how architecture can be a medium for critical activity.'[22] To paraphrase the filmmaker Jean-Luc Godard, not a just architecture, just an architecture.[23] Braidotti explains how to set desire for becomings at the centre of the political agenda:

> In keeping with their reading of advance capitalism as a supple and dynamic system, Deleuze and Guattari diversify their notion and practice of politics. Politics for them consists not so much in 'LA politique' (politics as usual, i.e. institutional or Majoritarian politics) as in 'LE politique' (the political movement in its diffuse, nomadic and rhizomic forms of becoming). This distinction between politics and the political is of crucial importance.[24]

Truth and falsity are not values that exist outside the constitutive problematic fields that give them sense. Ethics, framed in this way, is a problem of power and not of duty. An ontological event is to supersede epistemological law. Rather than relying upon *logos*, the emphasis shifts to the 'natural law' of *nomos*. In the undivided shared space of cosmos everything becomes a matter of dosage. The neo-materialist philosopher Manuel DeLanda explains the main tenets of Spinozian ethics where the moral dichotomy of good and evil is replaced by the concept that goes by the name of *pharmacon*:

> In an ethics of nourishing [joy] versus degrading [sadness] assemblages, real-life experimentation (not a priori theorization) is the key. To use an obvious example from environmental ethics: a little phosphorous feeds the soil; too much poisons it. Where exactly the threshold is varies with type of soil so it cannot be known a priori. But the normative statement 'do not poison the soil' is there nevertheless. Similarly for society: too much centralization poisons (by concentrating power and privilege; by allowing corruption; by taking away skills from routinized command-followers etc) but exactly how much is to be decided by social experiments, how else? [25]

A double bind is a concept proposed by the anthropologist and cyberneticist Gregory Bateson to account for a particular condition of *aporia*, which results from a kind of split loyalty or mutual determination.[26] We raise it to address a particular concern about the alleged tendency of some proponents of the affective turn to undermine intelligence in favour of instinct, the difference being that instinct presupposes instantaneous payoff, while intelligence is about a deferred higher efficiency. A possible consequence of pursuing a narrow instinct-driven interest may have an unintended effect in the long run. With its impulsive 'will to survive' (*élan vital*), humanism might indeed turn out to be suicidal, as the feminist philosopher Claire Colebrook cautions. To prevent this scenario she proposes to counter the old (Luddite) 'active vitalism' with the so-called passive vitalism, where the emphasis needs to be on the *non-organic* life as a dynamic creativity rather than on the *homeostatic* environment:

> Vitalism in its contemporary mode therefore works in two opposite directions. The tradition that Deleuze and Guattari invoke is opposed to the organism as subject or substance that would govern differential relations; their concept of 'life' refers not to an ultimate principle of survival, self-maintenance and continuity but to a disrupting and destructive range of forces. The other tradition of vitalism posits 'life' as a mystical and unifying principle. It is this second vitalism of meaning and the organism that, despite first appearances, dominates today.[27]

The existential territory is not a given. Rather, life forms actively construct and are constructed by existential niches (sets of affordances) that hold together as assemblages. The evolutionary biologist Richard Lewontin explains:

> This view of environment as causally prior to, and ontologically independent of, organisms is the surfacing in evolutionary theory of the underlying Cartesian structure of our world view. The world is divided into causes and effects, the external and internal, environments and the organisms they 'contain'. While this structure is fine for clocks, since main-springs move the hands and not vice versa, it creates indissoluble contradictions when taken as the meta-model of the living world.[28]

Passive vitalism

It should be easy enough for architects to empathize with the above 'deferred payoff reasoning' since their job is not merely allographic and tactical. It is also strategic, if not logistical, as in the case of urbanism and physical planning.[29] There is hardly anything immediate or instantaneous in architectural design. Architects don't (even) make buildings, they make drawings and models of buildings. But the analogy with artistic practices is simply far-fetched. The sociologist Richard Sennett rightly dismisses the cult of the artefact as implausible:

> Architecture forms a special case in relation to the ideal of integrity, for it comes into being in ways paintings, sculptures, and poems do not. The making of a piece of urban architecture is a messy process, involving an army of specialist designers and technicians at war with opposing armies of government officials, bankers and clients.[30]

Put succinctly, architectural design is action at a distance in a profound sense. If 'assemblage' has been the core concept of Deleuze and Guattari ever since *A Thousand Plateaus* (1980), then what they call a 'territory' is simply its limit condition, as in stratification:

> Just as milieus swing between a stratum state and a movement of destratification, assemblages swing between a territorial closure that tends to restratify them and a deterritorializing movement that connects them to the Cosmos. Thus it is not surprising that the distinction we were seeking is not between assemblage and something else, but between two limits of any possible assemblage, in other words, between the system of strata and the plane of consistency.[31]

Any deterritorializations and reterritorializations are to be considered as mere dimensions of the very assemblage, which is beyond the full control of the designer. Given the asymmetry between the *actual* territory and the *virtual* assemblage, it should not come as a surprise that: 'What holds an assemblage together is not the play of framing forms or linear causalities but, actually or potentially, its most deterritorialised [abstract] component.'[32] What gives integrity to an assemblage, in other words, is Nietzschean 'Eternal Return' which does not allow for the return of identity, since this would ultimately come down to a final stasis, but must instead stand for the eternal return of differentiation. 'All our potential futures are fully real (if virtual) as are all the non-actualized pasts, and yet the actualization of any event transforms the whole, always and eternally.'[33] In the words of Guattari: 'Repetition is not the law, the finality of something; on the contrary, it marks the threshold to "deterritorialization", the indication of a desiring mutation.'[34] He continues:

> Schizoanalysis … meets with the revolutionary struggle to the extent that it strives to free the flows, to remove the bolts – the axiomatics of capitalism, the overcoding of the superego, the primitive territorialities artificially reconstructed, etc. The work of the analyst, the revolutionary, and the artist meet to the extent that they must constantly tear down systems which reify desire, which submit

> the subject to the familial and social hierarchy (I am a man, I am a woman, I am a son, I am a brother, etc.). No sooner does someone say, 'I am this or that' than desire is strangled.[35]

Deleuze and Guattari's favourite example of the 'cutting edge of deterritorialization' is the 'refrain' (*ritornello*). 'In general sense, we call a refrain any aggregate of matters of expression that draws a territory and develops into territorial motifs and landscapes.' [36] They insist that it is the difference that is rhythmic, not the repetition.[37] 'Rhythm is milieu's answer to chaos.'[38]

To meet the challenge of the double bind, there needs to occur a fundamental change in the architect's role from a synaptic visionary – a psychological subject whose private meanings and public expressions are crucial to understanding his work and its effects – to a more humble explorer of the *machinic phylum* where resingularization may occur.[39] A paradigmatic example of a synaptic visionary is Ayn Rand's architect Howard Roark.[40] By contrast, the 'intensification of events' also known as *dramatization* can best be illustrated with an example of the Periodic Table. DeLanda explains, 'What constitutes Mendelev's great achievement is that he was the first one to have the courage to leave *open gaps* in the classification instead of trying to impose an artificial completeness on it.'[41] The sedentary pigeonholing has given way to the nomadic distribution. According to the topology *connoisseur* Bernard Cache, 'one of the great failings of architectural theory has been its inability to go beyond a theory of proportions, a striking case being Le Corbusier with his Modulor' which is a mereological issue.[42] Conversely, the architecture theorist Manfredo Tafuri identifies the great *mereotopological* merit of American urban planning since the mid-eighteenth century: 'In the United States, absolute freedom is granted to the single architectural fragment, which is situated in a context that is not formally conditioned by it. … Here urban planning [whole] and architecture [part] are finally separated from each other.'[43] The whole is not *of* the parts, but alongside them and in addition to them, ever open and divergent.

A determinant interconnection between obeying and commanding (empathy and abstraction) requires not surrendering to the matter but 'meeting it halfway'.[44] 'It is the concurrent organization of matter by the force of thought, and the reorientation of thought by material forces. It is the mutual penetration and destabilization of thought and matter … .'[45] Many a Deleuzian epigone will frown at such a proposal of semi-automatic mode of operation, as if immanence were only guaranteed by taking the architect out of the loop, together with the right angles and the rest of the 'superseded' toolkit. Very often one hears arguments in favour of processual automatism that the architecture theorist Robert Somol sums up as 'look, ma', no hands'. In his view, this is just not convincing enough. The process is just a device. It ought to become a technique to generate other effects that are not reducible to or explainable by the context of function arguments. Furthermore, while formalism certainly knows what probability means, it does not know what realization means and to presume otherwise is to commit a category error.[46] An event that is unforeseen in fact is unforeseeable in principle:

> The future doesn't consist of future possibilities. The future is real, when possibility … is only a fabrication made up after the real. The real future (as opposed to our toy-idea of a future) is made up of events, which emerge out of nothing that may anticipate them. Such events are real and create the possibilities that 'will have led' to them.[47]

Those opposed to the 'partnership with matter' also forget that the architect is but an effect quasi-caused by the 'conceptual persona' or 'aesthetic figure'. The former is the power of concepts and the latter is the powers of affects and percepts. 'Philosophy's sole aim is to become worthy of the event, and it is precisely the conceptual person who counter-effectuates the event.'[48] Counter-actualization is the highest power of the principle of sufficient reason (as an intrinsic genesis, not an extrinsic conditioning) in its turning against the principle of non contradiction. It marks the passage from the exclusive to the inclusive disjunction.

The 'architectural audience' does not come ready made either. We are in need of a people, Deleuze and Guattari say, who are yet to come. Not to address the one who is missing, but the one who will arrive.[49] Colebrook's distinction between active and passive vitalisms becomes crucial. In order to take a step forward we need not take a step back, as in the former, but start from the middle (*milieu*), as in the latter:

> Active In the beginning we created the world, we subjected ourselves to systems and now we have to *reclaim* the world we created.
>
> Passive In the beginning there is a 'system'. It is through the system that we think. One has to understand the *emergence* of the system.[50]

It is certainly not enough to replace the quasi-objective Cartesian space with the quasi- subjective *Umwelt*.[51] In everyday German *umwelt* means 'surroundings' or 'environment', but through the work of the German biologist Jakob von Uexküll the term has acquired the meaning of the 'phenomenal world'. Instead, we need to tap into the mutual becoming, of two transcendental illusions formerly known as *self* and *world*. The champion of the concept of radical auto-affection Raymond Ruyer takes this to be the most delicate point:

> We should vehemently deny the existence of a geometric dimension that provides a point of observation external to the sensory field. But we should affirm no less vehemently the existence of a sort of 'metaphysical' transversal to the entire field, whose two 'extremities' are the 'I' (or the x of organic individuality), on one hand, and the guiding Idea of organization, on the other.[52]

By contrast to the two paralogisms that bestow extensive properties of actual products on the intensive production process, we need to tap into the dynamic creativity or Ruyer's 'absolute survey' instead. It is always the difference – sub-representational will to power – that is the condition of identity and not the other way around.[53] The mechanicist part-to-whole relationship has to be supplanted by the one-all machinic concept of *multiplicity*:

> Multiplicities are made up of becoming without history, of individuation without subject (the way in which a river, a climate, an event, a day, an hour of the day, is individualized). That is, the concept exists just as much in empiricism as in rationalism, but it has a completely different use and a completely different nature: it is a being-multiple, instead of a being-one, a being-whole or being as subject.[54]

If metaphysics is concerned with the beginning/totality, and epistemology with foundation/ground, our task is to address consistency/consolidation. At the meso-level (formerly known as environment) the commitment to passive vitalism turns our attention to ecology, not as a tree-hugging pathos (the Gaia hypothesis), but as an ethos of irreducible complexity. By irreducible we mean non-transcendental, non-universal, non-eternal and non-discursive. This is how Lewontin underscores the emergent (yet constructed) wholes that could not be understood by being broken down into parts:

> Over the last three hundred years the analytic model has been immensely successful in explaining nature in such a way as to allow us to manipulate and predict it. It seems abundantly clear to us now that the holistic view of the world obstructs any possibility of a practical understanding of natural phenomena. But the success of the clock model, in contrast to the failure of obscurantist holism, has led to an overly simplified view of the relations of parts to wholes and causes to effects … Taken together, the relations of genes, organisms, and environments are reciprocal relations in which all three elements are both causes and effects.

> Genes and environment are both causes of organisms, which are, in turn, causes of environments, so that genes become causes of environments as mediated by organisms.[55]

In other words, synthesis is not analysis in reverse. As the dystopian novelist James Graham Ballard noted, 'the obsession with the specific activity of quantified functions is what science shares with pornography'.[56] By contrast, each concept ought to be related to the variables that determine its mutations, rather than construed *a priori* or a posteriori. Rationalism and empiricism are not opposed but co-constitutive.[57] It is high time to put the horse of *intensity* and its affective 'catalytic operators' before the cart of *intentionality* or 'aboutness' of reason. Society is *not* an ensemble of rational individuals who are each aiming at the maximization of profit. The unconscious investment of desire always counts for more than the conscious investment of interest.[58] Consequently, what architects create first and foremost are ethico-aesthetical *affordances*, a certain existence that is more than the idealist's representation, but less than the realist's thing.

The recomposition of what Guattari refers to as 'architectural enunciation' transforms the trade of the architect who becomes its relay by assuming analytic and pragmatic responsibility for the production of subjectivity.[59] We are in need of a practice that will reunite the quasi-objective theory of perception with the quasi-subjective theory of art, where 'particular situations' are not subsumed by 'universal forms'. According to the Whiteheadian scholar Judith Jones subjectivation is a creative act: 'the subject is not having emotional reactions to an object but is a subject in virtue of the provocation of reacting incorporation of objects in the coming to be of an entity which would not come to be unless those provocative objects [affordances] were working in it'. [60] What we are in need of is the architecture of immanence where the condition is no greater than the conditioned. In the words of the author of *Cyclonopedia* Reza Negarestani: 'proceeding becomes a matter of following a new choice of disequilibrium that opens up a new path or transit, and with that new constraints which bring into view new affordances of action'.[61] To rethink Hume's challenge is to be concerned not with the *epistemological* stability of logically necessary theories but with the meta-stabilities of contingently obligatory *ontological* processes of singularization themselves.[62] Not only will this keep us from 'cheating' by overcoding, but it will also release us from the bad habit of tracing the transcendental from the empirical. Most importantly, it will allow for the long overdue unyoking of coherence from congruence.

Notes

1 Deleuze, *Difference and Repetition*, 73.
2 Negarestani, *Torture Concrete*, 11.
3 Braidotti, *Transpositions*, 30. [emphasis added].
4 Bennett, 'How is it, then, that we still remain barbarians?', 654.
5 Simons, *Foucault and the Political*, 77.
6 'Ecosophy' is defined as a science of ecosystems. See: Guattari, *Chaosmosis*, 91.
7 Eagleton, *The Ideology of the Aesthetic*, 45.
8 'Parametricism: A term used in a variety of disciplines from mathematics to design. Literally, it means working within parameters of a defined range. Within the field of digital design, it refers broadly to the utilization of parametric modelling software. In contrast to standard software packages based on datum geometric objects, parametric software links dimensions and parameters to geometry. It therefore describes the incremental adjustment of a part that is able to impact on the whole assembly.' See: Parisi, *Contagious Architecture*, 265.
9 Rocker, 'Apropos Parmetricism', 100–1.
10 Schumacher, 'Parametricism with Social Parameters'. 'That parametricism "goes social" is not a concession to the prevailing winds of political correctness (that divert and dissolve the innovative thrust of architectural discourse). Rather, it is a sign of parametricism's maturity, confidence and readiness to take on the full societal tasks of architecture, i.e. it implies the inauguration of Parametricism 2.0'.
11 Guattari, 'The Postmodern Impasse', 11.
12 Gibson, *The Ecological Approach to Visual Perception*.
13 Gibson, 'The concept of the stimulus in psychology', 702. Presidential Address to the Eastern Psychological Association, New York, April 1960.
14 Guattari, *The Three Ecologies*.
15 Brassier, 'Concepts, Objects, Gems', 290.
16 'The affordances of the environment are what it offers the animal, what it provides or furnishes, either for good or ill. The verb to afford is found in the dictionary, but the noun affordance is not. I have made it up. I mean by it something that refers to both the environment and the animal in a way that no existing term does. It implies the complementarity of the animal and the environment.' See: Gibson *The Ecological Approach to Visual Perception*, 127.
17 Longo, 'The Consequences of Philosophy', 11/12.
18 For more information on ways of thinking about cognition that depart from standard cognitivist models see Protevi's blog.
19 Ingold, 'From Complementarity to Obviation', 267–8.
20 Deleuze and Guattari, *Anti-Oedipus*, 36.
21 Deleuze, *Difference and Repetition*, 139.
22 Bouman and van Toorn, *The Invisible in Architecture*, 15.

23 A paraphrased line from Deleuze's text covering a series of TV programmes made in 1976 by Godard and Anne-Marie Mieville. Deleuze adjusted Godard's formula, 'not a just image, just an image', in order to advocate experimentation as a way of escaping normalization according to dominant orders. See: Deleuze, 'Three Questions on Six Times Two', in *Negotiations*, 37–45.
24 Braidotti and Dolphijn, 'Deleuze's Philosophy and the Art of Life', 25.
25 DeLanda, '1000 Years of War'.
26 Bateson, *Steps to an Ecology of Mind*, 199–204.
27 Colebrook, *Deleuze and the Meaning of Life*, 137.
28 Lewontin, 'Organism and Environment', 159.
29 In contrast to *autographic* arts such as sculpturing, *allographic* arts are those capable of being reproduced at a distance from the author.
30 Sennett, 'The Technology of Unity', 563.
31 Deleuze and Guattari, *A Thousand Plateaus*, 337.
32 Ibid., 374.
33 Colebrook, 'Futures'.
34 Guattari, 'The Best Capitalist Drug', 150.
35 Ibid., 152.
36 Deleuze and Guattari, *A Thousand Plateaus*, 356.
37 Ibid., 346.
38 Ibid., 313. 'Chaos is not the opposite of rhythm, but the milieu of all milieus'.
39 Radman and Sohn, 'The Four Domains of the Plane of Consistency'.
40 Rand, *The Fountainhead*.
41 DeLanda, 'Deleuzian Ontology'.
42 Cache, 'Geometries of Phàntasma', 90.
43 Tafuri, 'Toward a Critique of Architectural Ideology', 13.
44 Barad, *Meeting the Universe Halfway*.
45 Negarestani, *Torture Concrete*, 5.
46 Poinceré's resolution of the three-body problem destroyed Laplace's myth of complete determination. See: Longo, 'The Consequences of Philosophy', 6/12.
47 Ayache, *The Medium of Contingency*, 21.
48 Deleuze and Guattari, *What Is Philosophy?*, 160.
49 Deleuze and Guattari, *A Thousand Plateaus*, 345.
50 Based on: Colebrook, *Deleuze and the Meaning of Life*, 126.
51 Uexküll von, 'A Stroll Through the Worlds of Animals and Men', 5–80.
52 Ruyer, *Neofinalism*, 99.
53 The expression 'will to power' is Nietzschean anthropomorphism for forces.
54 Deleuze and Parnet, 'Preface to the English Edition', viii.
55 Lewontin, *The Triple Helix*, 72, 100–1.
56 Quoted in: Crary, 'Eclipse of the Spectacle', 292.
57 Deleuze, 'On A Thousand Plateaus', 25–34.

58 Deleuze and Guattari, *Anti-Oedipus*, xviii.
59 Guattari, 'Architectural Enunciation', 237. 'Architectural enunciation doesn't only involve diachronic discursive components. It equally implies a taking consistency of synchronic existential dimensions or levels of ordinates.'
60 Jones, 'Provocative Expression'.
61 Negarestani, *Torture Concrete*, 10.
62 Hume's problem – also known as the problem of induction – is the problem of causal necessity or the potential changeability of natural processes themselves.

References

Ayache, Elie. (2015), *The Medium of Contingency: An Inverse View of the Market*. Basingstoke: Palgrave Macmillan.

Barad, Karen. (2007), *Meeting the Universe Halfway: Quantum Physics and the Entanglement of Matter and Meaning*. Durham: Duke University Press.

Bateson, Gregory. (1972), *Steps to an Ecology of Mind: Collected Essays in Anthropology, Psychiatry, Evolution and Epistemology*. London: Jason Aronson.

Bennett, Jane (1996), 'How is it, then, that we Still Remain Barbarians?: Foucault, Schiller, and the Aestheticization of Ethics', *Political Theory*, 24 (4, November): 653–72.

Bouman (1994), *The Invisible in Architecture*. London: Academy Editions.

Braidotti, Rosi and Dolphijn, Rick. (2014), *This Deleuzian Century: Art, Activism, Society*. Edited by R. Braidotti and R. Dolphijn. Leiden and Boston: Brill/Rodopi.

Braidotti, Rosi. (2006), *Transpositions: On Nomadic Ethics*. Cambridge: Polity Press.

Brassier, Ray. (2011), 'Concepts, Objects, Gems', in D. Attridge and J. Elliot (eds), *Theory after 'Theory'*, 278–93. New York: Routledge.

Cache, Bernard (2011), 'Geometries of Phàntasma', in *Projectiles*, 74–90. London: AA Publications.

Colebrook, Claire. (2015), 'Futures', unpublished paper.

Colebrook, Claire. (2010), *Deleuze and the Meaning of Life*. London: Continuum.

Crary, Jonathan. (1984), 'Eclipse of the Spectacle', in B. Wallis (ed.), *Art After Modernism: Rethinking Representation*, 283–94. New Museum.

DeLanda, Manuel. (2003), '1000 Years of War', in Arthur and Marilouise Kroker (eds), *CTheory*, http://www.ctheory.net/articles.aspx?id=383 (accessed 1 April 2016).

DeLanda, Manuel. (2002), Deleuzian Ontology: A Sketch; presented at *New Ontologies: Transdisciplinary Objects*, University of Illinois (30 March 2002), http://www.situation.ru/app/j_art_1078.htm (accessed 1 April).

Deleuze, Gilles and Parnet, Claire. (1987), 'Preface to the English Edition', in H. Tomlinson and B. Habberjam (trans), *Dialogues*, vii–x. New York: Columbia University Press.

Deleuze, Gilles and Guattari, Félix. ([1980] 2004), *A Thousand Plateaus*. Translated by B. Massumi. London and New York: Continuum.

Deleuze, Gilles and Guattari, Félix. ([1972] 2008), *Anti-Oedipus*. Translated by R. Hurley, M. Seem and H. R. Lane. New York, NY: Penguin.

Deleuze, Gilles and Guattari, Félix. ([1991] 1994), *What Is Philosophy?* Translated by H. Tomlinson and G. Burchill. New York: Columbia University Press.

Deleuze, Gilles. ([1968] 1994), *Difference and Repetition*. Translated by P. Patton. New York: Columbia University Press.

Deleuze, Gilles. ([1990] 1995), *Negotiations*. Translated by M. Joughin. New York: Columbia University Press.

Eagleton, Terry. (1990), *The Ideology of the Aesthetic*. Oxford, UK: Blackwell.

Gibson, James Jerome. (1960), 'The Concept of the Stimulus in Psychology,' *American Psychologist*, 15 (11, November): 694–703.

Gibson, James Jerome. ([1979] 1986), *The Ecological Approach to Visual Perception*. New York: Lawrence Erlbaum Associates.

Guattari, Félix. ([1989] 2013), 'Architectural Enunciation,' in A. Goffey (trans), *Schizoanalytic Cartographies*, 231–9. London: Bloomsbury.

Guattari, Félix (1995), 'The Best Capitalist Drug,' in S. Lotringer (ed.), *Chaosophy: Texts and Interviews 1972-1977*, translated by D. L. Sweet, J. Becker and T. Adkins, 141–53. Los Angeles: Autonomedia/Semiotext(e).

Guattari, Félix ([1986] 1996), 'The Postmodern Impasse,' in G. Genosko (ed.), *The Guattari Reader*, translated by T. Dufresne, 109–13. Oxford: Blackwell Publishers.

Guattari, Félix. (1995), *Chaosmosis: an Ethico-aesthetic Paradigm*. Translated by P. Bains and J. Pefanis. Bloomington: Indiana University Press.

Guattari, Félix. ([1989] 2008), *The Three Ecologies*. Translated by I. Pindar and P. Sutton. London: Continuum.

Ingold, Tim, 'From Complementarity to Obviation: On Dissolving the Boundaries between Social and Biological Anthropology, Archaeology and Psychology,' in S. Oyama, P. E. Griffiths and R. D. Gray (eds), *Cycles of Contingency: Developmental Systems and Evolution*, 255–79. Cambridge, MA: The MIT Press.

Jones, Judith, 'Provocative Expression: Transitions In and From Metaphysics in Whitehead's Later Work,' https://phenomenologymindsmedia.files.wordpress.com/2011/12/judith-jones.mp3 (accessed 1 April).

Lewontin, Richard. (1982), 'Organism and Environment,' in H. C. Plotkin (ed.), *Learning, Development, and Culture*, 151–70. Chichester: Wiley.

Lewontin, Richard. (2000), *The Triple Helix: Gene, Organism, and Environment*. Cambridge, MA: Harvard University Press.

Longo, Giuseppe. (2016), 'The Consequences of Philosophy,' in *Site 0: Castalia, the Game of Ends and Means | Glass Bead* (2016), http://www.glass-bead.org/journal/site-0-castalia-the-game-of-ends-and-means/?lang=enview (accessed 1 April).

Negarestani, Reza. (2014), *Torture Concrete: Jean Luc Moluene and the Protocol of Abstraction*. New York: Sequence Press.

Parisi, Luciana. (2013), *Contagious Architecture: Computation, Aesthetics and Space*. Cambridge, MA: MIT Press.

Protevi, John., '4EA Cognition', http://proteviblog.typepad.com/protevi/embodiedembeddedaffective_cognition/ (accessed 1 April).

Radman, Andrej and Sohn, Heidi. (2017), 'Preface: The Four Domains of the Plane of Consistency', in A. Radman and H. Sohn (eds), *Critical and Clinical Cartographies: Architecture/Robotics/Medicine/Philosophy*.1–20, Edinburgh: Edinburgh University Press.

Rand, Ayn. ([1943]1993),*The Fountainhead*. New York:Signet.

Rocker, Ingeborg M. (2011), 'Apropos Parmetricism: If, In What Style Should We Build?' *Log*, no. 21: 89–101.

Ruyer, Raymond. ([1952] 2016), *Neofinalism*. Translated by A. Edlebi. Minneapolis: Minnesota University Press.

Schumacher, Patrik. (2015), 'Parametricism with Social Parameters', in I. Lazovski and Y. Kahlon (eds), *The Human (Parameter)' Parametric Approach in Israeli Architecture*. Tel Aviv: ZEZEZE Architecture Gallery.

Sennett, Richard. (2000), 'The Technology of Unity', in P. Weibel (ed.), *Olafur Eliasson: Surroundings Surrounded: Essays on Space and Science*, 556–65. Karlsruhe: ZKM.

Simons, Jon. (1995), *Foucault and the Political*. London and New York: Routledge.

Tafuri, Manfredo. (1998), 'Toward a Critique of Architectural Ideology', in Michael K. Hays (ed.), *Architecture Theory Since 1968*, 6–35. Cambridge, MA: MIT Press.

Uexküll, von Jakob (1957), 'A Stroll Through the Worlds of Animals and Men: A Picture Book of Invisible Worlds', in Claire H. Schiller (ed. And trans.), *Instinctive Behavior: The Development of a Modern Concept*, 5–80. New York: International Universities Press.

Index